9/18

PRAISE FOR *ELIZABETH WARREN*

"If you wonder why Elizabeth Warren is profound yet always understandable, tough-minded yet soft-hearted, able to bring real life to Washington—and vice versa—read her life story by Antonia Felix. It will not only show us what a leader can be, but who we can become."

—Gloria Steinem

"Felix gives us an intimate portrait of an insecure girl growing up on 'the ragged edges of the middle class' who finds the grit to force her own limits. An irresistible read for anyone who cares about Elizabeth Warren's fight for America's hammered working class."

—Gail Sheehy, author of *Passages* and *Daring*

"Antonia Felix captures Elizabeth Warren's honesty, decency, authenticity, poise, and passion in this well-written biography. Altogether, the book illuminates a rising political star who fuses together a first-class intellect and temperament."

—Mark Green, author of *Bright, Infinite Future* and founder and CEO of ShadowingTrump.org

"*Elizabeth Warren* is a great read about a life of tenacity, grit, and perseverance that resulted in an iconic U.S. senator renowned for her warrior spirit on behalf of the public she serves."

—Richard Carmona, MD, MPH, FACS, 17th Surgeon General of the United States

"From its well-chosen opening epigraph to the end of its four trenchant appendixes (not to mention every page in between), Antonia Felix's biography of Elizabeth Warren is worthy of its stellar subject. If you're as much of a Warren fan as I am, you'll be grateful for this thoroughly engaging, gracefully written overview of the senator's life and work—thus far."

—Letty Cottin Pogrebin, author, activist,
and cofounding editor of *Ms.* magazine

"Elizabeth Warren is a dynamic leader, and Antonia Felix's beautifully written, detailed book captures the fighting spirit that has made Warren a progressive icon. From her humble beginnings in Oklahoma, Felix deftly chronicles Warren's extraordinary life, a true American success story."

—Congressman Eliot Engel (New York)

"Felix beautifully captures Senator Warren's determination, tenacity, and persistence, particularly in the face of the challenges she encountered when entering politics. Senator Warren's is a story with which everyone should be familiar—especially women with the drive to lead—and Felix's empowering book will inspire anyone interested in American politics."

—Lauren Beecham, executive director of womenwinning

"Antonia Felix's compelling biography deftly illuminates the social, economic, political, and personal factors that have shaped Senator Elizabeth Warren into a smart and compassionate champion for the average American. The impact and meaning of these trends over the last fifty years are brought into sharp focus through Senator Warren's story."

—Virginia Arthur, president of Metropolitan State University

"Engrossing...the life story of an amazing leader, teacher, and reformer as well as a detailed narration of the social justice issues that shaped her politics and passion. A great read!"

—Sandra L. Pappas, Minnesota state senator, senate president, and president of Forward Global Women

"A compelling, consuming story, exhaustively researched. Felix wonderfully documents Warren's world of achievement, including her academic pursuits that have had real-life impact on millions of average American families."

—Steven Jacques, national Democratic strategist and author of *Advance Man*

ELIZABETH
WARREN

HER FIGHT. HER WORK. HER LIFE.

ANTONIA FELIX

Published by Sourcebooks, Inc.
P.O. Box 4410, Naperville, Illinois 60567-4410
(630) 961-3900
Fax: (630) 961-2168
sourcebooks.com

Library of Congress Cataloging-in-Publication data is on file with the publisher.

Printed and bound in the United States of America.
LSC 10 9 8 7 6 5 4 3 2 1

To Stanford

I'm never tired of despair and desperation,
And I won't be quiet. I keep crying out that the house
Is being robbed. I want even the thieves to know.
—Robert Bly, "The Night the Cities Burned"

CONTENTS

INTRODUCTION

"To glorify democracy and to silence the people is a farce; to discourse on humanism and to negate people is a lie."

—Paulo Freire[1]

On the main streets of the Oklahoma towns of Elizabeth Warren's forebears, wooden buildings with tall, false fronts tried to make the structures appear larger than they actually were. All it took was a side-angled view to discover the deception. Similarly, through one particular decade of her career as a legal scholar, Warren gradually noticed the emptiness in the promise that the markets of American capitalism held potential prosperity for everyone. Behind that claim stood nothing but a tall tale: capitalism's promise of benefits for all did not hold true on the Main Streets where 99 percent of the population lived. Warren took a pivot in her life to tell that story and transform it into policy and reform.

My interest in writing about Elizabeth began in 2012 when I watched her televised speech at the Democratic National Convention.

As the warm-up to Bill Clinton, she stepped onto the blue stage to thundering applause and chants of *Warren! Warren!* The law professor, for the first time, was running for an elective office, the U.S. Senate seat from Massachusetts. She had staked her claim as a populist, similarly white-knuckled about standing up to the big banks as her favorite president, trust-buster Teddy Roosevelt. That night, she tapped into the post–financial crisis angst with her trademark mantra that rang true for the millions who'd lost their pensions and homes and jobs to a Wall Street free-for-all and felt no one had been held accountable for it: "People feel like the system is rigged against them. And here's the painful part—they're right."[2]

After Warren won her Senate election that year, I started a file that stayed on the corner of my desk for the next few years, crammed with articles and magazines that featured her photo on the cover. By the spring of 2017, she had become a brand-name populist who many had thought would run for president in 2016 and were now eyeing for 2020. My folder had also turned into a bona fide research project, and I was delighted to have a contract to write this book.

I looked forward to meeting people across the country who could give their unique angle of Warren's life as it had crossed theirs. The public sees Elizabeth in front of the camera on cable news, late-night talk shows, and in Senate committee hearings, and in each of those settings she has a message to convey or information to glean and little time to do it. The people I interviewed who encountered Elizabeth in various passages of her life have a longer view and described her as energetic, open, warm, genuine, unaffected, and kind. Her leadership style, according to those she mentored into law careers or who worked on her staff, seemed to fit the profile of the female leader—relational, collaborative, and encouraging.

In her book *Lean In: Women, Work, and the Will to Lead*, Facebook COO Sheryl Sandberg invited women to reach for more success by acting more like men, leaning in to grab opportunities and negotiate for better salaries. At the same time, however, acting "nice" and "concerned about others" would increase a woman's chances, according to one scholar she mentioned, which put the onus on women to throttle back their authentic selves to serve the biased expectations of men (and some women). That game-playing perpetuates rather than challenges the gender bias embedded in the workplace and in society in general, and Sandberg acknowledged this paradox. Elizabeth Warren is not one to reengineer her focused communication style or tenaciousness in order to adhere to expectations about what is "appropriate" for fighting for an issue.[3]

Since discovering her mission to put her expertise about the financial hardships of the middle class into practice, Warren has never lost the sense of urgency that first gripped her around the issue. She knew that about herself when she entered the Senate in 2013. "I came knowing that large parts of what I understood about how the Senate worked would never work for me," she told *Time* magazine in 2015. "I would not have that kind of time, but more importantly, America's middle class did not have that kind of time."[4] For Elizabeth Warren, the clock is always ticking.

Among the surprises that unfolded in Warren's story was the impact her bankruptcy research had on her evolution as a scholar and, as I frame it, a public intellectual who feels compelled to bring her work to the public square. Writing for general audiences instead of limiting her work to law journals was another form of teaching, which had been her goal since grade school. The more her research taught her about people whose financial peril brought them to the bankruptcy courts, the more she peeled away her own assumptions about America's most indebted and down-and-out. Her work changed her to the point that she shifted from a Republican to a card-carrying Democrat.

Another transformational piece of her story goes back to coming of age in the early and mid-1960s. Elizabeth was too young to be influenced and empowered by the feminism that was only beginning to sprout. Instead, like so many of her generation, she struggled with the clash between the Betty Crocker model of ideal female wholeness and her inner spark to get out in the world and try something. I found that struggle just as telling about who Elizabeth Warren is as the tale of her rise from a dusty, financially strapped Oklahoma childhood to academic and political prominence. She had to find her own way through those critical years when her heart was pulled in two directions with equal, searing force. There were no easy answers or foolproof road maps, only choices to make and the tenacity to work through them.

At about seven o'clock on February 7, 2017, a handful of senators were debating about President Donald Trump's nominee for U.S. attorney general, their colleague Jeff Sessions.[5] It had been a long day amid fevered weeks of arguments by Democrats against Sessions's confirmation, recalling his record of suppressing black votes when he was attorney general in Alabama in the 1980s and '90s.

That evening, Elizabeth Warren stood at the podium dressed in one of her signature buttonless suit jackets, this one blue, with collar slightly up, over a black top and pants. Twenty minutes into her talk, she began to read a letter written in 1986 by Coretta Scott King, Martin Luther King Jr.'s widow, to the Senate Judicial Committee. That year, the committee was deliberating about confirming Jeff Sessions as a federal judge, and Mrs. King's letter expressed her brief but pointed reasons against his confirmation. One sentence stated, "Mr. Sessions has used the awesome power of his office to chill the free exercise of the vote by black citizens."

Republican Senator Steve Daines from Montana, who was presiding as the chair, knocked his gavel three times to stop Warren from speaking. "The Senator is reminded that it is a violation of Rule Nineteen of the standing rules of the Senate to impute to another senator, or senators," he said, "any conduct or motive unworthy or becoming [sic] a senator" (the rule reads "unbecoming").

The process around Rule Nineteen is two strikes, you're out. First you get a warning, and if your "insults" to a fellow senator continue, you get told to sit down. "The rule," explained retired Senator Barbara Mikulski, "dated back to the early 1900s, when men used to come to the Senate floor, if they were working late, either drunk or making terrible, insulting comments about another senator's family, usually a spouse." They would nearly come to fistfights, she said, and this rule was made to calm down that kind of behavior. "Elizabeth was not carrying on in the way the rule prohibited," Mikulski said, "but was just speaking."[6]

"This is a reminder," Daines said, "you stated that a sitting senator is a disgrace to the department of justice." That was a line from a 1986 speech by the late Senator Ted Kennedy that she had read earlier in her remarks. Like King, Kennedy had denounced

Sessions's nomination for a judgeship. Daines explained that the rule applied to any type of words, from quotes to articles or other materials. "The senator is warned," he said.

"So can I continue with Coretta Scott King's letter?" she asked.

"The senator may continue."

Elizabeth kept reading, and about twenty-five minutes later was stopped again. Republican Senate Majority Leader Mitch McConnell claimed that Warren had violated the rule, citing a line from Mrs. King's letter. "The senator has impugned the motives and conduct of our colleague from Alabama, as warned by the chair," he said.

"The senator will take her seat," Daines said.

She appealed his ruling, and over the next hour and a half, the Republican-majority Senate voted to silence her.

After the tally, McConnell stood at a microphone and stated, "She was warned. She was given an explanation. Nevertheless, she persisted."

Overnight, *Nevertheless, she persisted* became the motto for the new era of solidarity over women's rights ignited by the women's marches that had taken place a month earlier. The rallying cry sounded coast to coast, producing thousands of tweets posted under the new hashtags #ShePersisted and #LetLizSpeak.

Elizabeth created her own viral sensation after the procedural vote that night, reading King's letter outside the Senate chamber in a live Facebook video. "The Republicans took away my right to read this letter on the floor," she posted, "so I'm right outside, reading it now." By the next day, the video had more than six million views.[7] After another full day of debate, the Senate confirmed Sessions's nomination in a 52 to 47 vote.

The phrase that will always be identified with Elizabeth Warren resonates with the vitality of women's determination, but what can easily fade is the fact that the words were conceived in a debate about race. Elizabeth Warren's work on race, which has been substantial in terms of the amount of research and writing she has done about the financial oppression of African American and Latinx people (as much as her writing on the economic straits of women), is often overlooked by those who profile and interview her. In an era of bitter immigration battles, exacerbated by a president who foments racial divisiveness, Warren's understanding of race is perhaps one of her strongest tools as a twenty-first-century leader.

The Great Recession still lingered for many when Massachusetts voters sent Elizabeth Warren to the Senate. She told them she would be their champion, and year by year, her consistent focus on issues that impact the household budgets of working people has strengthened her perception as that champion. Warren's grasp of the role of race in America is joined by her knowledge of working people's economic struggles and the forces that impact them, gleaned from a thirty-year-long career of scholarship and teaching in the law that focused on bankruptcy. People were angry at the big banks, whose risk-taking cost them their pensions, homes, and jobs, and Elizabeth became a focal point for answers, offered up in plainspoken prose.

She knows the kitchen table struggles because she lived them, and that story of a populist's evolution begins in Oklahoma.

ELIZABETH WARREN

HER FIGHT. HER WORK. HER LIFE.

1

HARDWARE, BISCUITS, AND FITTING IN THE SOIL

Evening and the flat land,
Rich and sombre and always silent;

…

Against all this, Youth,
Flaming like the wild roses…

—WILLA CATHER, "PRAIRIE SPRING"[1]

She was lucky to be tall for her age.

As a thirteen-year-old starting ninth grade at Northwest Classen High School in Oklahoma City, Elizabeth Ann Herring had skipped sixth grade and gone straight from the kiddie desks to the midcentury modern splendor of Oklahoma City's newest high school. She was as tall as her mother and not particularly confident about her looks, but the girl her family called Betsy, who grew up in Norman,

the university town twenty miles south, became a teenage freshman known as Liz in the fall of 1962.

The nearly three thousand students at Northwest Classen were
taunted by some as "silkies" for living in this middle- and upper-class
quadrant of the city where some homes had swimming pools and
lawns manicured by hired help.[2] Heading to the main doors every
morning, students passed the school mascot, a suit of armor complete
with feathered helmet and jousting lance, symbol of the Northwest
Classen Knights and serving as a daily reminder, perhaps, of the
fights ahead. Liz signed on to several groups that first year, starting
with the Cygnets pep club, which involved a hazing ritual designed as
the ultimate teenage girl's humiliation: newcomers wore mismatch-
ing clothes, colored socks, flats, and no makeup on pledge day. She
also joined the Junior Classical League, open to students taking Latin
and famous for the annual Roman banquet where the wrists of first-
year "slaves" were bound in white plastic chains as they served trays of
fruit. As a member of the Courtesy Club, she would spend every other
Monday playing hostess at school events. Her successful audition to
assess how well her personality, diction, and voice control would play
over the speaker system landed her in the Announcer's Club as one
of several who would read the school announcements every morning.
By the end of the first week, she had balanced out all these frills
by joining the debate team on the Forensic League. Joining up with
activities seemed a surefire way for a new kid to fit in.[3]

Northwest Classen had opened just nine years earlier and was
still considered the best high school in the city, a "dream school,"
as administrators called it.[4] The most qualified teachers, most with
master's degrees, had been pulled in from schools all over the city.

With seating arranged by alphabet, Liz spent the next four years sitting side by side in the same advanced-track classes with Katrina Harry. They went to school plays and football games together, ate hamburgers at the local drive-ins, and giggled over the corny dating advice a panel of senior boys gave in one of their family life classes. Their friendship sailed through those four years without a hitch, in spite of the one thing upon which they never agreed—politics. "She was very conservative back then," Katrina said. "I was from a family of Democrats—my dad was the campaign manager for U.S. Senator and former Oklahoma Governor Robert Kerr. Liz was not in favor of Lyndon Johnson's Great Society or welfare or any of that and was all over me for four years about the 'socialist' friends I kept. We joked around about it, and I called her an ice-cold Republican."[5] Liz was coming of age in a family that never discussed partisan politics, and when she reflected on her parents' party affiliation years later, she believed they had probably been populist Democrats, fond of President Franklin Delano Roosevelt. Two of her older brothers, however, were "dyed-in-the-wool Republicans." She recalled that her mother was a poll worker and brought her along to voting places each Election Day. Her first memory of someone talking about politics was from the time she was six years old, listening to her grandmother, Hannie Reed, talk about the Great Depression. Hannie said, "Franklin Roosevelt made it safe to put money in banks, and he did a lot of other things, too."

The politics of Oklahoma were undergoing a major shift during Elizabeth's teenage years. Democrats had ruled the state since statehood in 1907, but in 1952, Oklahomans began voting for Republican presidents. With that undercutting of support for the national party,

Democrats began to lose their hold on governorships, starting with the election of Henry Bellmon, the state's first Republican governor, the year Liz started high school. From there, Republicans began winning U.S. Senate and House races as well as more seats in the state legislature. Since that pivotal time in the 1950s, Oklahoma has made a complete turnaround from a Democratic stronghold with a state motto of *Labor omnia vincit*, "Labor conquers all," to its status today as one of the most conservative states in the country.[6]

Coming of age in the south in the 1960s also meant witnessing the civil rights movement firsthand. In 1963, while the nation was tuned in to the violence in Birmingham, Alabama, where Commissioner Bull Connor set police dogs and fire hoses on peaceful black protesters and Martin Luther King Jr. was sent to jail, desegregation was underway in some of Oklahoma City's restaurants and hotels. Clara Luper, a black history teacher at one of the city's segregated black high schools and adviser for the city's NAACP Youth Council, had famously organized lunch counter sit-ins with black children at the Katz Drug Store downtown in 1958. After her success in desegregating the store, she led many other peaceful protests, including one at an amusement park just two miles up the road from Liz Herring's high school. The Wedgewood Village Amusement Park had been closed to blacks since it opened in 1957, and in the summer of 1963, Clara set up protests with white and black pro-integration marchers.[7] The protests ultimately convinced the owner to open the gates to blacks that August, the same month as the March on Washington. By the time Liz graduated in 1966, the nation had seen the bombing of Birmingham's Sixteenth Street Baptist Church; the assassination of President John F. Kennedy; the murders of Mississippi civil rights workers Chaney, Goodman, and Schwerner; the passage of the Civil Rights Act; and the Selma to Montgomery March.

Integration came to the Oklahoma City school district during Liz's senior year, at least among the faculty, as announced in a local paper: "Youngsters in five all-white schools will find a Negro teacher on the faculty for the first time. Two Negro schools also will have their first white teachers."[8] The new teacher at her school, William Wedgeworth, taught industrial arts and advised the Amateur Radio Club and Electronics Club. Liz did not have Mr. Wedgeworth as a teacher, since the shop class he taught was for boys only.

One of the faculty who made a lasting impression on Liz was her sophomore English teacher, Judy Garrett. Her self-possessed mix of calm and confidence fed Liz's desire to be a teacher and came through as they read *A Tale of Two Cities* and *Julius Caesar* and listened to Mrs. Garrett's story about getting a glimpse of the Beatles during a European trip.[9] "Liz was really young for high school," Judy said, "but she was probably the brightest student I've ever taught. She was a little bulldog-type person, always questioning; she was so far ahead of the others. It was delightful to have her in class because she always kept me on my toes."[10]

Judy figured that because Liz was younger, she may not have felt like she "fit in the soil," but she stood out academically and was a strong communicator, always making her point in logical sequence—one, two, three. No irony is lost on the fact that Judy, who gave Liz advice about being her own person, was forced by school policy to quit when she became pregnant. "You could not wear pants," she said, "and you could not show that you were pregnant. That really sums up the era."[11]

The Herrings lived one mile away from Northwest Classen, just a block within the dividing line that put them in the school district. The two-story, colonial-inspired house on Northwest Twenty-Fifth Street looked at least twice as big as the house they had left in Norman, with two white pillars at the doorway standing on a set of semicircular, red-brick steps. It was an attractive house with white paint and black shutters that matched the steeply pitched roof. Houses along the block did not follow any particular style—a colonial could stand next to a stocky house built of bricks from the red clay soil of the region—but the front yards were roomy and well-kept. Her high school friend Joe Pryor, who later made a career in real estate in Oklahoma City, recalled Liz's neighborhood as lower middle class. Not as upscale as other neighborhoods around the high school, but not working class either.[12]

Defining the middle class has never been an exact science, but descriptions usually revolve around income. While economists have different ideas about the boundary lines, one popular formula puts the middle in a range between the poorest 20 percent at the bottom and the wealthiest 20 percent at the top. Liz's parents had their own criteria, and regardless of how strapped they were financially, they always considered themselves middle class. "For them, the distinction was they used good English, and they didn't say 'ain't,'" the adult Liz, known as Elizabeth, said many years later. "Those were important indicia of middle-classness of my folks."

Liz later described her family as living on the "ragged edge of the middle class," at times barely getting by.[13] "We grew up on the same path," said her classmate Joe Mallonee, who lived a few blocks away. "The homes in those neighborhoods ranged from small two-bedrooms with no garage to mansions. Where we lived by the mall, it looked nice from the outside, but we didn't have the money to pay the bills."[14] The mall was Shepherd Plaza, the city's first enclosed shopping center, which opened just a block and a half away from the Herrings' house when Liz was a sophomore. She learned how to drive in that parking lot, weaving her dad's old Studebaker up and down the rows.[15] Joe felt a kinship with Liz through their need to start working early on. He stashed money away to buy nice shirts, and she bought fabric to sew her own blouses, sleeveless pullover jumpers, and dresses. "Kids like me and Liz," he said, "were always trying to keep up."[16] For Liz, working early on meant starting to wait tables at her Aunt Alice's restaurant at age thirteen, sewing dresses for her aunts throughout high school, and keeping up the babysitting she'd begun in Norman as a nine-year-old.

The Herrings were Methodists in heavily Baptist, Bible Belt Oklahoma. Liz's mother taught Sunday school at the May Avenue United Methodist Church near the high school, and the churches, like the schools, were either white or black. Northwest Classen students only interacted with black students when they played against them in basketball, baseball, football—or debate. "Oklahoma City had a large black population," said Karl Johnson, Liz's debate partner for three years, "but in our part of the city, they were virtually invisible. They literally lived on the other side of the tracks."[17] As debaters, however, Karl and Liz had regular encounters with black students. "We debated those kids from Douglass High School and made friends with them," he said.[18] They also debated black students in out-of-state tournaments, and Karl felt that those experiences outside the boundaries of their white middle-class school and neighborhood broadened them in a way that nothing else in high school could have.

Joining the debate team was a commitment to hours of research and practice every afternoon after classes. Divided into two-person teams, debaters dealt with two levels of competition—first between their own teams to see who was good enough to represent the school in tournaments, and next as competitors in those tournaments. The two top teams at Northwest Classen were a mix of both genders—from Liz's sophomore through senior years, she and Karl Johnson made up the A team, which had the most wins, and Jeanette Yeager and Joe Pryor were the B team.[19] Their coach, school counselor Dick Mitchell, was a demanding and respected mentor. "He didn't suffer fools," Joe Pryor said, "and you knew you had earned your spot. You won on merit, nothing else. We all wanted to please him."[20]

Liz made the move from novice debater in her freshman year to the top team in her sophomore year. During her first year in debate, the top team had been Karl Johnson and Joe Pryor. But Liz had stood out and made a strong impression on Karl. "At the end of the year, I had to do something very difficult," he said, "and tell Joe that I wanted to be Liz's colleague for the next three years. Our skills meshed perfectly."[21] The fact that all these freshmen were the best debaters on the team revealed that Liz's incoming group was exceptionally bright, and Liz's younger age was never a factor. "She was our equal," Karl said, "and we all gained a lot of confidence over four years."[22]

Joe remembered Liz as very self-directed, unlike himself, admittedly a typically distracted male teenager. "Two things separated Liz as a top debater," he said. "She was intense about her research and outstanding at rebuttal. She could take apart an argument extremely well."[23] Fifty years later, when he saw her on television questioning someone during a senate committee hearing using meticulous research and always steering the process back to her exact points, he recognized the same person from debate class. He also recalled that her successes never went to her head. As she and Karl racked up trophies from tournament wins year to year, she "never tried to act superior," he said, "but she certainly could have."[24] The teams often studied in the main library downtown, which held all the political and policy magazines like the *Economist* and *U.S. News and World Report*. Even during those hours, out of sight of Mr. Mitchell or anyone else who might have been keeping score, Liz kept up the pace. "If you had a discussion with her," Joe said, "you better bring the goods."[25]

Debate challenged and stretched them. "You got to travel to meets with kids in speech, debate, and drama who were at the top of their class, very smart and talented kids," Karl said. "The entire experience was formative, life changing. It made my life what it is."[26] Now a managing partner in Albuquerque, New Mexico, where he practices Indian law and commercial law, Karl started his career as a legal aid attorney on the Navajo Reservation and then joined the faculty of the University of New Mexico School of Law. The spark for teaching and practicing Indian law came in high school, when he took a bus ride through the Deep South to attend a debate tournament. In their junior year, he and Liz had an opportunity to go to a major debate tournament in Miami Beach, Florida, but since they couldn't get an adult chaperone to sign on, Liz couldn't go. Karl teamed up with a senior, Andrew Mason, instead, and even though they didn't win, the trip was cathartic for Karl.

Their Greyhound bus stopped at every station between Oklahoma City and Miami Beach, and Karl witnessed Jim Crow society at its most pervasive. As the son of a prosperous general manager of a car dealership in Oklahoma City, his debate trips were the only occasions to leave his upper-middle-class neighborhood or high school to witness the stark realities of segregation. "It was an absolute eye-opener," he said.[27] He came back a changed person, more radicalized than he had already become under the influence of the civil rights movement and Vietnam War. Liz did not undergo the same radicalization as her close friend Karl during those years, but that did not mean that her youthful conservative mind-set was fixed and inflexible. Through the next decades of her further education and development as a teacher and scholar, her outlook evolved.

Forensic debates, unlike the "debates" between political candidates aired on TV, are tightly structured and demand that both sides respond to each point made by the opposition. In the pre-word-processing or laptop era, debaters showed up with stacks of index cards containing quotes from government documents, journal articles, and other sources to draw upon as evidence in their arguments and rebuttals. While listening to an opposition team member, they took flowchart notes on legal pads to track the points they needed to address. Preparing for competition meant learning that year's issue inside out, since they had to be ready to either defend the topic or argue against it in any given tournament. Then, like now, four years of debate wires a teenager for logic, for looking at all sides of an issue, for backing up what she says, for the quick wits of thinking on her feet, and for speaking with impeccable clarity.

The national debate topics those years—free trade, socialized medicine, nuclear weapons—allowed them to delve into the nuts and bolts of policy issues that are still hot topics today, and their conversations revolved around politics and current events. "Debate," Joe Pryor said, "got us out of the confines of our place and into the world that was waiting for us."[28]

Being on the top team didn't ensure that Liz could make every tournament or student congress. Tight finances at home sometimes put a wrench in her plans, but very few of her classmates knew it. "Most of the students on the debate team came from families where the dad was a professional," said Joe Mallonee.[29] For them, money wasn't an issue when it came to meals and lodging at out-of-town competitions. But Liz's situation was different, since her dad worked retail at Montgomery Ward and earned a lower-middle-class salary. Joe recalled that Liz had to miss debate tournaments at times because she couldn't afford the hotel room.

Studying policy issues did not leave much time for a social life, but the debate team also delivered on that front. In her first year, Liz dated another member of the team, Jim Warren, a seventeen-year-old junior. Jim was a math whiz who got top grades in everything, worked on the school council, and was a member of the Key Club, a group that did community service around the city. They seemed to balance each other—Liz was positive and energetic, always in a good mood, and Jim was more subdued. Karl described Jim as the quiet type, a salt-of-the-earth, great guy who happened to be really smart—"burning hot smart in physics and math."[30] While he was very smart, Karl recalled, his persuasive skills weren't as strong because he was a little more withdrawn. "His debate was heavy on logic and short on emotion," Karl said. Regardless of Jim's slightly inferior gifts of persuasion, his math prowess would land him a very interesting—even historic—job in the years to come.

Liz didn't consider herself pretty, she wrote in *A Fighting Chance*, but her yearbook photos say otherwise.[31] Her brunette bangs drew attention to her light eyes, her smile was bright and genuine, and her overall expression was cute, charming, and attractive. She experimented with her hair, sometimes growing it to her shoulders, but never wore it in a stiff early 1960s "do" that was popular with many of the girls. She sewed her own clothes and didn't fuss over her looks. "She wasn't a froufrou girl," Katrina said. "If she remembered to put a lipstick in her purse, that would really be something."[32]

Since Jim lived four doors down from Katrina, Liz would meet him there and spend a lot of time at Katrina's house. "They were a perfect couple, intellectually matched," Katrina said.[33] But the romance didn't survive long. When Jim became a senior the next year, he made two changes—wearing black-rimmed glasses and breaking up with Liz. "He was the first boy I'd ever dated—and the first to dump me," Liz said.[34] The breakup, along with the family troubles she would endure in high school, may have brought Mrs. Garrett's Shakespeare, at least one line of *Julius Caesar*, closer to home: "This was the most unkindest cut of all."

Liz and Karl won a national tournament their senior year, bringing home a tall, gold-cup trophy for first place in cross-examination debate at the Bellaire Tournament in Houston. In her four years at Classen, she discovered her talent for fighting with words, becoming, as she put it, "the anchor on the debate team."[35] The competitive pressure and intellectual challenge taught her that she had the self-discipline to master complex subjects on her own. Before she graduated, she understood that losing an intellectual battle during a round didn't mean she was beaten—the greater lesson was about challenging herself and never giving up. "Debate let me stretch as far as I could go," she said.[36] Her wins gave her confidence, something she could take with her and build upon, unlike the trophies behind glass that remain to this day in the Northwest Classen lobby, gathering dust.[37]

As much as Liz came to know the rewards of being masterfully prepared, she also learned how to stay calm under fire and use a loss as an opportunity to be better next time. That resiliency showed up on both sides of her family line, starting with her parents, who met during tough times in Oklahoma.

Liz's parents were both from Wetumka, a town in Eastern Oklahoma with a population of about twenty-one hundred in 1928, the year they met. Pauline was fifteen, and Donald was four years older, a self-trained pilot with a passion for airplanes who worked summers at Herring Hardware, the family business. Elizabeth described her teenage mother as a girl who played the piano and loved to sing, "a whisper-thin, dark-haired beauty who was lively and funny."[38]

Donald married Pauline, his "Polly," in January 1932, smack in the throes of the Dust Bowl and Great Depression. Oklahoma felt the brunt in decimated crops, job losses, and bankruptcies, all of which changed lives in every corner of a small town like Wetumka. In the early 1930s, half the state's teachers were not paid, and the Wetumka school term was cut back to a mere four and a half months.[39] Drought dried up the fields, and locals talked about winds whipping the dusty soil into dunes so high along the barbed-wire fences that cattle could walk right over them. Even though the worst dust storms were in the Oklahoma Panhandle, towns in the east also had their share, like the big duster that hit Wetumka in April 1935 and created a visibility of zero that shut down the town.[40]

Wetumka did its best to keep spirits up. In 1933, with hotels closing down and businesses going bankrupt, one of the Ford dealers held a draw to give away a new automobile to boost community morale. In front of a big crowd gathered on Main Street, a girl named Miss Geneva was selected to dip her hand into the hopper and pull out the winner, someone who turned out to be in dire straits and did not own a car. A couple of years later, a new building project put a few electricians back to work to extend wiring out to a farm on the outskirts of town. The property was selected as a Civilian Conservation Corps (CCC) camp for young black men, built as part of President Franklin D. Roosevelt's New Deal to create jobs during the Depression. The CCC program put millions of men to work on environmental projects around the country and was considered one of the most successful work-relief programs of the New Deal. As one of three segregated CCC camps in Oklahoma, the Wetumka camp put the men to work planting trees, reseeding farmland, and building hundreds of miles of erosion-resistant farm terraces. Since the town was segregated and workers had no recreational options in the camp, the downtown Nusho Theater movie house closed the doors to everyone but the black CCC workers on Thursday nights. Years later, the CCC site became a German POW camp where about four hundred German prisoners lived and were sent out to work on Wetumka farms.[41]

Elizabeth described the Great Depression as a "constant presence" in her family's story, an era that brought trouble from without and within.[42] Her Aunt Bee told her about the day her local bank failed and drew a crowd to the locked front doors. Bee, who was still single at the time, was living with her elderly parents and bringing home a salary from her secretarial job. Her father, Liz's grandfather, Harry Reed, lost everything he'd saved from his lifetime of construction work, and even after Bee's pay was cut in half, it was all they had to survive on. Bee didn't approve of her mother's habit of using their scarce cash to feed the jobless men who appeared at the back door every morning. Across the country, millions of men and thousands of women took to the rails in search of work and stopped in small towns along the way to earn a meal or two by working odd jobs. Elizabeth's grandmother, Bethania "Hannie" Reed, never turned away these strangers but instead doled out biscuits and plates of grits or whatever else she had on hand. Bee fought her on it and became so frustrated that one day, she stood down her mother at the stove and yelled, "Stop feeding these bums! We don't have enough for ourselves!" That outburst haunted Liz's Aunt Bee from that day, and decades later at her mother's deathbed, she tearfully told her how sorry she was for it.[43]

Through this time, Herring Hardware stayed afloat thanks to an inventory as diverse as a general merchandise store. Farm machinery sales may have been down, but people stopped in for other necessities like furniture, rugs, paint, horse-drawn buggies and wagons, refrigerators and stoves, radios, saddles, harnesses, kitchen appliances, tires, and even caskets.[44] The store had been in the family since 1910 when Liz's great-grandfather, John Herring, bought Lumley's Hardware. Known to everyone in town as "Uncle Jack," John saw a lot of the world before settling in Eastern Oklahoma. Born in Cornwall, England, he came to the United States with his parents when he was six years old.[45] While he and his wife raised their family in Billings, Montana, he traveled the world as a sales representative for the International Harvester Company. After moving to Wetumka, he got into the competitive hardware business, joined the Wetumka Masons, and became active in town affairs such as directing the cornet band that entertained the town with outdoor concerts. In 1920, he opened a second store about ninety-five miles east of Wetumka in Sallisaw for his son Frank to run.

John's father, also named John Herring (Liz's paternal great-great grandfather), was born in Tintagel, a Cornwall town on the cliffs overlooking the Atlantic that has held a magical spell on the British since the twelfth century. Around 1135, Geoffrey of Monmouth released the *History of the Kings of Britain*, introducing the legend of King Arthur and the name of his birthplace, Tintagel.[46]

Great-grandfather John Herring's son Grant—Elizabeth's paternal grandfather—ran Herring Hardware in Wetumka and extended credit to his impoverished customers throughout the Depression. Liz grew up hearing her father's stories of how many of these towns-folk left Oklahoma and headed west, lured by advertisements for jobs in California's lush agricultural regions.[47] Many may have tried to erase the Dust Bowl misery they left behind, but some never forgot their roots—or their debts. "Twenty years later," Elizabeth wrote, "my grandfather would still get an occasional envelope with a few twenty-dollar bills and a handwritten note: 'Grant, we finally got ahead a little. Put this on my account, and let me know if I owe you more.'"[48]

By the time Liz's dad was thirteen, Herring's was the largest hardware store in town.[49] The oil boom was still on, bringing some stability to the state's economy during the Depression. A few years later when Donald was dating Pauline, his grandfather John got lucky with some land he'd bought in Oklahoma City. Wells were cropping up all over the capitol since the Oklahoma City Oil Field opened within the city limits in the spring of 1930. In June, the Mid-Texas Petroleum company completed building an oil and gas well on John Herring's property with prospects of producing twenty-two thousand barrels a day and tapping into eighty million cubic feet of natural gas.[50] After Mid-Texas No. 1 was up and running, a newspaper in Sallisaw, where John's son Frank (Elizabeth's great-uncle) ran the second hardware store, reported, "Frank Herring stated this week that while many of his father's friends had felt that he had made a bad purchase when he came into possession of the Oklahoma City lots, the senior Mr. Herring now has the last laugh—and the best."[51]

Mid-Texas No. 1 was one of the 870 producing wells that dotted the city landscape in 1932, the peak year for the Oklahoma City Oil Field. That year, the city's wells produced a combined sixty-seven million barrels, and the field remained one of the most productive in the country for the next forty years.[52]

Liz's father, Donald Herring, was studying engineering at Oklahoma A&M College in Stillwater when he married Pauline Reed in 1932. One hundred miles northwest of Wetumka, the university kept him away from home except for summers, when he came back to the family and his job at Herring Hardware. For years, he had been working at the store during school vacation days and summers, learning the ropes of retail commerce from his father, manager Grant Herring. In a small town like Wetumka, everyone knew the families who ran the stores and businesses and political life. Pauline's father, Harry Gunn Reed, who had come south from Illinois, was a builder who had begun putting up small houses and one-room schoolhouses when the region was still Indian Territory. His wife, Bethania, a native of Missouri who came to the area in a covered wagon as a teenager, raised their large family in which Pauline was the youngest.

Harry Reed's grandfather, Rev. Joseph H. Reed, was a Methodist minister and Illinois state representative who had migrated to Illinois from Ohio in 1838 with his wife, seven children, and parents in a covered wagon to stake out a homestead. He was forty-five when he set up his family in Madison Township in the southeastern section of the state and is credited for naming Richland County after suggesting it be named after the county in Ohio from which he and many others came.[53] Joseph, Elizabeth's maternal great-great-grandfather, was a member of the Whig Party when he served in the Illinois General Assembly from 1845 to 1847, not far behind another Whig, Abraham Lincoln, who finished his last term in the assembly in 1842.[54]

Pauline was studying at the teacher's college in Ada, about fifty miles from home, while Donald was at A&M. They were in love and planned to marry, but Donald's family rejected the match.[55] As Elizabeth later described the situation, Pauline's family included Native American ancestors on both her mother's and father's sides, and the Herrings "made it clear that they did not approve. They looked down on my mother and her family, and when my father announced that he wanted to marry my mother, his parents were adamantly opposed."[56] That deep-running enmity crushed any chance the couple had of a wedding, so during spring semester of 1932, they left for Holdenville, twenty miles away, to be married by a Methodist minister in a ceremony witnessed by two people, including the minister's wife. When they came home, their elopement made the *Wetumka Gazette*:

> The marriage of Donald Herring and Miss Pauline Reed, two of Wetumka's most popular young people, came as a surprise to many of their friends when they returned from Holdenville late Saturday afternoon and announced their marriage.[57]

When Elizabeth was very young, she learned about her parents' elopement by pestering her mother about her wedding dress. She relayed that conversation in an interview for the *New Yorker*:

> I said to my mother, "What did your wedding dress look like? Tell me about your wedding dress."
>
> And my mother stiffened up and said, "I didn't have one." I couldn't imagine how you couldn't have one. And I couldn't leave this alone and I could remember asking—even though you're asking something that's going to upset your mother—so I'd ask again... "So, was Aunt Bea [sic] your maid of honor, or was Aunt Max your maid of honor, or did you pick Aunt Alice?" Because she had these three sisters and I thought, What a quandary! What a problem! How do you pick? And she said, none of them. And finally

my mother said to me, "Your Daddy and I loved each other very, very much, but we couldn't get married, so we ran away and got married, and we didn't have our family with us."[58]

The Herring and Reed families never mended their rift and, as Elizabeth recalled, were rarely seen in the same room again, even though they continued to live in the same small town of roughly two thousand people. "As kids, we got it: There was Daddy's family and there was Mother's family," she wrote. "We saw Mother's family all the time. But visits with Daddy's family were infrequent, planned long in advance, and always very stiff."[59] The situation robbed Pauline of the embrace of her husband's family, but it never stifled the Reeds from talking about their Native American ancestry. Liz and her brothers grew up listening to their aunts, uncles, and grandparents tell stories about how the grandfolks met in Indian Territory and had Cherokee and Delaware heritage. Those ancestral claims surfaced during Elizabeth's Senate campaign in 2012, when her opponent, Scott Brown, and others accused her of using her minority status to get jobs in academia. That story is told in a later chapter, but the background of family claims to Native American heritage, particularly among Oklahomans, sheds light on why Elizabeth stood her ground to defend her family's stories.

The history of the region has made white claims of Native American ancestry especially prevalent in Oklahoma. President Andrew Jackson's 1830 Indian Removal Act began the forced migration of the Choctaw, Seminole, Creek, Chickasaw, and Cherokee from their lands in the southeast to the region west of the Mississippi that had begun to be called Indian Territory. These tribes were known collectively as the Five Civilized Tribes for their assimilation of some aspects of European/American culture and intermarriage with whites. The Cherokee removal, known as the Trail of Tears, in which four thousand Cherokees died, was followed by another movement of tribes who, already forced into Nebraska and Kansas, were removed once again and sent south to Indian country. In fact, as sociologist Laurence French wrote, "the Trail of Tears was played out dozens of times during the nineteenth century with other tribes that were eventually removed to Indian Territory."[60]

In the late 1800s, railroad expansions and the discovery of oil in Oklahoma Territory created a burning push for statehood. Oklahoma became the largest oil-producing region in the world, and in 1890, the federal government divided the region into Indian Territory and Oklahoma Territory, with Indian Territory reduced to slightly more than half of the eastern section of the original area. In the land rush of 1899 (still before statehood), homesteaders staked their claims across the nearly two million acres that the government had opened to settlement in what were called the Unassigned Lands, nonpopulated areas that the Creek and Seminole Indians ceded to the government after the Civil War. (Those who cheated the rush by crossing the border before the gunshot that launched the official run were labeled as "sooners," which gave Oklahoma the nickname the Sooner State.[61])

Native American leaders tried to avoid joint statehood by convening the Sequoyah Convention and drawing up a constitution for their own state. The U.S. Congress refused to consider the statehood bills advanced on their behalf and instead confirmed the joining of the two territories into the state of Oklahoma in 1907.[62] The Native Americans left an indelible mark with their Sequoyah Constitution, however, since many elements of it were incorporated into the Oklahoma Constitution. According to the Oklahoma Historical Society, the two shared many similarities, including "an underlying Populist distrust of elected officials."[63]

This history reveals why many Oklahomans share stories of Native American heritage, probably more than those from any other state. Census figures estimate that 4.5 million Americans identify themselves as Native Americans or Alaskan Natives, yet only two million are actually enrolled in tribes.[64] Since the Cherokee Nation is the largest tribe in the country, with the leadership of its 355,000 citizens located in its capitol in Tahlequah, Oklahoma, family stories of Cherokee ancestry are the most common.[65] This is not to say that any such claim is not true, but Cherokee membership is limited to those whose ancestors appear on specific rolls that were drawn up in the nineteenth and twentieth centuries. In the 2012 Senate campaign controversy over Elizabeth Warren's claims of Cherokee heritage, Elizabeth never said that she or anyone else in her family had tribal membership, a separate issue from heritage.[66]

In a 2012 article in *Indian Country Today*, Gene Norris, a genealogist with the Cherokee Heritage Center, explained, "When the U.S. federal government took the U.S. federal population Census for 1900, Indian Territory was divided into two sections— non-Indian population and Indian population—[and] 61 percent of the Cherokee Nation's population were not legally considered Cherokee but U.S. citizens who had migrated from other states such as Arkansas, living in the Cherokee Nation." In the same article,

Myra Vanderpool Gormley, a certified genealogist specializing in Cherokee and Native American history, stated that there are "various Indian rolls from about 1885 that identify Indians by tribe and name. Most of them pertain to Indians living on reservations and not in the general population." These rolls include the Final Rolls of Citizens and Freedmen of the Five Civilized Tribes in Indian Territory, a roll covering 1898–1906 commonly known as the Dawes Rolls, and the 1924 Baker Roll of the Eastern Band of the Cherokee, which was a compilation of several older rolls.[67]

The editors of *Indian Country Today* wrote that "oral history does carry some weight in genealogical circles,"[68] and genealogist Megan Smolenyak Smolenyak (the double name is correct) explained in the *Atlantic* that as an Oklahoma native, Elizabeth Warren's family stories were "wildly common."[69]

By the time Donald Herring registered for the draft in 1940, he and Pauline had two boys, Don Reed and John, ages six and three. They had survived the Dust Bowl 1930s, and Elizabeth would grow up hearing her mother's stories about raising a baby during those years. She would put Don Reed to sleep and drape a wet sheet over his crib to protect him from the dust. When she came back a couple of hours later, Elizabeth said, "the sheet would be dry and stiff and covered with caked mud. And that's how they lived."

By 1940, the leading sentiment among Americans was to stay out of the war raging in Europe, and congressmen had come to blows on the House floor over whether or not the country should institute a draft in peacetime.[70] Germany had invaded Poland, Holland, Belgium, France, Denmark, and Norway and was bombing London when the Selective Service and Training Act passed and was signed by President Franklin Roosevelt in September 1940. At the signing ceremony he said, "We must and will marshal our great potential strength to fend off war from our shores. We must and will prevent our land from becoming a victim of aggression."[71]

Donald, who loved flying, hoped to join the army air force, but at nearly twenty-nine, the army considered him too old to be a fighter pilot, according to Elizabeth's recollection of the family story. He was selected to serve as a flight instructor instead and assigned to the air fields in Muskogee, a larger town in eastern Oklahoma about seventy-five miles northeast of Wetumka.[72]

Throughout the war, the center at Hatbox Field graduated more than thirty-seven hundred pilots, and soldiers at Davis Field were trained for aerial photographic reconnaissance missions. Davis was also the airport where supplies were flown in for nearby Camp Gruber, a massive infantry and tank division training camp where four thousand civilians worked and nearly forty-five thousand troops were trained by the end of the war.[73] After hearing her parents' stories, Elizabeth imagined how her father left for work each morning in his leather flight jacket and trainer's cap tilted to one side. "Daddy loved to fly," she wrote, "and these were good years for them."[74]

The Herrings' third son, David Lee, was born in the last year of the war, and Donald looked forward to putting his years of experience into a new career. "When the war finally ended," Elizabeth recalled, "Daddy desperately wanted a job flying the new passenger planes for one of the fast-growing airlines like TWA or American. But that didn't work out either."[75] Like the army air force in 1940, the airlines were looking for younger men. He and Pauline talked about going home to Wetumka, where he could work at the family store, but when his father told him there wasn't work for him, he scrambled to make another plan. He moved the family to Seminole, a small town about a half hour drive west of Wetumka, where he and a partner set up a car lot. Donald worked in the garage, and his partner wore the dual hats of salesman and front office clerk. Seminole's oil boom days had come and gone years before the war, leaving it once again a small town on the Rock Island line. Donald's bad luck didn't end with his new business—one day, his partner cleared out the cash and left town.

Elizabeth was born not long afterward on August 6, 1949, while her father was working a string of postwar jobs. Whatever riches, if any, Donald's grandfather, John Herring, earned from the oil wells on his property, they did not trickle down to Donald. Elizabeth's brothers were four, twelve, and fifteen, and the family soon settled in Norman, just south of Oklahoma City. The home of the University of Oklahoma since its founding in 1890, Norman was a bustling and growing college town of about twenty-seven thousand people. Donald and Pauline took out a mortgage for a tiny, two-bedroom, blond-brick house on W. Haddock Street, part of a new addition inching its way onto the prairie. Five posts held up the roof overhang to create a narrow porch facing the gravel street, and out back, the garage was converted into a bedroom for the boys. Set on a corner lot, the backyard looked out onto the sparse yards of the other houses down the block and gave plenty of room for the sandbox Donald built with a frame above for a swing to hang upon.

The train tracks were a quarter mile away to the west, a reminder day and night of the Santa Fe Railroad that created the town along its north-south route through Indian Territory. The railroad had already built a station house and plotted out the town at right angles to the tracks in time for the land rush, after which Norman became a town overnight. The tracks also marked the east-west divide that identified the political leanings of the town since its earliest days. The east side, which tended to be Democratic, won the fight over where the county courthouse would be built, and in a hotly contested debate, the Republicans won the battle for the location of the university west of the tracks. By the 1950s, the town and its carefully planted trees had surrounded the Collegiate Gothic university buildings that once stood like giant board game pieces on the flat, naked plain.[76]

Liz, or Betsy as her family called her when she was a little girl, started school eleven blocks from home at Woodrow Wilson Elementary, an imposing red-brick schoolhouse with a Gothic arch entrance. Cherrie Birden, who was three years older than Betsy and principal of the school in the 2000s, recalled that the town was so bursting with postwar children at the time that the overcrowded school held some classes in nearby homes.[77]

Betsy's most memorable year at Wilson was second grade, when she found her calling. At a time when few women worked outside the home, her teacher, Mrs. Lee, was moved one day to have a little talk with her about what girls could do when they grew up. In that brief conversation, Betsy learned for the first time that she had options. "She took me aside to say that, if I wanted to, I could *do something*," Elizabeth wrote. The idea percolated inside her for weeks, and later that school year, she strode up to Mrs. Lee's desk and declared that she would be a teacher, like her. Mrs. Lee said, "Yes, Miss Betsy, you can." Mrs. Lee didn't leave it at that but instead gave her a chance to try things out by letting her work with the lower-level reading group. She found herself in the reading corner, surrounded by classmates as they read aloud and listened for her to chime in when they stumbled. The thrill she felt each time she helped someone "get it" lit a fire in her, and from then on, she played teacher every chance she could get with the kids in the neighborhood.[78]

Another who made a lasting impression during her girlhood days seemed to magically snap out of the TV set and onto the front sidewalk of Wilson Elementary. Norman's most famous native son, actor James Garner, paid a visit to see family in the late 1950s and spent some time saying hello to the kids at his old elementary school.[79] Garner's pre-Hollywood name was James Bumgarner, which made him the great-grandson of Levi Briggs, one of the town's most prosperous businessmen in its first decades. Briggs owned whole blocks of Main Street and had a stake in several cotton gins in towns throughout the state.[80] Garner was the dashing star of the TV western *Maverick* at the time, and the sight of him—better yet, the fleeting touch of his hand on her shoulder—made Betsy realize that life held astounding possibilities, even for folks from Norman.[81]

For as long as she could remember, her mother's sister Bessie Amelia, or "Aunt Bee," babysat her and gave her special gifts, like a new dress at the start of every school year. Dresses were for school and church; the rest of the time, Betsy tore around in play clothes that faded in the Oklahoma sun. She was an active girl, carousing with the other kids and her little dog Missy on the lawns of Haddock Street hard enough to break her nose twice.[82] When spring days heated up and school vacation was near, children in tornado country learned the shifts of color that spelled danger in the skies. Watching thunderclouds creep in from the southwest, especially in April and May, sometimes revealed an eerie green cast to the sky—hail and tornado weather. Three tornadoes hit Norman during Betsy's childhood, none of them strong enough to kill or injure anyone but real enough to set the sirens blaring hours after she had gone to sleep.[83] Up in Oklahoma City, forty-one tornadoes would dip down in the fifteen or so years she lived in the state. The worst during her high school days were two category F3 (out of F5) twisters that blasted concrete buildings into ash.[84]

While Betsy grew up in Norman, her two oldest brothers finished school and left for the military, first Don Reed into the air force, and then John after him. David Lee joined the army a few years later after the family moved again. Don Reed would make a career of the air force and fly 285 combat missions in Vietnam, serving in a way his father had dreamed of doing during the Second World War.[85]

Betsy babysat and never tired of talking about becoming a teacher, an idea that riled her mother, who was raised to believe that women who worked were just unfortunate souls who couldn't find a man and settle down. Pauline couldn't make much headway urging her daughter to be more girly, to curl her hair once in a while or play with makeup. She wanted Betsy to get the ridiculous notion of teaching out of her head, since no one in their family had finished college, and besides, a girl's highest goal should be to marry a good man who would give her financial security.[86] The message about a woman's place came through loud and clear, not just during tense conversations with her mother but from everywhere she looked. Women in Norman—except her teachers—were in their kitchens, in church with their families, at the grocery store with their children in hand. The dads were behind the counters at the post office and drugstores or out of sight until they pulled into their driveways at six o'clock. No girl could prevent that message from getting beneath her skin.

Pauline's wish for Betsy's future as a happy, well-married young woman led her to convince Donald that they should move to the city where Betsy could attend an excellent high school. Education, as well as good pronunciation, was one of the family's criteria for being middle class. Betsy was eleven years old when they left Norman for Oklahoma City and started over again. Donald found a job selling carpet at Montgomery Ward, and Pauline sketched out where to plant roses in the front yard of the white two-story house. The old Studebaker stood in the driveway in front of the "new" used station wagon Donald bought for Pauline, the nice family car with air-conditioning and leather seats.[87]

The Shepherd District was a solid step up from their neighborhood in Norman, but within a year, Donald faced another hard knock. Working on the car one day, he suffered a heart attack that put him in the hospital for a week. He was fifty-four years old, and his recovery kept him home long enough to see the bills start to pile up. As the weeks went by, the Herrings fell behind on their car payments and lost the station wagon. When Donald was finally well enough to go back to work, Montgomery Ward downgraded him from his salaried position to a commission-only job selling yard supplies and lawnmowers. His smaller paycheck took a toll on the overstretched family budget, and he and Pauline bickered and fought under the strain.[88]

No one needed to spell out the details for Liz—who now went

by the more grown-up name among everyone at school—to understand that things were falling apart. Bill collectors called, and her mom cried in the kitchen and behind her bedroom door. One day, as Liz rode along with her mom and Aunt Bee to look at a house for rent in another neighborhood, a small, dusty place planted on cinder blocks, she wondered, *Are we poor? Are we losing our house?* At home, she listened to her mother yell at her father and caught the gist of her mother's bitterness over Donald's inability to provide for them. She also saw her parents drink more, "a lot more," she later wrote.[89] "The bottom just fell out for us."[90]

Pauline was determined to keep the house and had to face facts. Unless she went to work, the situation would only get worse, and they would be headed backward again, maybe even forced to find a rental outside the school district. She put on her best black dress and heels one day and walked down the block and around the corner to Sears, where they were hiring, and landed a full-time, minimum-wage job taking catalog orders over the phone. Her income saved the mortgage and got them caught up, but even with two incomes, there wasn't money to spare.[91]

Now a student at Northwest Classen High School, Liz earned spending money by babysitting and, on long school breaks, working for her mother's sister Alice in Muskogee.[92] In a 2017 speech, she shared her aunt's story and the waitressing job that came from it:

> When I was thirteen, I started waiting tables at my Aunt Alice's restaurant. Aunt Alice had been widowed in her early fifties. She hadn't worked before Uncle Claude died, but she pulled up her socks and did what

she knew how to do—cook. The place didn't make a lot of money, but she lived in the back of the restaurant, and she got by. I spent summers and holidays working for her and living in the back myself, and I saw first-hand the kind of commitment and energy it takes to launch a small business and to keep it going. Six days a week, from early morning until late evening, Aunt Alice did everything from arguing about the produce delivery to filling in for the dishwasher who didn't show up. On the seventh day, we scrubbed floors on our hands and knees and got ready for the next week.[93]

Liz was private about her home life those days, even among her close friends, but Katrina knew one thing—Liz idolized her brothers, gushing with pride when she brought up their military careers.[94] Other than that, her friends did not learn much about her family. "There were two sides of her," her friend Joe Pryor said, "one very personal side that was her own and that you couldn't reach, and another that made her very easy to talk to."[95] She tried to hide the fact that her parents struggled with money, making a silent agreement with her dad to get dropped off in the rusty Studebaker a block away from school.[96] Everyone else seemed to have a shiny new car, and she imagined herself the only student from a family with money problems. Instead of bringing friends over after school, which would bring up the question of why her mom was gone at work, she spent time at Katrina's, especially when she was dating Jim, who lived nearby.[97] The tension around money lightened somewhat but never completely lifted in the Herring household, and Liz seemed to internalize her mother's fear of losing everything. "I [was] afraid of being poor, really poor," she said.[98]

Her wobbly sense of security lived side by side with her confidence in her intellectual strengths. When she challenged herself, she won. When she gave something 100 percent, it paid off. The formula worked again and again, and not just in debate. In her senior year, she studied for the national exam for the Betty Crocker Homemaker of Tomorrow award and took the test in December. Far from a lightweight exercise about liquid measurements and proper table settings, the knowledge and attitude test was based on a program covering ten subject areas, from the psychology of relationships and child development to money management and community affairs, developed by General Mills and taught at the school.[99]

The Betty Crocker program brought up discussions about women's roles that reflected the postwar ideal of the modern American housewife. Senior-class girls with ambitions for careers were compelled to wrestle with statements about the ability of women to achieve "completeness" as homemakers, such as this from the 1966 teaching aid booklet:

> The homemaker realizes the value of continuing education. She can increase her efficiency in the home with knowledge of time- and energy-saving devices and conserve human resources. She can continue to develop as a responsible and well-informed citizen in community and nation. She can make profitable use of leisure time through creative adult education and the library. As a result of her innate desire for

on-going education, she fulfills herself as a complete personality—intellectually, culturally, and spiritually.[100]

To students who had read Betty Friedan's *The Feminine Mystique*, published three years earlier, this idea may have sounded like a dictionary definition of what Friedan was challenging. The "complete" fulfillment that the Betty Crocker life map described above promised did not exist, according to Friedan, since life is about realizing one's full potential. Friedan would likely argue that a path toward such a potential would involve more than reading library books between household duties.

As a young woman, Liz battled the conflicting messages coming from her mother and culture and those arising from her inner self.[101] As she struggled with the contrast between the Betty Crocker ideal and her desire to teach—a desire for doing meaningful work—she had yet to benefit from the feminist writings soon to come. Scholars began looking closely at women's historical roles in the world of work and shed light on the development of the homemaker role and its less-than status in American society. The depiction of homemaking in Liz's 1950s and 1960s was a far cry from the way white women's work in the home had been portrayed before the Industrial Revolution.

Before industrialization, women were equal partners in the economy of the family, making everything from scratch—growing crops for her baking and cooking, spinning yarn and cotton for sewing clothes, churning butter, and making soap and medicines. This work was indispensable to life and not considered beneath other occupations done by white men. Only when industrialization redefined the value of work as that which made a monetary profit for the business owners did this status change. As industries began making the products that had been the woman's domain—and for the most part shut women out of those factories or paid them pittance wages—women were left with the lowly tasks of housework.

Since housework did not create a profit, it was considered inferior to wage work and the less-than view of "women's work" stuck. The Betty Crocker program was one more example of how women were taught that the work of human progress went on outside the home. It bolstered the concept of women as housewives, models of universal womanhood who were "naturally" separate from the world of work—and through the lens of the economy, naturally inferior. All this refers to America's white women; black women's history of doing outside work during and after slavery gave rise to the virtues of self-reliance and assertiveness. This contrasted with the virtues of "feminine weakness and wifely submissiveness" that society expected of white housewives. As Angela Davis wrote, black women escaped that label through their history of "work, work, and more work."[102]

The Betty Crocker program quote above perfectly illustrates how white, middle-class womanhood was defined by the time Liz was in high school. A fulfilled woman was one who efficiently managed the home, her leisure time, and her responsibilities as a citizen while never contributing to the world through her work or career. She educated herself to become a more interesting and engaging spouse. Liz, who had dreamed of a teaching career since girlhood and was performing better than most of the guys on the debate team, had to grapple with the way that these realities about herself conflicted with the ever-present expectation that marriage was the ultimate goal.[103] Some of the test questions hit this issue squarely on the mark, such as Test Item 13:

Many teen-aged girls are faced with deciding between an early marriage and continuing their education. Which of the statements below is supported by research evidence?

A. Happier marriages result when the wife has considerably less education than her husband.

B. Excessive education for the wife will result in marital discord and tension.

C. The more education a couple has, the more apt they are to have a happy marriage.

D. The education of the wife is irrelevant to the success of her marriage.[104]

Correct answer "C" implies that college is a good thing, but only in terms of what the homemaker can bring to her relationship with her husband.

The Betty Crocker Homemaker of Tomorrow program made senior girls think about important issues they would face in life, which was significant. The downside was that the program assumed women's greatest fulfillment came from homemaking, a role that would always occupy a lower rung in society because a person's value was based on what she contributed to the profit-making part of the economy. One of the gifts of the feminism that began in the late 1960s was replacing that deeply embedded assumption with the idea of freedom—women's freedom to choose between homemaking and career without casting a negative label on either choice. Liz grew up in the prefeminist mind-set and matured as an intellectual, educator, and politician in the feminist era, to the point that she hates being asked questions about being a "woman" senator.[105] Those questions are often framed around the idea that women's leadership is freakishly unusual, a radical accomplishment. By not playing into that, she steers the mind-set toward female leaders as natural and normal.

Liz's hopes for a teaching career did not wane in high school, and Pauline continued to chide her about it. The pain this brought apparently ran deep, compelling Elizabeth the senator to share the following scenario in a brief, autobiographical section of *This Fight Is Our Fight: The Battle to Save America's Middle Class*:

> Whenever she heard me talking about my dreams of teaching, my mother would break into the conversation and explain to whomever I was talking to, "But she doesn't want to be an old-maid schoolteacher." (You could almost hear the fright music playing in the background.) Then she would turn to me, pause, and narrow her eyes. "Right, Betsy?"[106]

The issue of women and careers came at her from all sides. Being the star debater motivated her to discover everything she was capable of, while her mother's discouragements threatened to make her second-guess herself. The Betty Crocker program brought the conflict into higher relief with its discussion questions about women with careers: "Is it possible for a woman to do an adequate job of homemaking and have a professional career outside the home? What attitudes and abilities are important to consider?"[107]

However insightful or even irritating the process may have been, Liz spent enough time on the materials to earn the highest score on the one-hundred-question test and win the Betty Crocker gold-heart pin. Another senior girl in Oklahoma had the highest score statewide, however, and won a scholarship and a chance to win the national award.[108]

In *This Fight Is Our Fight*, Elizabeth also recalls that the friction between her and her mother came to a head one evening during her senior year when they were arguing about college. The fight became a one-sided shouting match, with Liz standing in stony silence and Pauline yelling insults—*What makes you think you're so special? Do you think you're better than the rest of us?* Liz stomped up to her room, and her mom followed, and when Liz finally shouted back—*Leave me alone!*—her mom slapped her hard across the face.

Liz threw some clothes together in a bag and ran out of the house. Her dad found her hours later at the bus station, shaking and red-faced from crying. He sat down beside her and told her how awful he felt after his heart attack, so ashamed of being useless that he almost walked away from all of it, from them. She asked what made him change his mind. He held her hand and told her that things looked up, little by little: her mom got a job, and the bills got paid.

Then he turned to her and said, "Life gets better, punkin."[109]

Liz kept to her plan and sent off for applications to the two colleges she'd learned had strong debate programs, Northwestern in Illinois and George Washington University (GW) in Washington, DC.[110] Her friend and fellow debater Andrew Mason, who had graduated and was a freshman debater at GW, told her that the university had a very good debate scholarship. For all of her attempts to hide this process from her mother, she finally had to come clean in order to get access to her parents' tax returns for the financial section of the applications. Talking it over at the kitchen table, Liz argued that colleges had scholarships, but Pauline repeated what she had said for years—they couldn't afford it.[111] Liz persisted, pleading to at least be able to apply to those that offered full scholarships. Donald listened quietly to their back-and-forth and finally broke in, asking Pauline to let Liz try.

As she transferred her parents' financial information to the applications, Liz got another reality check about their hanging-by-a-thread situation. The low income listed in their returns ramped up her anxiety that she may really be different from everyone else at school, an imposter among the well situated and secure. She may be *poor*.

That anxiety blew down the tracks the day she received her acceptance letter from GW, complete with a full scholarship. Pauline was proud to tell her friends that Liz was going to college, but she couldn't help adding that she doubted the girl would ever marry.[112] Even though she was hardheaded about Liz's choices, Pauline showed her love in tangible ways. She had considered quitting her job, but when Liz got accepted at GW, she stayed on at Sears to help pay some of her college expenses.[113] None of them imagined what Liz's future held, but Donald and Pauline, according to Liz's friend Joe Mallonee, "knew they had an exceptional child."[114]

Liz graduated from Northwest Classen in the spring of 1966. She was sixteen years old, with the school's Grady Memorial Debate Award and a cluster of trophies in the lobby's glass cabinet to show for her past four years.[115] Out in the wider world, *The Sound of*

Music won best picture at the Academy Awards, Ronald Reagan was running for governor of California, and five thousand U.S. Marines had just driven the North Vietnamese back over the demilitarized zone in Operation Hastings, the largest battle of the war to date.[116] Antiwar protests were rampant in cities all over the country, including Washington, DC, but Liz's strongest focus on current events would revolve around the issues taken up by the George Washington University debate team.

2

GREAT EXPECTATIONS

"Law is an advanced degree in thinking."
—Elizabeth Warren[1]

Students who do well in debate often think about careers in international studies, politics, or law. Liz was not interested in any of those but instead still dreamed of teaching and majored in education when she got to Washington, DC. Her debate scholarship covered room, board, tuition, books, and spending money. "It was sort of the equivalent of an athletic scholarship," she said, "but one that actually a girl could get, even though there weren't very many girls in debate, either."[2]

George Washington University had one of the handful of elite debate programs that produced championship teams year after year. They debated archrivals like Georgetown and Dartmouth as well as teams across the country, competing in weekend-long tournaments that, over the course of the semester, required as much preparation as several classes combined.[3] The GW coach, George F. Henigan, was among the founders of the American Forensic Association and "one of the debate gods," said Bill Toutant, a member of the team with Liz. "George Washington University was a very big debate school, a rigorous program," he said. "They would not send you out on a tournament unless you had a good chance."[4]

George Henigan's son, Dennis, debated in high school and grew up idolizing his father's debaters. After weekend tournaments, they would come to the Henigans' house in a Virginia suburb, laden down with trophies. "It was a Sunday night ritual," Dennis said. "They would review the judges' comments in our living room, praising some judges and condemning others like baseball players complaining about umpires."[5]

Being selected for the university's prestigious debate scholarship marked Liz as an exceptional talent among a lot of very smart young men and women. The team included, for example, Andrew Mason, her friend from high school who would become an internationally renowned economist and professor at the University of Hawaii.[6] Her debate partner, Greg Millard, the only black student on the team and an American studies major, became a Peabody Award–winning documentary writer, poet, playwright, and cultural affairs commissioner in New York City Mayor Ed Koch's administration before dying from a long illness at age thirty-seven.[7]

Washington, DC, was the ideal place for researching the debate topic Liz's freshman year: "RESOLVED: That the United States should substantially reduce its foreign policy commitments."[8] Debaters were easy to spot on campus, carrying around their long, gray metal boxes full of index cards. During practice in the afternoons, they took to the floor one by one to immediately respond to arguments thrown at them. "Then," Bill Toutant said, "when you were in actual debate, the thirty to forty seconds you had to respond seemed like a luxury."[9] Bill, who won the Top Novice Debater Award his first year, later became a composer, professor of music theory and composition, and dean at California State University, Northridge.

The debaters had a brilliant rhetoric teacher and mentor in coach George Henigan, and he was deeply admired. "They could tell that he cared so much about them as people," Dennis Henigan said. "In the days when there was a lot of student activism, he was very liberal and sympathetic to the antiwar movement, but he expressed a lot of concern about the more radical students, worrying that they might get arrested and in trouble." Dennis, an attorney, was a champion debater in high school and has spent most of his career at the Brady Center to Prevent Gun Violence. Reflecting on the U.S. Senator that Liz became, he recognized his father's imprint on her strengths as a speaker. "She knows how to explain the most complicated issues in simple, ordinary language that people from various backgrounds and education levels can understand," he said, "and how to be convincing. She reflects everything my father taught about persuasion."[10] Being mentored by Coach Henigan, who nurtured the talent and disposition for hard work that Liz brought to GW, helped her develop her trademark clarity as a speaker.

Seventeen-year-old Liz had never been east of Oklahoma before she moved to Washington to go to college. With access to one-dollar student tickets for the Lisner Auditorium, she saw her first Shakespeare play, ballet, modern dance, chamber music, and symphony orchestra concerts.[11] At the National Gallery of Art,[12] she visited her first art museum. Those experiences, along with events involving her Kappa Alpha Theta sorority, were like a crash course in Western culture. "They changed who I am and what I do," she said, "and made me forever after a strong supporter of the humanities."[13]

During her second year, she decided to change her major and entered the bachelor of science program in speech-language pathology and audiology so that she could work with children with speech and hearing disabilities. She envisioned teaching children with special needs in public schools and kept on track to earn a teaching certificate as well.[14] The debate team was onto a new topic about guaranteed minimum income, an alternative social safety net that has been discussed since Sir Thomas More envisioned it in *Utopia* five hundred years ago. The national debate issue (written out, as always, in the style of a legislative motion), "RESOLVED: The federal government should guarantee a minimum annual cash income to all citizens," plunged Liz into research about both the necessities and bureaucratic challenges of social welfare systems, issues that are still relevant today.[15] The guaranteed income idea resurfaced in the mainstream when Tesla cofounder Elon Musk and Facebook founder Mark Zuckerberg started talking about a universal basic income (UBI) as one answer to the job-loss challenges in a world of expanded automation. In this latest dialogue about the concept, guaranteed income is seen as an efficient way to help people retrain for new jobs or start their own businesses.[16]

As Liz studied these issues, along with her general education courses and classes for her major, such as phonetics and language development, a familiar face popped back into her life. Jim Warren, who had broken up with her four years earlier in high school, was now a "math geek" at IBM working on the Apollo space missions in Houston.[17] He was established in an exciting career and ready to settle down, and Liz was more than flattered when he proposed. "He seemed so sure of himself," she said, "so confident about what life should look like."[18] His proposal was an irresistible pull into the security she had never known. Two months later, she let go of her scholarship and dropped out of the university, trading in one dream for another. In *This Fight Is Our Fight*, she looked back at how her nineteen-year-old mind-set, weighed down with insecurities, won the day:

> For nineteen years I had absorbed the lesson that the best and most important thing any girl could do was "marry well," which roughly translated into "find a decent man" and "get some financial security." And for nineteen years I had also absorbed the message that I was a pretty iffy case—not very pretty, not very flirty, and definitely not very good at making boys feel like they were smarter than I was. Somewhere deep in my heart, I believed that no man would ever ask me to marry him. When Jim popped the question, I was so shocked that it took me about a nanosecond to say yes.[19]

Back home in Oklahoma City, life sizzled in the glow of her happiness—she was in love, elated, walking on air. The wedding details hummed along, first with a date put on the books at the family church, May Avenue United Methodist, and then invitations.

Her mother hauled out the sewing machine when Liz came home with a few yards of white satin and set out to create a sheath wedding gown with short, puffy sleeves and a white bow at the empire waist. The veil she chose floated out of the back of a small, nurse's cap-like hat.[20] She picked out a pair of short white gloves as the final touch, and on November 3, 1968, her father walked her down the aisle.[21]

Liz signed on with an office temp agency a week after she and Jim moved into an apartment in Houston, and Jim got back to work at IBM.[22] That year, NASA was deep into the Apollo 11 mission that would land the first man on the moon in 1969. Jim had started working for IBM four years earlier, right after graduating from college, and IBM programmers worked with the computing and data processing system that IBM provided to NASA's Manned Spacecraft Center. This system, called the Real-Time Computer Complex (RTCC), was involved in directing every phase of the Apollo missions, and IBM personnel manned a few chairs in the mission control center, identified by the IBM logo stitched on the back of their jackets. The RTCC computed the solutions to problems so quickly that bugs were fixed virtually in real time.[23]

Jim and Liz likely watched the Moon landing of astronauts Neil Armstrong and Buzz Aldrin on July 20, 1969, with the same pride as all the other IBM and NASA people involved in the mission. The Apollo 11 mission flight director, Gene Kranz, later wrote about the role that IBM's people played as the lunar module *Eagle* descended:

> The systems information that we used to make the go, no-go decisions was developed by IBM, and the ultimate go, no-go decision [that day] was provided to

me by computers operated by IBM engineers within NASA's Mission Control Center. Without IBM and the systems they provided, we would not have landed on the Moon.[24]

Jim later worked on the antiballistic missile defense system, "poring over spreadsheets and hunting down bugs," Elizabeth wrote.[25] In the meantime, she answered phones and did clerical work in her temp job assignments, chatting over coffee breaks about wanting to be a teacher. In one of those offices, a supervisor mentioned that she should check out the University of Houston.[26] It was an inexpensive public university that attracted working adults. Jim's first response was that they couldn't afford it, but she convinced him that with tuition only fifty dollars a semester, she could pay her own way on a part-time job, gas included.

She transferred her credits from George Washington University and took up where she had left off, studying speech science, language disorders in children, and the anatomy of speaking and language. Just as her plan was running smoothly and with only two classes left to complete, she learned that IBM was transferring Jim to New Jersey, and she thought she might have to drop out again. Her department, however, assured her that she could finish with correspondence courses.[27] They packed up and left Houston for north central New Jersey.

Jim bought a small house in a woodsy neighborhood of Rockaway, New Jersey, called White Meadow Lake.[28] Between studying and mailing in her assignments, Liz took on fix-up projects, refinishing floors, wallpapering, and retiling the bathroom.[29] Soon after finishing her courses, she received her diploma for a bachelor of science degree in speech pathology and audiology, and with her new credentials in hand, she looked for work in the Rockaway area.[30] Having just turned twenty-one (but still looking like fourteen, she noted in *A Fighting Chance*), she landed a job as a speech therapist for children with special needs.[31] Her mornings now began with a twenty-mile drive up I-287 to Riverdale Elementary School, where she helped children who had suffered from brain injuries or ailments that left them with speaking or hearing problems.[32] Since she was hired on an "emergency" teaching certificate, she enrolled in two graduate education courses to work toward her certification.[33] Her new career started strong, but the speech pathology track, with all its fits and starts, was not, it seemed, meant to be. The Riverdale position only lasted one school term—the principal, who could see by the end of that first year that she was pregnant, did not hire her back.[34] Times had not changed a lot for female teachers since her days in Mrs. Garrett's English class.

Amelia Louise was born in the autumn of 1971, named after Aunt Bee and Pauline's middle names. Jim did not want Liz to work full-time now that a baby had come, so she let go of her plan to search for another school job.[35] For the next couple of years, she ricocheted between loving every second of her life as a mother to feeling restless about what else she could do. "Amelia and I went everywhere together… I loved her until my chest hurt and my eyes filled with tears," she said. "I wanted to be a good wife and mother, but I wanted to do something more."[36] Jim told her to give full-time motherhood a chance—they would have more children, and she'd love it.[37] She felt ashamed of her desire to take on something else in the world beyond him and her daughter and their home, but she kept casting about for ideas.[38] *What about engineering?* She sent off for applications at schools that promised bright futures building bridges, waterworks, or satellites.[39]

Liz's restless years as a young wife and mother in the late 1960s and early 1970s reflected the soul-searching of the women's movement that carried on outside the cocoon of her family. Even though she wasn't involved in the outer trappings of that movement, her struggle to make peace between her love of her family life and her drive to do something in the world was being discussed out loud in society. She was connected to other suburban women through the question at the heart of *The Feminine Mystique*: "Is this all?"

On a trip back to Oklahoma for Christmas, she met up with some of her friends from debate and told them about her restless life in the green New Jersey suburbs. The guys said she should go to law school. Of all of them, they said, she should have been the one to go. *You'll love it.*[40] She talked it over with Jim, and after some reluctance, he agreed. School sounded more reasonable than going back to a full-time teaching job. Even though she had never even met a lawyer, she felt that the possibilities were endless, because at the end of the day, every kind of lawyer helped people. As she scheduled a slot for taking the Law School Admission Test (LSAT) and rounded up applications, she called her mother to share the news about her plan. Pauline's reaction didn't surprise her, since she had never warmed to the idea of women seeking careers, but it still stung. Pauline lectured her about staying put as a wife and mother instead of becoming one of those perpetually unhappy "crazy women libbers."[41]

She applied to two schools, Rutgers and Columbia. One was

located in downtown Newark and cost $460 a semester, and the other sat across the Hudson and charged $1,600.[42] Columbia was Ivy League, a gold-plated ticket, but as out of reach as Tranquility Base. On Amelia's second birthday, Elizabeth stepped into her first class at Rutgers School of Law, affectionately known as the "People's Electric Law School" for its activist, antiestablishment vibe.[43] By the time she enrolled in 1973, Rutgers had taken several actions to infuse socially conscious energy into legal education, including dramatically increasing its number of students of color and women. Rutgers Law professor Paul Tractenberg recounted that the 1970s were "a time of vast energy, enthusiasm, and engagement at the school. It was a time when many faculty members and students worked collaboratively to grapple with the great issues of the day: the growing opposition to a war that seemed to many ever more wasteful, hopeless, and immoral; the growing belief that attention, energy, and resources had to be devoted to curing the ills and gross inequalities within the United States, and the growing awareness that law and constitutional processes could be instrumental in achieving social and political justice here and abroad."[44]

In response to the civil unrest of the 1960s and race riots that hit Newark in 1967, Tractenberg wrote, the law school had taken up the demands of the Association of Black Law Students and revamped its curriculum to more reflect the legal needs of urban America. Tractenberg chronicled the black students' indictment of the school for not offering a program that dealt "legitimately with the legal demands of contemporary society"[45] but instead continued to emphasize theory over practice and ignore aspects of the law that impacted people of color. The school responded by adding new classes such as Social Legislation, Urban Poverty, Consumer Credit and the Poor, Work of the Juvenile Court, and two new required first-year classes, Legal Representation of the Poor and International Law and Just World Order. The vast expansion of legal clinic programs that gave students hands-on experience offering free legal aid to Newark residents became a model for other law schools.

Rutgers Law also responded to the times by taking action to racially diversify the school, opening the doors to a wider range of students. The new approach considered an applicant's business and professional experience, community involvement, leadership potential, and personal recommendations in addition to their LSAT scores. In this move, one of the first affirmative action programs in the country, Rutgers also made a strong appeal to women, and Liz enrolled in the midst of a dramatic increase in the number of female students. The school had recently launched the *Women's Rights Law Reporter*, the first journal of its kind and led by one of Rutgers' two female professors, Ruth Bader Ginsburg.[46]

By 1977, the year after Liz graduated, women made up the majority of the student body—a first for any law school in the country.[47] Many were mothers whose children had reached school age, freeing up their daytime schedule, but Liz was determined to get started, even with a toddler in tow. She was surrounded by a supportive group of friends that included Patricia Nachtigal, who would become the general counsel and senior vice president of Ingersoll Rand. They spent many hours a week studying in the Warrens' living room, and Patricia recalled that within their close group of friends, someone was always happy to take care of Amelia if Liz's babysitter got sick.[48]

The shifts in the social climate played out in their classrooms, where women felt empowered to react to stodgy sexism. Liz recalled an episode from early in her first year when a male professor began giving an imaginary example of a conflict that involved "the guy's secretary, a typical dumb blond." One woman instantly booed at the remark, and the rest of the room soon followed. In the mayhem, "the professor looked up quickly and then actually staggered back as if he had been hit," Liz wrote. It was a moment of electrifying, this-is-how-the-world-changes clarity.[49]

The seventies saw an explosion of insights about the plight of women in the law, thanks in large part to a study about sexual discrimination in the field by a group at New York University. As discussed in an article by Cynthia Grant Bowman, the study reported that in 1970, women applying for positions in New York law firms routinely heard comments such as "We don't like to hire women," "We hire some women, but not many," "We just hired a woman and couldn't hire another," "We don't expect the same kind of work from women as we do from men," "Women don't become partners here," and "Are you planning on having children?" In talks with researchers outside the study, women also said that interviewers at law firms had asked them about their use of contraceptives. The study found that firms were refusing to interview female law students, preventing their contact with clients, holding company events in places that excluded women, and committing other acts of sexual discrimination that violated Title VII of the Civil Rights Act.[50]

After the NYU group finished the study, they teamed up with other researchers at Columbia Law School and filed a complaint against ten major New York law firms that eventually became a full-blown class-action lawsuit. More complaints sprang up around the country while the New York suits were being settled, and in the end, the New York firms agreed to new, pro-women hiring practices. This opened the floodgates, and the number of female lawyers in firms across the country jumped from thirteen thousand (4 percent) in 1970 to sixty-two thousand (12.4 percent) in 1980. All this seemed to bode well for Liz's graduating class of 1976, but many women who poured into firms during the 1970s did not experience the careers they had hoped for.

A follow-up article revealed that instead of breaking into the field on equal ground, they were passed over for challenging assignments and stymied from promotion. After a few years among older male partners who never got comfortable working with women, lacking mentors to help them navigate the territory, and feeling unenthused about sharing in "male pastimes such as golf and dirty jokes," things went sour. The decade did not appear to change long-standing mind-sets, and without that fundamental shift, women felt that the future would only bring more of the same. As one female lawyer reflected:

> Sooner or later they will find a woman who will conform to their requirements: that you have to sound like and be like and appear like all of the other [female associates] who walked before... But it is not going to really be a breakthrough for women. What it means is that there will be a woman partner when she conforms to the male stereotype personally and professionally and that's not social progress.[51]

In the first minute of her first class, Liz got a wake-up call about the demands of the rite of initiation called a three-year law degree program. She and the rest of the twenty students waited for their professor to look up from his stopwatch, and at exactly the top of the hour, he called on a student named Miss Abramson.

"What is 'assumpsit'?" he asked.

Miss Abramson was silent, and Elizabeth looked around to see that everyone else had the same blank look. She figured the professor had stepped into the wrong class. He asked another student, and when that brought on more silence, he asked another to read the first word in the case they were assigned to read. "Assumpsit," the student said. The professor kept grilling until he got to Nancy Newman, who knew the term backward and forward. Elizabeth left the class shaken, feeling like an alien in the foreign land of I Wasn't Prepared.[52] She had been here before, however. As a teenager, she had read articles still warm from the copying machine about the intersection of tax brackets and social security taxation and the role of international humanitarian laws in proposing nuclear disarmament policy. The first read was always a brick wall, but she had a knack for making tough, new learning one of the most enjoyable processes in her life. She was born with both a motivation to force her own limits and the focus required to do it, two of the secret ingredients to experiencing *flow*. Absorbing herself in three-pound legal casebooks during that intense state, when hours fly by like minutes, made studying law sheer pleasure. "I loved it," she said. "I loved every subject and every one of my teachers. It was a place that taught me to pull up my socks and *try*."[53]

She plugged in at Rutgers Law, thriving on the intensity and optimism. Her friends recognized her gifts as well as her seemingly tough financial situation—why else would she come to school with offshoots of her spider plants to sell or show up at a potluck with a penny-pinching dish like chicken gizzard casserole?[54] Her fellow student Edith Payne, who would become a judge on the New Jersey Appellate Court, described her as wickedly smart in class, "clearly an academic star," and at the same time someone who appeared to be in "dire" financial circumstances.[55]

Her coursework, writing, and, maybe most impressively, mix of intellect and upbeat personality made her stand out. Her peers and professors loved to have conversations with her. Professor Calvin Johnson recalled that his colleague the late John Payne once remarked about how much he positively enjoyed talking to her. "She shot up like a rocket," Johnson said, "and got adopted by some very bright people, including Allan Axelrod, one of the best professors at Rutgers."[56]

Axelrod taught contracts, commercial law, property, and bankruptcy and was the first to hold an endowed chair at Rutgers, the highest recognition a university can bestow on a professor. He brought a sense of humor and broad range of passions such as literature and classical music to his work and was admired for his ability to discuss areas outside his specialties, such as constitutional law, with as much brilliance as he commanded in his own areas.[57]

In a memorial to Axelrod after his death in 2008, students recalled how he arrived in class armed with newspaper clippings and lighthearted anecdotes to show how property law worked in the world. He was known as playful and irreverent, a skeptic of the heavily prevailing "law and economics" movement in law studies that analyzed legal issues through the science of economics.[58] Rutgers

Law professor Howard Latin wrote that Axelrod "always considered social and legal problems in light of his concern for others, especially the incapacitated or downtrodden.[59] This concern for the welfare of less fortunate and gifted people was more important to Axel than the musings of his prodigious intellect or the ideological dogmas of scholars." Professor Ruth Bader Ginsberg called him "the very best, the most elegant yet informal of classroom performers, the least self-regarding of professorial types."[60]

Calvin Johnson believed that Axelrod's mentorship had a crucial impact on Elizabeth's future success. "Axelrod was the best of the best," he said, "a very subtle mind and soul. I think he was one of the influences that made her the sophisticated scholar she quickly became."[61] Elizabeth confirmed this in her own reflections about Axelrod. She first heard about him from her first-year torts professor, Robert Carter, who insisted she take Axelrod's classes.

"Professor Carter had told me, 'You've got to take Allan Axelrod as soon as an opening comes up.' I said, 'What does he teach?' and he looked at me with just this disgusted look and said, 'It doesn't matter—take him if he's teaching the phone book.' I took every class he taught." She credits Axelrod as the reason she ended up teaching commercial and bankruptcy law and for expanding her notion of "neutrality" in law. He made her think more about the value, or lack of it, in the concept of a theoretical state of indifference, or neutrality, which ignores issues that could be subject to bias or prejudice. "He changed my life," she said. "He taught me how multidimensional the world is and about how neutrality is an illusion." Axelrod helped her understand that real-life interactions between people and companies and organizations don't exist in the perfect vacuum of indifference that legal theory describes. "It really is always about winners and losers," she said, "and how those who know, those who start with power, those who start with resources can do so well in that world."[62]

In addition to introducing Elizabeth to Axelrod, Robert Carter was the mentor who first suggested to Elizabeth that she could become a law professor. In November of her first year, he took her to lunch—"Lunch with a professor, I mean, wow!" she thought at the time—and said, "You know, you could be a teacher."

"No," she said, "I'm going to law school."

"I mean a law teacher, a law professor," he said. "You've got it in you."

The idea absorbed her thoughts the rest of the day. "I can remember driving back down Route 280 in my little blue Volkswagen," she said, "and I said it out loud for the first time, 'Professor Warren... Boy, wouldn't that be an amazing thing.'"[63]

Liz found her pace and kept it up for three years while raising Amelia. She got to school, prepared from studying the night before, and each class seemed to go by in the blink of an eye. The energy of the discussions and ideas felt like riding on a roller coaster, she said, climbing and twisting and turning and falling. After classes, she rushed to the babysitter's house to pick up Amelia by two o'clock, the cutoff time she had paid for, and then drove home while shaking Amelia's foot to keep her awake until she could put her down for a nap. With the baby drowsing in her crib, Elizabeth walked to the bedroom and fell across the bed with her book bag still hanging from her shoulder. "I fell instantly to sleep for maybe half an hour," she said. "It was as if my brain had been so stretched out of shape by four hours of law school that it needed time to just pull back into some semblance of normal." She woke up to make dinner, spend time with Jim and Amelia, and then study for classes the next day.[64]

In her second year, she worked at the kitchen table on her first formal law article, "Busing: Supreme Court Restricts Equity Powers of District Court to Order Interschool Busing," which was published in 1975 as a student piece in the *Rutgers Law Review*.[65] This was also the year for the traditional interview at a law firm to set up a summer associate job. On her third interview of the day at Cadwalader, Wickersham & Taft on Wall Street, the partner put her on the spot— for a millisecond. Looking up from her resume with a disappointed frown, he told her he'd found a typo on it. "Should I take that as a sign of the quality of the work you do?" he asked. She didn't skip a beat and said, "You should take it as a sign that you'd better not hire me to type." He laughed and sent her on her way. (She scoured her resume word by word for the typo afterward but didn't find one.)[66]

The firm gave her the job, and that summer, she rode in on the train five days a week to work in the skyscraper offices of the oldest firm on Wall Street. At one point during those ten weeks, a partner pulled her aside with a piece of advice she keenly recalls to this day. "You know," he said, "being a summer associate is all well and good, but take a deep breath. Try to figure out if you think these guys are ever going to make a woman partner."[67]

His words took some of the dazzle out of the firm's high-flying atmosphere of prestige, possibilities, and money. She earned what she called an "astonishing" income that summer, a windfall that allowed them to buy a second car and send Liz to the orthodontist. When she returned to her final year of law school in braces, she looked even younger than when she'd begun.[68]

That fall, she became pregnant with her son, and she was forced to mix the joy of that with the frustration of lowering the odds of a successful job search. While most of her friends were getting offers, she would show up for a first interview and never get a call to come in for a second. On graduation day in June 1976, eight months pregnant, with a headache and swollen feet shoved into her best shoes, she panted in her chair and tried to keep from fainting.[69]

She brought Alexander James Warren into the world in mid-July, when firecrackers and stray fireworks were still popping on the heels of the bicentennial celebrations that had lit up the skies on the Fourth. Amelia was four years old, Jim had a good job, and she felt that her family was perfect. She knew she was lucky—this was supposed to be enough. But law school had been a heart-revving train ride, and once the brakes kicked in, she struggled to adjust. "I thought that the three years I'd been in law school were gone," she said in a speech in 2011. "I'd stepped off the career track that was really not open to women, and I thought I'd given it all up." She considered it the hardest moment in her life, turning her back on the world of ideas and a profession that could make things happen. Without getting a job right out of school, she thought the world that had just opened up to her was now closed off. It felt like "I just kissed it all goodbye," she said.[70]

After settling in to the pattern of quieter days and a few sleepless nights during Alex's first months, she reignited her resolve and studied for the bar exam. She passed and put out her shingle in the front yard to announce that there was a lawyer on the block. The sign, extending out of the colonial lamppost just above the hedge, read: ELIZABETH WARREN: ATTORNEY AT LAW.[71]

As clients trickled in for real estate closings, incorporation filings for budding entrepreneurs, and lawsuits, word filtered down to Rutgers Law that one of its stars was floundering.[72] "Axelrod heard that she was trying to make a go of it," Calvin Johnson recalled. "He went to Peter Simmons, the dean, and said, 'Hire this woman as a writing instructor. She's smart as a whip and she'll do good for the school.'"[73]

Dean Simmons invited her to come in and talk about a last-minute opening for a legal writing instructor. "It was clear she was an imaginative, warm, empathetic human being," he recalled about the interview. "And very smart—her academic work at the school was exemplary."[74] He gave her the one-night-a-week class, very part-time and just at the instructor level, but a position that gave her a place in the institution. In that spring semester of 1977, her students sauntered in from the cold after a full day of work and learned the craft of persuasive writing, how to format legal citations, and the fine points of each section of an appellate brief. Elizabeth made the most of her position by using the library to research a new article, a piece about tax law that was published in the *Rutgers Law Review* the following year.[75] Raising a baby and a preschooler, keeping meals on the table, writing, and teaching—"my life bubbled over," she wrote, "and it was thrilling."[76]

In her second semester of teaching, Jim learned that he would be transferred again, and she felt another wave of regret about leaving a situation she loved. Among Jim's options, however, was

Houston—home of her alma mater, which also had a law school. She mailed off a letter expressing her interest in teaching and listing her experience.[77] Jim had a few weeks to make his decision, and as the time came near in early 1978, Elizabeth received a call from a professor at the University of Houston Law Center. Eugene Smith asked the standard first-call interview questions about her research interests and teaching philosophy and then called back the following week to invite her to the campus for an interview. She recalled that visit on campus as a time of telling stories, having a good time, and talking "a little bit about law, but not a lot." Eugene Smith had undoubtedly heard the details of her performance as a student and teacher at Rutgers Law, and her on-site interview confirmed her reputation.[78]

Houston Law Center hired her, launching her tenure-track career in 1978 as an assistant professor assigned with directing the legal writing program and teaching contracts.[79] Houston was the first of Elizabeth's four career academic positions, and she never forgot that it all started at a public law school in Newark where she came of age as a bright, gifted thinker. "It took an unsure kid, married at nineteen and now with a baby on her hip, and put me to the test to figure out who I was and what I could do," she said. "Law school opened a thousand doors for me."[80]

3

TOUGH LOVE

In the whole human race
there is no greater criminal
than a man without money.

—BERTOLT BRECHT, LIBRETTO, *RISE AND FALL*
OF THE CITY OF MAHAGONNY[1]

Elizabeth's five years at the Houston Law Center were a time of evolving scholarship and major life changes. When she arrived in 1978, she doubled the number of full-time female professors, joining Irene Merker Rosenberg, a specialist in juvenile justice and criminal law who would become the first woman at the school to receive tenure.[2]

Being one of only two women on the full-time law faculty was not unusual, since women made up a very small percentage of law professors in the 1970s. Early in the decade, only twenty-two women across the country were tenure-track law professors. The majority of women who got hired by law schools either were librarians or held bottom-rung teaching appointments. However, affirmative action programs of the 1970s that brought more women into law firms also saw an upsurge of hiring in law schools. Feminists in the American Bar Association (ABA) led a successful campaign for a resolution that urged law schools to "make substantial efforts to recruit, hire, and promote women professors." That and other actions, according to the ABA, increased the percentage of women on law faculties from about 4 percent in 1972 to 10 percent in 1978. Yet according to researcher Kelly Weisberg, that one in ten figure "did not accurately reflect the overall picture of women in the law faculties." The gains occurred in a small number of schools, and many schools still had not hired any women. By 1980, in spite of the uptick, "half of all law schools employed two or fewer women," Weisberg found.[3]

In short, as a twenty-eight-year-old, tenure-track female law professor, Elizabeth was treading new ground. While she developed a strong professional relationship with her mentor, John Mixon, another contracts professor whom she credits for teaching her how to teach law, another male colleague consistently made her uncomfortable to the point of full-blown harassment.[4] Eugene Smith, who recruited and hired her, had only been on the faculty for four years but had taught at two other law schools before coming to Houston. A polio victim, he had weak arms and "walked like a crab," John Mixon wrote in *Autobiography of a Law School: Stories, Memories and Interpretations of My Sixty Years at The University of Houston Law Center*, but he could drive a car and, of course, take on the demands of a teaching career.[5] Gene "lusted openly" after Elizabeth, Mixon wrote, "but she would have none of it."[6] He added later that Gene had a reputation for making sexual overtures.[7]

In 2017, with prominent women from many fields sharing their sexual harassment and assault stories in the wake of the Harvey Weinstein scandal and high-profile cases that followed it, Elizabeth shared her story of Gene's advances on NBC's *Meet the Press* on October 22. Appearing in a special report in which four female senators talked about the sexual harassment they had experienced in their careers, Elizabeth said:

> I was a baby law professor and so excited to have my first real teaching job and there was this senior faculty member who, you know, would tell dirty jokes and make comments about my appearance.
>
> And one day he asked me if I would stop by his office, which I didn't think much about. And I did. And he slammed the door and lunged for me. It was like a bad cartoon. He's chasing me around the desk, trying to get his hands on me.
>
> And I kept saying, "You don't want to do this. You don't want to do this. I have little children at home. Please don't do this." And trying to talk calmly. And at the same time, what was flickering through my brain is, "If he gets hold of me, I'm going to punch him right in the face."
>
> After several rounds, I jumped for the door and got out. And I went back to my office and I just sat and shook. And thought, "What had I done to bring this

on?" And I told my best friend about it. Never said a word to anyone else. But for a long time, I wore a lot of brown.[8]

She told the *Boston Globe* that she tried to handle it on her own, "just to stay out of his way and to be as far away as I could… Years later I feel bad that I didn't speak up… I did the best I could at the time."[9] Peter Linzer, who joined the Houston faculty a year after Elizabeth left, recalled Gene Smith as a "good old boy" with a bottle of whiskey in his desk drawer. "Liz Warren's story is an example of a young, vulnerable woman being treated badly," he said.[10]

Her NBC segment ignited a controversy around the previous telling of that incident that had appeared in John Mixon's book. He had written that Elizabeth and Gene Smith laughed during Smith's behind-closed-door action and that Elizabeth was "amused by the pursuit."[11] After the NBC story aired, he told a reporter that in retrospect, he felt he had written about that episode too lightly in his book.[12] Elizabeth, while agreeing that John's phrase "she would have none of it" was a good description of how she felt during the office episode, disagreed with his portrayal of her and Gene as good friends in his book. Elizabeth's and John's very different perspectives of the incident highlighted the nature of the male lens that prevented him—and likely many others—from sensing the signs of vulnerability, pain, and coping that his colleague had gone through.

Women in the 1970s who wanted to share their workplace harassment stories wrote them up in letters that poured into the *Ms.* magazine office by the hundreds every month, but it would take a

Hollywood scandal nearly forty years later to break the silence in a social media #MeToo movement that rippled across the country and the world.[13]

Throughout her years at Houston—for the most part very happy, productive, and successful years—John Mixon was a positive male figure on the faculty who took Elizabeth under his wing. "Each teaching award I received later on was thanks to his guidance," Elizabeth said.[14] She and John spent many lunches at the Casa Dominguez restaurant talking about the strategies that worked well for John. He found real benefits in starting out the first week by discovering what students knew and didn't know and focusing on that, as well as coming into each class with clear objectives while also being flexible.[15] "John was amazing," she said. "He would take me out to lunch and very gently help me see my own classes from new perspectives. I remain in his debt."[16]

"She was a very keen student of teaching methods," Mixon wrote.[17] Teaching the first half of a contracts course was easy, he said, but the concepts in the second half were not. Under the pressure of teaching this complex course for the first time, Elizabeth found John a calm, steady mentor. She told Julius Getman, author of *In the Company of Scholars: The Struggle for the Soul of Higher Education*, "He just talked to me. He was calming, like the first stage of a mantra, or like psychotherapy. He was like that, calming…yet very intense about teaching."[18]

Those conversations were an oasis in a schedule that took on a breakneck pace. Teaching law and all the activities that went with it—department meetings, student advising, and researching and writing—demanded long days and take-home work in the evenings.

Elizabeth's commitments cut into her personal life, but she pushed herself to strike a balance by doing what mothers do while raising young children: leading a Girl Scout troop, bringing cookies to bake sales, teaching Sunday school.[19] She felt Jim's disappointment in the way he looked at his watch when meals were late or when, later at night, she was still at the table grading papers.[20] They never argued, she said, but the fact that she was working—*really* working in a career job—seemed to be pulling them apart. "I thought he felt I had reneged on our unspoken deal that he would work and I would take care of the house and children," she wrote. "I also thought he was right."[21]

Amelia was seven years old and in school most of the day, but Alex, her blond, brown-eyed two-year-old, would not adjust to being carted off every morning to babysitters and day care. One day, while picking him up at day care and finding him sitting miserably on a cot in a wet diaper, she felt near the breaking point. Child care was an endless circus of sitters and neighbors who canceled and day cares that didn't care enough. Alex was unhappy, kicking and fighting her every day and waking her up in the middle of the night crying, seeking the comfort of her and their rocking chair. As she held him that night after the sad pickup at day care, she realized she was failing her son.[22]

Soon after that, Aunt Bee called to ask how things were going. The house was quiet with the children in bed, and Elizabeth broke down. She told her she couldn't do it, couldn't teach and take care of Amelia and Alex. She cried and choked out what a terrible job she was doing, so terrible that she had to quit. Her aunt listened until Elizabeth blew her nose and calmed down and then said she could be there in two days. That Thursday, she showed up at the airport with half a dozen suitcases and her Pekinese, Buddy.

The house settled into a home where Aunt Bee, now seventy-seven years old, was a constant presence for Alex, tended to Amelia if she got sick and had to stay home from school, and turned the kitchen into a hub of comfort.[23] She relieved Elizabeth of a mountain of pressure, but the household was far from perfect. The distance between her and Jim rose up one evening as she stood by the sink doing dishes. She smelled his cigarette and turned to see him looking at her from the doorway. Then it just came out. "I asked him if he wanted a divorce," she said. "I'm not sure why I asked. It was as if the question just fell out of my mouth. I was shocked that I'd said it."

Jim, in his understated way, simply said, "Yes."[24] They talked it over for a few days, and Jim was gone by the next weekend. They had agreed he could take the bedroom furniture and some of the pictures from the walls, so the bedroom stood empty except for a twin bed she pulled in.[25] As they worked through the legal separation, there were moments of thinking they may be able to work things out, but they didn't. Without arguments or drama, they made decisions about child support and visits.[26]

Back in Oklahoma City, Liz's parents had sold the house and moved to the apartment complex where Donald worked as a maintenance man. The duties were strenuous at times for a man of sixty-seven, but he received free rent as part of his compensation. Elizabeth imagined them close by instead, retired and with nothing to do but play with their grandchildren. She felt she needed them, and soon after her separation from Jim, she called to tell them that and invite them to Houston. She would buy them a house of their own, she said, and they could have a new adventure living outside Oklahoma for the first time in their lives. They took her up on it and headed south, leaving the Sooner State behind.[27]

The summer after her first year of teaching, Elizabeth attended a seminar on law and economics, the field that applied economic thinking to legal practice. Understanding this approach and applying it to her earliest articles would have an impact on her job trajectory and, in later years, allow her to critique the model.[28] Over time, she became critical of its usefulness when it was applied to bankruptcy law, her area of specialty.

In law and economics theory, law is seen as a tool for creating "efficiency," a concept used in economics.[29] In an efficient system, resources are used to serve each person or organization in the best way—while also minimizing waste and inefficiency. This is a zero-sum game, in which any change in the system that will benefit one stakeholder will harm another. The theory also assumes that everyone makes decisions in a rational way, thinking through the costs and benefits and choosing the best outcome for themselves. Critics of the law and economics approach point out that these "theoretical" people often do not reflect how consumers make decisions in the real world.[30]

The law and economics training Elizabeth took in the late 1970s is reflected in her earliest law journal articles written during her time at Houston. Her introduction to the field took place during a national push to shift the thinking in law schools more toward the right.[31]

The Economics Institute for Law Professors summer program designed by scholar Henry Manne (pronounced MAN-ee) was part of a thrust by the John M. Olin Foundation to expand conservative ideas through think tanks, books, and law schools.[32] As Jason DeParle wrote in the *New York Times* in 2005, the foundation "has spent three decades financing the intellectual rise of the right." In his interview with the foundation's longtime director, James Piereson, DeParle traced the ideas that turned into law seminars for law professors and judges. "Liberal academics don't like American capitalism, American culture, and they don't like American history," Piereson said. "They see it as a history of oppression. There are some people who are prepared to spend large sums of money to address this problem."[33] Piereson believed that law schools had a disproportionately strong impact on public life and saw the law and economics approach as a tool for making that impact more conservative.

The foundation spent $68 million on law and economics programs,[34] including donating $18 million to Harvard Law School to launch the John M. Olin Center for Law, Economics, and Business in 1985.[35] "I saw it as a way into the law schools—I probably shouldn't confess that," Piereson told DeParle.[36]

As Jane Mayer chronicles in *Dark Money: The Hidden History of the Billionaires Behind the Rise of the Radical Right*, the Olin Foundation began its inroads into law schools by funding grants to Henry Manne, one of the founders of the law and economics movement who had learned his free-market economics at the University of Chicago Law School.[37] The grants, which began in the early 1970s, allowed Manne to create his own training programs, starting with the Economics Institute for Law Professors at the

University of Rochester in New York. The Chicago Law School described the institute as a place where, "for the first time, law professors were offered intensive instruction in microeconomics with the aim of incorporating economics into legal analysis and theory."[38] Manne moved his training program to the University of Miami in 1974, where he founded the Law & Economics Center. At the same time, he set up a generous scholarship program, named after and funded by Olin, that brought in PhD economists to study law. To some, perhaps in retrospect, the intensive summer seminars in law and economics for law professors were known as "Manne Camp."[39]

Piereson admitted that law and economics courses were a central project of the Olin Foundation's goal of shifting law schools to the right through their faculty. "Economic analysis tends to have conservatizing effects," he said.[40]

"Early on," Elizabeth's Houston colleague John Mixon said, "she went to a law and economics course taught by Henry Manne where they undertook to impose Chicago Law on law school teachers. This was before Elizabeth formed her own notions about the justice aspect of contract law and the social utility of it." In her early writing, he said, she was "learning the technicalities of this essentially right-wing law."[41]

For a Texas law professor just finished with another semester, the Manne institute that summer of 1979 felt like a reward, a vacation launched by a flight over the Gulf to the edge of the Florida coastline, sparkling on the Atlantic. The two dozen lawyers gathered in the presentation room with coffee and fresh-squeezed orange juice seemed relaxed, dressed in polo shirts and shorts. That first morning, Elizabeth kept eyeing the tall guy in glasses in the row in front of her. Sitting with his chair turned and legs stretched out, he looked to be over six feet, she thought, and those taut legs were a distraction. As she took notes on the difference between fairness and the "optimal operation" of an economy, she scoped the room for someone who looked approachable enough to ask about the man in the big glasses. At the first break, she checked around and learned that he was Bruce Mann, no relation to the instructor, since his name was spelled without the *e*, and that he was a legal historian with a focus on eighteenth-century America. He also played a lot of tennis.

At lunch, she introduced herself and made small talk until getting to the point: *Will you give me a tennis lesson when we're done here this afternoon?* He politely said yes, and they met up a few hours later. She discovered that his penchant for the Revolutionary War era lined up with his ancestry of a long line of Massachusetts families and that he was an Ivy Leaguer with a law degree and PhD in history from Yale. He got through his college years like she had, earning scholarships, taking out student loans, and working part time—but in his case, mostly teaching tennis. As reluctant as he was to give someone lessons on his brief getaway from Connecticut, where he taught law at the University of Connecticut School of Law, he didn't regret it. The attraction was mutual. She was bright-eyed and lit up a room, and in spite of her horrible backhand, she looked great on the tennis court.[42]

Bruce recalls a slightly different version of their first meeting. "I saw Elizabeth talking to someone and I was just immediately drawn to her," he told a Boston journalist. She was "lively, beautiful, engaged, smart—she just radiated energy," he said.[43]

They were both law professors, but that's where the comparison stopped. "If I was a hard-charging, go-to-the-mat-for-whatever-you-believe kind of professor, he was more of a scholarly, camping-out-in-the-archives-poring-over-an-old-legal-manuscript kind," she wrote.[44] She was vivacious, and he was soft-spoken. Elizabeth fell in love, and after the start of the new school year, on a visit to Connecticut, she sat in the back row of one of his classes. Years later, she told the story of that eventful day on her Facebook page:

> I proposed to Bruce in a classroom. It was the first time I'd seen him teach, and I was already in love with him, but watching him teach let me see one more thing about him—and that was it. When class was over and the students had cleared out, he came up to me and asked, somewhat hesitantly, "Uh, what did you think?"
>
> "What can I say? Will you marry me?"
>
> He stared back at me. It was not the first (or last) time that I gob smacked him… He blinked a couple of times, then jumped in with both feet. "OK."
>
> To make sure the deal was sealed, I smiled and said, "Good. Let's do it."[45]

They weighed their options—should she pack up her family and move to Connecticut, or should he leave his tenure-track post and join the clan she'd gathered around her in Houston? She had made roots with her young children, and Bruce had seen firsthand how much she loved the life she had pulled together with her family and career. The decision wasn't hard. He gave his resignation after just two years on the tenure track, and the last thing on his schedule in Connecticut was a wedding.[46]

Elizabeth didn't have the time or inclination to sew that summer, so she bought a white sundress, and on July 12, 1980, after just turning thirty-one, she married Bruce in Hartford. It was a perfect day, not too warm, with summer clouds prancing toward the north…just right.[47]

Houston Law offered Bruce a one-year position with a clear message that it was temporary, and that year, Elizabeth took on the role of associate dean.[48] She got her first taste of administration and made a statement by setting up a swing in her office. Instead of holding meetings with colleagues or students behind her desk, she swayed forward and back in the swing. "She had a bit of whimsy," John Mixon said. She sailed along and may have stayed longer but was advised that if she wanted to rise up the ladder as a scholar, she had to leave administration and continue her research, get published in journals, even start on a book.[49]

That year, she and Bruce were searching the country for professorships that would put them in the same school or at least in the same city. Then, out of the blue, they both received invitations to be visiting professors at the University of Texas at Austin School of Law (UT). As visiting professors, they would be under watchful eyes, considered for full hiring.[50] They sold their house and moved west with Alex, now five years old, and Amelia, who was starting fifth grade. Renting a house in case the move was temporary, they left Elizabeth's parents and Aunt Bee comfortable in their Houston homes. At UT, Elizabeth was still Professor Warren—she had kept her last name after marrying Bruce to make things simpler for Alex and Amelia.[51]

By the time they were putting down temporary stakes in Austin, Elizabeth was gripped by a new issue that impacted contracts and other areas of the law. In 1978, the overhaul of bankruptcy law ushered in the first revision of the code in forty years and made it easier for individuals to file and troubled companies to "reorganize," as bankruptcy is commonly called in business.[52] Anxious to delve into bankruptcy law, she asked the dean at UT if she could teach a course in it, even though she had never taught it before.[53] The revised code was so new that no one had published a textbook on it yet, so she would be starting from scratch.

The dean approved, and she came up with a game plan for the course: they would study each section of the law, working backward, thinking through the reasons lawmakers made each of the changes.[54] In a lecture she made several years later at the University of Wisconsin, Elizabeth spelled out the basics of bankruptcy law as it worked before some major changes were made in 1978. "The new [1978] law," she wrote, "made bankruptcy relief more readily accessible to families in financial trouble."[55] The U.S. Bankruptcy Code is divided into sections called *chapters*—Chapter 7, she explained, is a form of bankruptcy that allows people to wipe out most of their debt, while Chapter 13 *reorganizes* debt by setting up a payment plan for paying back some of it.

Families in financial trouble can file a petition in bankruptcy, pay a filing fee, disclose all their assets and liabilities, and have most of the debts discharged. If they own a home or a car, they are likely to continue paying on those obligations because, even if they are no longer personally liable, they will lose the home or the car (the collateral) if they do not make their payments. Certain debts—child support, taxes, and student loans are the most notable—are not dischargeable and must be repaid notwithstanding the bankruptcy.

About 70 percent of all debtors choose a chapter seven, or liquidation, which concludes with a discharge in about six weeks. The remaining 30 percent agree to make payments over a three- to five-year period, usually on the house, the car, and, in some cases, the credit card debt. Chapter thirteen has become more attractive to debtors because it offers them several incentives, such as an expanded discharge, an opportunity to strip down a lien against a car or other personal property, and a chance to catch up on mortgage payments by paying an arrearage.[56]

Credit card companies and businesses, she added, had a vested interest in weakening bankruptcy laws because written-off debts cut into their profits.

She realized that her fascination with bankruptcy was, to some extent, personal.[57] Having watched her parents suffer and argue through the hard times that put them on the brink of losing everything, the fear that rambled through their lives those years still haunted her. People who had lost a lot and made a tough choice to get a fresh start were like kin in a way. She could imagine the guilt and shame they went through as they signed the papers, and the idea would not let her go. But the scholar in her, steeped in the law and economics theory that tended to tip the balance of "efficiency" toward the benefit of companies over consumers, set up a conflict in her motivation to study the subject. To make things even more complicated, a guest speaker in her class that year revealed a huge gap in the academic understanding of bankruptcy.

The renowned bankruptcy scholar who had advised Congress during its revision of the code, Stefan Riesenfeld, surprised her with his response to a student's question about who filed for bankruptcy protection. "He said that the people who filed were mostly day laborers and housemaids who lived at the economic margins and always would," Elizabeth wrote. She followed up with a question of her own, asking how he knew this. Expecting him to cite studies, she was bowled over when he simply replied, "Because everyone knows that." To his irritation, she continued to pursue it, but in the end, she realized that there were no facts about filers, just assumptions.[58] That opened a huge door to potential research.

Texas had selected four visiting law professors that year, and all of them were outstanding. Professor Patricia Cain, who taught federal tax law at UT, recalled that the situation put the faculty at odds over who they should hire, and they struggled to make a decision. To complicate it further, she said, UT had a bit of a tough history of hiring partners. The school ruminated long and hard each time a pair came up, trying to measure if the spouse of the selected candidate was up to snuff. "As a result of all the conflict among the faculty," she said, "we decided to hire none of them."[59]

Back at the University of Houston, Elizabeth returned to her research and classroom teaching. By that time, in the fall of 1982, she was one of Houston Law's award-winning professors, having received its Outstanding Teacher Award the previous year. That recognition was the first of several teaching awards she would receive in her career.[60] Developing her ideas with the law and economics she had studied with Manne, she continued working on a paper titled, "Trade Usage and Parties in the Trade: An Economic Rationale for an Inflexible Rule," which was published with its several illustrations of supply and demand curves in the *Pittsburgh Law Review* in 1982.

The "Trade Usage" article caught the eye of one of the leaders in the law school over in Austin. Russell Weintraub, who passed away in 2012, was an eminent scholar of international business law who had been at UT for nearly twenty years and held the Powell Chair in Business & Commercial Law. "Russell Weintraub read that article and said she'd be very good at law and economics and we need to hire her," said Professor Calvin Johnson, the John T. Kipp Chair in Corporate and Business Law at UT. Calvin sat through the department's second evaluation of Elizabeth and recalled that the hiring committee made a good presentation of her strengths and gave her plusses for being "a hard-headed numbers woman." Being a woman was a plus, because law schools were on the hot seat to hire women, but "she was hired primarily because Russell really loved a piece on law and economics she had published," Calvin said.[61]

Elizabeth accepted the permanent job offer from the University of Texas, and this time, the entire extended family moved to Austin.

Bruce and Elizabeth bought a new house and set up Elizabeth's parents and Aunt Bee in a side-by-side duplex. Aunt Bee's Pekingese had died and now there was a cocker spaniel, and Amelia and Alex had a new golden retriever puppy named Trover. While the move to one of the best law schools in the country was a thrilling step in Elizabeth's career and Austin a lively, music-filled city in which to live, the downside was that Bruce did not get hired with her.[62]

Bruce had his own success in landing a job at the Washington University School of Law in St. Louis, but being a distance couple was tough.[63] They kept searching, but it can take years for academic couples to find jobs together. He rented an apartment in St. Louis and flew back to Austin every week, making a connection in Dallas, which cut into his precious time with the family. He was a devoted dad, making the trips in time to coach Alex's soccer team and go to Amelia's school events, and he and Elizabeth tried to create as normal a life as possible over the next four years as they taught in separate schools.

Mark Gergen, Elizabeth's colleague at UT who taught at the school for twenty-three years before becoming a professor at Berkeley Law School, recalled that the holdup for Bruce at Austin was due to the fact that he had not yet published his first book. "Law historians aren't like other law professors," Mark said. "With legal scholarship, you can do one big article a year, but if you're doing a history of law in eighteenth-century Connecticut, that's a lot of archival work, a lot of writing."[64] History projects take years, and until Bruce got the book done, Mark said, people at Texas didn't want to pursue hiring him.

"The decision by Texas to hire her and not her husband Bruce was painful and made their personal lives difficult during that separation," Patricia Cain said.[64] She underwent the same thing when she was hired at UT Law and the school decided not to make an offer to her spouse, Jean, who was also a law professor. "Liz and I had something in common, and that helped us understand each other's position better," said Patricia.

One of the handful of women on the UT faculty when Elizabeth arrived, Patricia was hired in 1974 when the law school happened to be under investigation for violating Section VII of the Civil Rights Act that prohibits sex discrimination in hiring. "It was hard," Patricia said. "There weren't a lot of female students—maybe 25 percent by my second or third year." Elizabeth and Patricia shared stories about their law school days, previous positions, and some of the obstacles they'd faced as women in the law. Patricia, now a professor at the Santa Clara University School of Law after teaching at UT for seventeen years, evolved as a scholar to become one of the nation's foremost experts in federal tax law and sexuality and the law, a field involved in taxation and estate planning for same-sex couples. After graduating from law school, her experiences with law firm interviews echoed those revealed in discrimination studies during that era. In one incident, a male partner from one of the country's major firms asked her in an interview what kind of birth control she used. "I wasn't going to tell him that I'm a lesbian, but I complained about the question," she said. She asked him why he wanted to know, and he said, "What if you get pregnant in the middle of a big case?" She answered, "What if you fell down the stairs and got a lobotomy in the middle of a big case?" They hired her.[66]

In one conversation, Elizabeth informed Patricia about the roles that she, Elizabeth, and some of the other female faculty took on at UT, something Patricia had not noticed. "She said she was the kid sister to them," Patricia said, "and Barbara Aldave was the mother." Patricia then understood that this was just the men's way of perceiving their female colleagues. Patricia recalled her experience at UT in the seventies and eighties as wonderful in many ways, yet not without discrimination. Her colleagues were terrific personal friends and genuinely supportive, such as when she was in the hospital for weeks with a life-threatening disease and they all took care of her. However, the men did not give her the respect they gave to their male colleagues. When Charles Wright, one of the most distinguished men on the faculty, who had argued thirteen cases before the Supreme Court and been a consultant to President Richard Nixon's counsel, held his casual discussions in the faculty lounge, she was always left out.

"Charlie Wright," Patricia said, "would routinely challenge professors in the lounge, telling someone, 'I just read this case in your field—what do you think about it?'" This was his way, she said, of giving professors a chance to prove where they stood in their field and engage with him. "He never asked me a question like that," she said. "We talked about football."[67] Although Charles was a magnificent man in many ways and treated her kindly, she said, he clearly did not treat her as an equal to male faculty.

Liz was highly respected at UT and didn't suffer from gender discrimination, Patricia said, but she did suffer because they didn't hire Bruce.

Elizabeth began a phase of scholarly research on bankruptcy at UT that launched her into a specialization that ultimately led to government work and politics.[68] At the beginning, she came to her central question—who is really filing for bankruptcy?—with a mindset not unlike the elderly expert who had visited her class. She had grown up in a family that had gone broke more than once but had never filed for bankruptcy, so she thought, *We pulled our belts tighter. Why didn't they pull their belts tighter?*

> This was back in the early eighties, and I'll tell you what I set out to prove. I set out to prove they were all a bunch of cheaters. My take on this, my thrust, what I was going to do, [was] to expose these people who were taking advantage of the rest of us by hauling off to bankruptcy and just charging debts that they really could repay, or who'd been irresponsible in running up debts.[69]

By the end of the eighties, when her bankruptcy project was published as a book, the findings revealed a completely different story: "I did the research, and the data just took me to a totally different place," she said. "These were hardworking middle-class families who by and large had lost jobs, gotten sick, had family breakups, and that's what was driving them over the edge financially."[70]

The study with her fellow law professor Jay Westbrook and UT sociology professor Teresa Sullivan, which they named the Consumer Bankruptcy Project, became the largest study of its kind.[71] They set out to take a close look at the predictions made in law and economics studies about bankruptcy that, in spite of being "simplistic and untested," were used to guide the decisions of lawmakers.[72]

Next, they wanted to find out about the occupations, income histories, home ownership, and other aspects of the people who filed, to add a social element to the study. They also looked at the way the process worked through the legal system by talking to lawyers and judges and, unlike most other studies, paid as much attention to the creditors—the credit card issuers, finance companies, banks, etc.—as to the debtors.

The team began their work in the summer of 1982 with a pilot study to help develop their methods, visiting a bankruptcy court in San Antonio. Over the next six years, they would gather and analyze 250,000 pieces of information from twenty-four hundred bankruptcy files, and the findings became talking points on TV shows and in boardrooms for years on end. Bringing this information to the public in an accessible way in the book *As We Forgive Our Debtors: Bankruptcy and Consumer Credit in America*, the team started a national conversation about bankruptcy and shattered the stereotypes of bankruptcy filers as deadbeats and, as Elizabeth had assumed, "a bunch of cheaters." [73]

As the study developed and Elizabeth learned about the "very real pain, anger, deceit, fear, and relief that color each bankruptcy file," as well as the devastating financial situation of so many working Americans, one question kept coming up: Why?[74]

With the first study, the team revealed the situations of people who failed financially and the workings of the bankruptcy process. For their next study, they tried to find out why—what forces came together in the country to cause four hundred thousand people to file bankruptcy in 1986 and twice as many a decade later? The second study, published in 2000 as *The Fragile Middle Class: Americans in Debt*, discovered those forces and offered a new portrait of the middle class.[75] The journey through these studies shifted Elizabeth's perspective of the free-market system, which she long believed was the ideal framework for a strong economy. Over the years, however, as she discovered how those markets were becoming more and more favorable to those at the top, she questioned the mantra that the markets, if left alone, could bring the best results for everyone. "At some point," John Mixon said, "Elizabeth realized that that was not consistent with her own value structure."[76]

Bringing an empirical or research-based framework into the law was not the norm at the time, since law is an academic field grounded in theories and concepts. But when fields like bankruptcy law—which are ripe with assumptions about human behavior that could be false—test those assumptions with feet-on-the-ground research, they can change society. Julius Getman, who came to UT Law during Elizabeth's last year on the faculty, wrote about the importance of the kind of real-world research her team was doing. Professor Getman pioneered empirical research in his area of labor law and reflected in 1992 that "in law it is possible to count on the fingers of one hand the major empirical research of the last decade. Similarly, major research is surprisingly rare in political science, international affairs, economics, women's studies, and African studies. In all of these areas, much current controversy and thinking exist that could be resolved or clarified through carefully designed field research."[77]

The bankruptcy and secured credit fields of law in which Elizabeth specializes, Mark Gergen explained, are dominated by people like Allan Schwartz at Yale Law School who are steeped in a law and economics approach. "Their scholarship tends to use fairly rigorous models of human behavior and ends up being pro-creditor. Liz and Jay were kind of the leading opponents of that way of approaching bankruptcy."[78] They did empiricism, but law and economics people would criticize it as soft empiricism, he said, empiricism that went out and talked to people and talked about the human consequences of these policies.

In an article about a law and economics legal education and middle-class values, John Mixon wrote that "morality, justice, fairness, and integrity" exist in people but are dismissed in the models learned in a law and economics program.[79] By advancing "self-interest and extreme individualism," this kind of education portrays government and its regulations as the enemy and leads to the kind of self-interested decisions that caused the recession of 2008.[80] That critique helps highlight the value of the socially conscious Bankruptcy Project. The study that had made Elizabeth an academic star forced people to consider the moral and human cost dimensions of bankruptcy—it exposed the human fallout of a system that kept widening the gap between the haves and have-nots.

4

EVERYWHERE YOU WANT TO BE

"Middle-class societies don't emerge automatically as an economy matures; they have to be created *through political action."*

—Paul Krugman[1]

The dusty old courtroom in San Antonio where the Bankruptcy Project team started their pilot study offered up a premonition of what they would discover. As Elizabeth sat in the back watching the hushed goings-on, she noticed that the people filing up with the lawyers didn't look like ragged deadbeats or shifty characters. The men and women of all colors and sizes looked like the same crowd you'd see walking out of church on Sunday morning or stepping into a PTA meeting. But these normal-looking folks were standing before the judge to admit financial failure, their last effort in some kind of downhill struggle that Elizabeth knew too well. A sense of trauma sucked the air out of the room. "I didn't stay long," Elizabeth said. "It was like staring at a car crash, a car crash involving people you knew."[2]

The chill of that first impression was like a tap on the shoulder from the Ghost of Christmas Future warning that their findings would not be pretty. Over the next two decades, Elizabeth, Teresa, and Jay's discoveries would turn America's ideas about the supposedly stable middle class upside down.

The models they were testing had caused an outcry from creditors who claimed that the new bankruptcy rules of 1978, which made it easier for people to file for bankruptcy, were driving up the rate of bankruptcies.[3] They also argued that the new code enticed people who could actually afford to make payments (in a Chapter 13 filing) to instead take the easy way out and file for Chapter 7. They were working hard to convince Congress that this was true, but Elizabeth, Teresa, and Jay's studies proved that it was not. Their work showed that the entire premise of the law and economics approach was suspect. The incentive approach in economic models predicts how people will respond to carrots and sticks put out to influence their behavior. However, the carrots and sticks are not designed through research and experiments but by "armchair theorists" imagining how people will behave. As Elizabeth and her team described it, this imagining is like theorists sitting around and saying, "Suppose you're on a desert island, and you have a nickel, and I have a banana…"[4] Instead, the Bankruptcy Project used actual facts to find out if the new code was luring people who could pay into taking the easy way out, and the data found that it was not true. This was one lesson of the Bankruptcy Project's work.

Elizabeth's skilled understanding of law and economics allowed her to point out the differences between predictions and facts using the jargon of the field. Economics had become "a discipline central to government planning and political debate," the team wrote, and lawmakers were writing laws "designed to influence conduct by incentives (carrots) and disincentives (sticks), usually economic ones."[5] As a "hard-numbers woman," she knew what the models were trying to say and how they swayed opinion on the volatile subject of bankruptcy.[6] She knew how to reverse engineer a slogan about deadbeats to its source in an economic model.

Her "coconspirators" in the project, who would form a long-lasting team, were stars of the UT faculty. Professor Jay Westbrook, the current Schmidt Chair of Business Law, was a partner in a DC law firm specializing in commercial law and international business litigation before joining UT Law, where he became an acclaimed bankruptcy scholar. Professor Teresa Sullivan was a young sociologist with a mastery of statistical analysis. She would spend twenty-seven years at UT before moving on to the University of Michigan and then becoming the first female president of the University of Virginia. Elizabeth described Teresa's meticulous attention to every technical twist in their data. "It is her stated goal to make our work absolutely unassailable," she said, "its statistical validity unquestioned: in short, that the data reflect fact, or as close to fact as fallible humans can make it."[7]

At both her first teaching job in Houston and then at Texas, Elizabeth took her teaching as seriously as her research.[8] Her students were going into a profession that would give them power over people's money, businesses, and lives, so she rightly felt a responsibility to form capable lawyers. If someone did not work, she was not afraid to flunk them.[9] The other duties that came along with the job also stretched her leadership skills—while serving as the chair of the tenure and promotion committee at UT Law, she had the unfortunate task of not approving someone for tenure. "She handled that delicate task well," her colleague Mark Gergen said. "She's a very strong person, and she was a strong advocate in appointments and for hiring and promoting people." She looked for good scholars doing work that focused on issues that mattered to people, he said. "At Berkeley, we call that social justice—we didn't call it that in Texas."[10]

She was also the faculty adviser to the Women's Law Caucus, the student organization that helped women build professional networks and gave them opportunities to do community service.[11] Student leaders of the caucus admired Elizabeth as one of the few women on the faculty, a prominent scholar, and a committed teacher and mentor, but they also recognized that speaking out about women's issues was not on her agenda. Jay Westbrook observed Elizabeth's routine urging of the faculty to hire more women as her style of advocating for these issues. She wasn't strident about it, but instead "would do so with a wink and a smile." The grindingly slow process of bringing women into the law may have brought her to the decision early on that this was not her fight—not her biggest fight. But her cutting-edge research on bankruptcy law led to a new understanding of not only the plight of middle-class families, but specifically women's financial challenges. She, like all empirical researchers, hoped that her findings would perhaps find their way into policy and make positive changes in society.

By 1986, Elizabeth and Bruce had been working in separate states for three years and were still eager to find positions in the same school. The dream situation finally came up that year when the

University of Pennsylvania Law School first reached out to Elizabeth and then separately to Bruce. Penn made a formal offer to hire them both that included its full support of Elizabeth's ongoing Bankruptcy Project research. By then, Bruce's growing notability in his field included more articles in peer-reviewed journals and the completion of his first book, *Neighbors and Strangers: Law and Community in Early Connecticut*, to be published the following year.[12]

UT Law responded to news of Penn's offer by offering Bruce a position. "We finally tried to hire Bruce because the book came out," said Mark Gergen, "and it was a good book, but by that point, Penn was looking at the two of them, and it was too late. We were kicking ourselves—we should have hired Bruce a couple of years earlier."[13]

Aunt Bee, who was now a sprightly eighty-six, was enthusiastic about moving to Philadelphia, and there was plenty of room for her in the old stone house that Bruce and Elizabeth found about five miles from the Philadelphia campus. But Donald, in his early eighties, and Pauline, seventy-eight, didn't share her sense of adventure. They weren't up for relocating to a strange part of the country but instead wanted to go back to Oklahoma. After a few weeks of trying to convince them otherwise, Elizabeth accepted the fact that she would not be able to keep the tight-knit clan together. It made sense that her parents wanted to stay in the south and closer to their sons, especially Don Reed, whose wife, Nancy, had died from leukemia a few years before. Don Reed and his wife and sons had finally settled in Texas after decades of moving place to place for Don Reed's military career. As an air force pilot, he had served multiple missions in Vietnam and risen to the rank of lieutenant colonel, and now he and his boys were on their own in Grapevine, just outside Dallas.[14]

Elizabeth's other two brothers were still in Oklahoma, John in his fifties and still working construction, and David piecing together work after his once-booming oil rig supplies business was hit hard by the oil bust of the eighties. Elizabeth and Bruce bought Donald and Pauline a house in Oklahoma City just a few blocks from David and planned to visit as often as they could.

At the start of the fall term in 1987, Amelia was sixteen and already scoping out colleges. Eleven-year-old Alex was as tall as his mother and a "full-fledged computer geek," Elizabeth said, and hooked on *Star Trek: The Next Generation*, which he, Elizabeth, and Bruce watched together religiously. As Elizabeth began setting up her office in the law school, it was no surprise that she was one of only three women on the faculty. These included torts and insurance law professor Regina Austin, a black scholar who was invited to be a visiting professor at Harvard two years later.* At that time, Harvard Law was embroiled in a fierce dispute over its lack of women and minorities on the faculty, and in the final semester of Regina's year, students staged overnight sit-ins in the law school dean's office.[15] When Regina did not receive an offer to join the faculty, Derrick Bell, Harvard Law School's first black professor, considered it the final straw and announced he would take a leave of absence without pay in protest. "I cannot continue to urge students to take risks for what they believe if I do not practice my own precepts," he said.[16] Derrick was one of the leading intellectuals of his generation, the father figure of critical race theory, a legal movement that explored the relationships between race, racism,

---

* Torts, like contracts, is one of the major areas of law that involves civil (noncriminal) acts that cause injury or harm to others.

and power. When Regina returned to Penn, she was promoted from associate professor to full professor.[17]

The report card for female law faculty in the 1990s showed growing numbers of assistant, associate, and full-time professors, but by the end of the decade, the percentage of tenured women nationwide was still pathetically low at 6.4 percent.[18] Alix James, a Penn Law student who took Elizabeth's bankruptcy course, recalled that the administration and faculty "were in all kinds of hot seats about their failure to have women on the faculty. They were under a huge amount of pressure to hire women, and to be able to get Professor Warren, one so qualified, was a win for sure."[19]

Although there was a glaring awareness and even some bitterness over the issue, Elizabeth did not talk about it. "She never communicated in any way that she felt that her opportunities were going to be less because she was a woman," Alix said. "She left all those issues on the side. They were not part of her persona. She was about teaching law and making good lawyers." Alix, who after graduating from Penn Law became the CEO of the sports and weather instruments company Nielsen-Kellerman, enjoyed the bankruptcy class, which was held in a stadium-style room with a podium front and center. "It's a topic that could have been crushingly dry and technical," she said, "and focused solely on the mechanics of bankruptcy, but she had a very well-articulated theory of why bankruptcy is a good thing to have available as a legal recourse and the balance that was involved in that." She recalled that Elizabeth explained the process with passion and was very engaged with the students. "That was one of the first classes I took in which the professor gave a lot of real-world examples. Professor Warren did a great job of illustrating in a very practical way what it meant when a company filed bankruptcy, all the considerations that went into the best possible outcome for a functionally failing business."[20]

Alix also attended Elizabeth's small lunch group for students who thought they might want to teach law. She recalled that Elizabeth was practical about her advice, balancing her passion for the teaching part with the other demands of the career. "She talked about the challenges of having to publish and survive in a political academic environment, which was what I had seen my dad have to do, and I ultimately decided I didn't want to go that route, to be in that small fishbowl."[21] The women appreciated that Elizabeth volunteered her time for these mentoring sessions, and some of them did choose to teach. Marci Hamilton, for one, clerked with Supreme Court Justice Sandra Day O'Connor after law school and became an endowed chair professor at the Benjamin N. Cardozo School of Law in New York. Now back at Penn Law as a professor, she is one of the country's leading experts on church-state and constitutional law and has successfully challenged the constitutionality of the Religious Freedom Restoration Act at the U.S. Supreme Court.[22]

In her eight years at Penn, including the year she spent as visiting professor at Harvard Law, Elizabeth produced an astonishing amount of work. Her output included sixteen articles in major journals including the *Yale Law Journal, University of Chicago Law Review*, and *Harvard Journal of Law & Public Policy*, four book chapters, and five books—not counting the accompanying teachers' manuals and supplements. Several of these works were cowritten with Teresa Sullivan and Jay Westbrook as they continued their bankruptcy research together.

She sparred with scholars with point-by-point responses to their opposing views on bankruptcy law, perhaps most famously with University of Chicago Law School professor Douglas Baird. In her 1987 *University of Chicago Law Review* article, written in the spirit "of the old 'Point-Counterpoint' segment of television's *60 Minutes*,"[23] Elizabeth throws down the gauntlet: "Baird presumes that there can be a simple answer to explain all of bankruptcy, and that the relationship between statutory law and modification of the behavior of debtors and creditors is known and can be predicted in new circumstances. I see bankruptcy as a more complex and ultimately less confined process."[24] Here, she took the offense position to the theoretical nature of law and economics, in which assumptions and predictions—instead of real-world facts—analyze what is happening in the world. She sums up their differences with a stinging critique of the entire theoretical approach that had become the mainstay of much legal scholarship:

> Mine is not an entertaining (or, I suspect, popular) position for an academic. I cannot claim that bankruptcy, at its heart, is an intellectual construct or that I can reason to a meaningful conclusion by doing nothing more than thinking hard about logical consequences derived from a handful of untested assumptions. I would like to endorse something that requires only library time and yellow legal pads to uncover ideal solutions to legal problems. The trouble is that I can't do it.
>
> But I do not think Baird can do it either. The certainty of Baird's position is a fiction... [He] simply makes the debate a shadow game that offers little real illumination.[25]

So, Professor Warren, legal scholars around the country likely thought, *tell us how you really feel.*

The associate professor who'd learned her law and economics at a summer Manne Camp retreat and experimented with it in her early writing was now a vocal critic of its limitations. In terms of bankruptcy law, she felt there was too much at stake—the middle class was crumbling due to the forces behind hundreds of thousands of bankruptcies, and she called on her fellow scholars to "get about the business of asking harder questions, looking for better evidence, and approximating better answers."[26]

The Bankruptcy Project wound up seven years of work during Elizabeth's first year at Penn, and in 1989, the story hit the bookshelves. In *As We Forgive Our Debtors*, Elizabeth, Teresa, and Jay admit up front that their findings had stumped them all along the way. Their analysis of fifteen hundred bankruptcy cases filed in 1981 in Pennsylvania, Illinois, and Texas forced them "to rethink our own understanding of bankruptcy."[27] The facts shattered the two most common stereotypes that bankrupts were either (a) members of the chronically underemployed lower class, or (b) better off but clever enough to manipulate the system.

The long-term study uncovered that bankrupt debtors are "right out of Middle America," spanning a typical cross section of the general population.[28] And, like Middle America, half of the debtors are homeowners. Contrary to another stereotype, less than 2 percent of bankrupt people are "credit card junkies" with massive amounts of credit card debt relative to their income.[29] The team also learned that debtors are employed in middle-class jobs—but in the lower-earning segment of those jobs, earning about 25 percent less than average.

Another finding focused on lenders: because they are able to charge high interest that brings enormous profit, creditors lend to people at or below the poverty line and to those who are already deeply in debt. This tied into a discovery that Elizabeth would continue to write about in upcoming books and articles, learning that single women are the poorest of all the debtors, "at the bottom of the economic basement."[30]

In *As We Forgive Our Debtors*, the research team concluded that the bankruptcy laws are doing what they set out to do, serving "people in serious, even hopeless financial trouble, who need either a fresh-start discharge from their debts or at least some protection from their creditors and a breathing spell while they try to repay."[31]

The Bankruptcy Project dissolved Elizabeth's assumptions about bankruptcy filers. The truth, she found, was that the people who went bankrupt were driven over the edge financially after losing a job, getting divorced, or falling ill, and they looked like most of the rest of the country. That new knowledge transformed Elizabeth's vision and planted the seeds of her desire to deliver that message to an even wider audience. She kept writing and teaching as she planned the next study with the team. *As We Forgive Our Debtors* was published at a time when more than seven hundred thousand families had filed for bankruptcy in a single year—more than double the number since her career began—and she was ready to devote another decade trying to find out why.[32]

As the first married couple on the faculty at Penn Law, Bruce and Elizabeth were a unique package. And while history and bankruptcy may have sounded far-flung from each other in the course catalog, some of Bruce's writing in legal history intersected with Elizabeth's area of the law. While he worked on a piece called "Failure in the Land of the Free," for instance, his trove of stories must have sparked many conversations in front of the fireplace in the old stone house.

In that article, he wrote about the changing mind-set toward debtors in the 1700s, opening with a statement that spoke to any era: "Whether a society forgives its debtors and how it bestows or withholds forgiveness are more than matters of economic or legal consequence. They go to the heart of what a society values."[33] While the early years saw "insolvent" souls thrown into prison for violating the moral code of God, the "Great Creditor," he wrote, this attitude was forced to change with the times.[34] As business and commerce grew, so did the risk of failure:

> Farmers and planters, artisans and shopkeepers, traders and merchants borrowed against anticipated profits to finance the undertakings that they knew—not hoped, but knew—would create them. Not surprisingly, some faltered while others soared. After all, crops fail, prices fall, ships sink, warehouses burn, owners die, partners steal, pirates pillage, wars ravage, and people simply make mistakes. Economic growth enabled more people to fail owing greater sums of money to larger numbers of credits than had previously been possible… For the first time one finds people arguing against imprisonment for debt and for bankruptcy laws.[35]

Just as Elizabeth's writing shed light on the experiences of modern people in debt, Bruce's articles brought the troubles of a much earlier generation to life. In "Tales from the Crypt: Prison, Legal Authority, and the Debtors' Constitution in the Early Republic," Bruce described the justice system in a New York debtors' prison built in the 1750s. The barred-window prison that had been described as "this unhappy mansion," a "human slaughter house," "that dismal cage," and a "loathsome store-house" had its own rules that, in one case, punished a man for writing a letter that could have brought harm to another prisoner.[36] The man was kicked out of his room for his "crime":

> For seven weeks, he lived in the stairwell. Finally, as fall approached, Narine petitioned to be readmitted to the hall, reciting "the great injury of his health from the impure smell from the [waste] Tubs and the night air," the "approaching inclement season," and the fact that his trunks and baggage were obstructing the stairs. He admitted his "improper Conduct and behavior" and was restored to the membership by unanimous vote. The debtors could not banish errant members from the prison, but they could expel them from their community.[37]

Bruce's descriptions of New York's earliest poor reflected the situations Elizabeth was sharing about America's bankrupt families, many of whom felt shamed and shunned after their financial lives fell apart. The bankrupt middle-class people in her studies endured self-blame and humiliation while also hearing the message loud and clear from antibankruptcy forces in the lending industry and Congress that they didn't deserve a handout in the form of Chapter 7 or 13.

In the spring of 1990, Penn Law recognized Elizabeth's achievements by appointing her the William A. Schnader Professor of Commercial Law, making her the first woman to be given an endowed professorship at Penn Law. The dean, Colin S. Diver, said in his announcement, "We are fortunate to have in our midst a scholar of such renown and a teacher of such gifts as to make the choice of the person to fill the Schnader Professorship so clear."[38] During her time at Penn Law, she was twice awarded the Harvey Levin Award for Excellence in Teaching, as well as the Lindback Award for Distinguished Teaching.[39] *As We Forgive Our Debtors* "caused a mild stir, at least in academic circles," Elizabeth said, and in 1990, it was awarded the Silver Gavel Award of the American Bar Association. Life was good and getting better.[40]

With both of their careers on the rise, Harvard came calling in 1992. The law school offered both Elizabeth and Bruce visiting professorships for the school year to start that fall, and with their positions secure at Penn, it was a win-win invitation to spend a tryout year at Harvard Law.[41] Rather than stay in Philadelphia alone, Aunt Bee spent that year in Oklahoma City with Pauline and Donald, and Amelia was already out of the house studying history at Brown University in Providence, Rhode Island. Elizabeth, Bruce, Alex, and the golden retriever, Trover, moved up to Cambridge, where Alex transferred to a new high school and joined the football team.[42]

Elizabeth and Bruce stepped into Harvard Law a year after the school had graduated a student named Barack Obama, a thirty-year-old who had made his mark as the first black president of the *Harvard Law Review*. The year they were teaching, Barack married another Harvard Law grad named Michelle Robinson over in Chicago.[43]

Elizabeth received her own proposal in the second semester of her visiting year, an offer for a tenured position. But since they did not extend an offer to Bruce, she turned it down. She felt settled in Philadelphia and loved what she was doing at Penn—without Bruce, the timing just didn't seem right.[44]

Before the family headed back to Philadelphia, her students gave her something they hoped would remind her of them and Harvard for a long time, a golden retriever puppy named Good Faith.[45] The fates seemed to have whispered to them about the perfect gift, because two days after Elizabeth and Bruce returned home, their beloved Trover died. "I called Daddy," Elizabeth said, "crying so hard that he couldn't make out what I was saying… And he started to cry too."[46] Trover had been part of the family for ten years, and Good Faith somehow knew it was time to come aboard.

The dean at Harvard called from time to time, letting Elizabeth know the offer was still open, but she still did not accept.[47] Their lives had been disrupted more times than she could count—but Amelia had kept score, telling friends that she attended nine public schools before graduating from high school.[48] Now she was a young woman with the blue eyes and prairie-wheat-colored hair of her mother, working on an MBA at the University of Pennsylvania's Wharton School, just a block from Penn Law.

When Alex left for college, the house was quieter, and in July, Bruce took Elizabeth out to dinner for their anniversary, as he always did. He gave her fourteen roses, one for each year they'd been married, and the next day, she dried them in the oven, like she always did, and poured the dry flakes into a sachet to hang on her closet door.[49]

The year 1995 brought the worst spring Oklahoma City had ever seen, an April so bad, the entire world still remembers it. Just after 9:00 a.m. on April 19, walls shook and windows rattled all over the city when a bomb ripped through the Alfred P. Murrah Federal Building downtown and left 168 people dead. The attackers were homegrown, two radical right-wing survivalists.[50] None of Elizabeth's family were harmed, but the city took a long time to heal. It was the year of the O. J. Simpson trial and an internet browser called Netscape that flickered on thick screens and called up a website called Amazon. com for the first time.

Television ads showed the many places credit cards were accepted—"Visa: everywhere you want to be"—as lenders were unleashed from usury laws (laws that protect consumers from excessively high interest rates) and free to set new fees and interest-rate increases that brought profits they'd never seen before. The number of bankruptcies kept increasing at the same time, up to eight hundred thousand a year, one more every twenty-six seconds.[51] One day, when Elizabeth worried out loud about where all this was going, Bruce asked her what she was going to do about it. She let that sink in for a while, and the next time she yelled at the car radio to set somebody straight about "credit card junkies," Bruce turned to her and said, "Take the Harvard job."[52]

"Penn was a terrific school," Elizabeth wrote, "but Bruce argued that if I wanted people to listen to my ideas, I might as well shout from the highest mountain I could find."[53] Bruce, who had been building his reputation at Penn for eight years, was willing to be a commuter and travel up to Massachusetts as often as he could.

Her offer was still waiting with Harvard Law's dean, Robert C. Clark, and she accepted. Her endowed position, the Leo Gottlieb Professor of Law, came with a six-figure salary and other compensation that made her the third-highest-paid person at the university.[54]

She grew up, like her father, afraid of being poor. "His response was never to talk about money or what might happen if it ran out—never ever ever. My response was to study contracts, finance, and most of all, economic failure, to learn everything I could. My daddy stayed away from big sores that hurt. I poked at them."[55] At forty-six, she was long free of the money fears that had troubled the first half of her life. She was the teacher she knew she would become in second grade, the woman hidden between the lines in a Betty Crocker study guide.

An interviewer once told her, "You started out teaching a night class at Rutgers and ended up at Harvard—you must have been terribly ambitious."[56]

"I'm not even slightly ambitious," she said. "I loved what I did, and I worked hard at what I did, and I tried to accomplish something where I was. Every time I did that, a door seemed to swing open somewhere else, and I walked through it."

5

THE TWO-DIMENSIONAL SCHOLAR

"The intellectual's role is...to challenge and defeat both an imposed silence and the normalized quiet of unseen power wherever and whenever possible."

—EDWARD W. SAID[1]

The crimson-red block letters of Harvard are as iconic as, well, Harvard. Movie scenes filmed on sidewalk cafés in Harvard Square, a legacy as the oldest university in the country (established in 1636), and an epic lineup of alumni (including five Harvard Law School graduates currently serving on the Supreme Court) reflect the university's bedrock status in the culture. Joining the faculty of Harvard Law School not only put Elizabeth at the top of her profession, but also brought her to the birthplace of how American legal education is taught today.

In the late 1800s, Harvard shaped the way law schools taught, including the courses taught in the first year and the case method of teaching, both of which became the standard in schools through-out the country.* In place of lectures, the case method involved reading the decisions of actual court cases and discussing them in class. Dissecting several cases revolving around the same subject allowed students to understand the underlying principles that affected the court's decisions. Harvard defined the purpose of legal education as learning to "think like a lawyer," as educational scholar Bruce Kimball explained.[2] After thirty years of teaching, Elizabeth described this in a similar way, summarizing the law degree as "an advanced degree in thinking."[3]

Harvard has always left a large footprint on the legal world and is consistently rated number two among American law schools, following only Yale. In the past fifteen years, Yale, Harvard, and Stanford have been rated the top three, in that order, according to a study of the average *U.S. News & World Report* rankings.[4]† A comparison of Yale and Harvard law schools, starting with the relative size of both, offers insights into Harvard's place in the Ivy League terrain.

An incoming class at Harvard Law is typically about 550 students, while a new class at Yale is about 240. Yale's smaller enroll-ment makes it more competitive to get into, but that smaller scale offers a more intimate, collegial, and relaxed way to study law than students may experience at Harvard. The larger class sizes at Harvard create a more institutional and competitive atmosphere.[5]

Douglas Peterson, a Harvard Law School graduate who studied economics as an undergrad at Yale and now serves as the general

---

* Contracts, property, torts, criminal law, and civil procedure.

† Rankings are based on assessments by judges, lawyers, and deans of other schools; students' Law School Admission Test (LSAT) scores; graduate employment rates; student/faculty ratio; and other criteria.

counsel of the University of Minnesota system, likens the difference between the two law schools to the distinctions between New York and Paris. "Harvard is more New York because it's a larger institution and more tied into the mainstream in many ways, even though it has its radical elements running right alongside it," he said. "Yale is like Paris, more creative and a little harder to define." It's not that one school is politically more left or right, he explained, but more that Harvard is more disciplined and classic, while Yale is more freethinking and creative. "But both places have thought and research that spans the political spectrum," he said.[6]

Elizabeth taught some of her classes in Austin Hall, the stately red sandstone law building constructed in 1883 with arches, columns, and a Romanesque revival–style turret.[7] Below the mock courtroom on the second floor, the large classrooms of the main floor included Austin West, with its grand floor-to-ceiling fireplace.

The year 1995 was an interesting one to move to Boston. It would be a winter like no other, burying the city in a record-breaking 107.6 inches of snow. The weather didn't help the already troubled Big Dig—the major public works project that had overtaken downtown since 1991. Officially known as the Central Artery/Tunnel Project, the Big Dig would replace the crammed overhead highway that cut across the city with a much wider underground roadway, create a new second tunnel to Logan International Airport, and construct a new bridge across the Charles River.[8]‡

---

‡ Bostonians didn't know that they were headed for fifteen years of downtown construction and a final price tag that was nine times more than the estimate ($24 billion, counting the interest on loans). By the time it was finished in 2007, the Big Dig was compared to the Panama Canal and Channel Tunnel in scope and achieved its mission of decongesting a major New England thoroughfare and beautifying the city.

During her seventeen years as a professor at Harvard, Elizabeth's students found her tough yet engaging in the classroom, personable and empathetic, and a generous mentor. Chrystin Ondersma, who is now a professor at Rutgers Law School, first heard Professor Warren at a Harvard lunch lecture where Elizabeth was talking about the Socratic method. "I wanted to be a law professor and was coming from a radical feminist viewpoint," she said, "and she was very persuasive. She said that if we care about diversity and equality, the Socratic method is the way to go. Otherwise it's two white guys dominating the discussion." Elizabeth told them that they would be doing a disservice to their students if they didn't teach each of them this skill of thinking on their feet.[9] (Traditionally, a law school professor called on just one student with a tough question and then spent most of the class grilling him with ten or twenty more to draw out several facets of the issue.)

Chrystin's mom waited tables and her dad sold vending machines back in Michigan, and she said that being at Harvard was always intimidating. "It reminded me of one of my professors at another university who used to say that when he was at Yale, he felt like a hobo who wandered in to the Ritz Carlton," she said. The first time she went to Elizabeth's office, she got a softer impression of the place. "I had just gotten this dog, and the vet told my husband and I that it was going to die, and I burst into tears," she said. "She got choked up because she was so close to her dog that passed away, and she told me the whole story. Instead of making me look stupid, she was so comforting, saying, 'Even if your dog has a short life, she had a great life.'" Chrystin had come to discuss her plan to study critical race theory, but Elizabeth took a half hour to talk about studying commercial law instead. "She said I needed to devote myself to bankruptcy and commercial law because they are dominated by folks on the right," Chrystin said.

She took all Elizabeth's courses and was her teaching assistant (TA) in bankruptcy and contracts classes. "As a TA," she said, "my main job was to help her make sure that she called on every student every day. I kept track, and five minutes before the end of class, I gave her a stack of cards with the names she hadn't called on, so she could be sure to get to them." At one point in the semester, Elizabeth invited the whole class over for dinner and made her Aunt Bee's peach cobbler recipe.

Elizabeth helped Chrystin learn the ropes of working with a national bankruptcy database and advised her about the job offers she received in her third year. Chrystin had flown all over the country for interviews with her nursing baby in tow. The only thing she knew was that she wanted to take an offer from one of the public universities. Elizabeth looked them over and said, "Rutgers."[10]

First-year students got a dose of the unnerving first-class-day treatment Elizabeth went through at Rutgers. Joe Kennedy III, who would become a congressman from Massachusetts in 2013, recalled his experience in a Senator Warren campaign piece:

> I had only one goal on my first day of law school: to escape unscathed. But roughly three seconds into my very first class, I got called on.
>
> "Mr. Kennedy. What is the definition of assumpsit?"
>
> My stomach sank. "I don't know," I said meekly to my professor.

"Mr. Kennedy," she said. "You realize assumpsit is the first word of your reading?"

It went on from there, and I didn't do any better.

I never showed up unprepared for Professor Elizabeth Warren's contract law class ever again.

Elizabeth was the toughest teacher on campus, but the wait list for her class was a mile long.[11]

Douglas Moll took Elizabeth's secured credit class in the enormous classroom called Austin West. "She randomly called on students, and there was a back row in her class where people would hide," he said. "If you weren't prepared, you would sit below the desks where she couldn't see you." She was as personable in the classroom as she was everywhere else, he said, and very energetic. "She brought a lot of energy into the class. You're not going to win teaching awards if you can't make the material interesting."[12]

Candidates for university teaching jobs prepare a formal presentation commonly known as a "job talk" for their interview, after which the committee asks questions. Now a professor at the University of Houston Law Center, Douglas recalled how Elizabeth spent hours helping him prepare for his job talk there, even though he had graduated from Harvard Law three years earlier. He planned to present a paper related to a credit issue Elizabeth had written about, and she gave him pointers about the paper as well as how a job talk works. "She was incredibly helpful," he said. "She sent me materials I could use in my presentation and connected me to some of her colleagues who gave me more information. She had millions of demands on her time and didn't have to help me at all."

One of Elizabeth's students from UT Law took up her teaching method when he later saw her in action at Harvard. Professor Ronald J. Mann of Columbia Law School, one of the country's leading commercial law scholars, was a visiting professor at Harvard while she was on faculty, and he credits her for helping him manage a problem in today's classrooms. "One of the big debates in the academy in the past ten to fifteen years is whether you should allow laptops in the classroom," he said. "If you're boring, the students will just read emails and news stories, and it's hard to have an engaged conversation." If you don't let them have technology, however, he explained, you're taking away their "method for retaining information." The tactic Elizabeth used, calling on every student every day, demanded that everybody be more on their toes because they're likely to get called on and want to know the answer. He completely adopted her method and has seen that although people are still writing down what they think is important, they are moment-to-moment engaged because they know they could get called on. "It's an effective way to not tell students what they have to do," he said.

"She had always been a very successful classroom teacher," he said but added that law professors aren't hired because they're good teachers. "You can get hired at places like Penn and Harvard because of the success and importance of your scholarship, not your teaching," he said.[13]

A Harvard student who has become one of Elizabeth's friends, coresearchers, and coauthors, Katherine "Katie" Porter, is currently a professor at the University of California, Irvine School of Law. Katie sat in the first row in Elizabeth's bankruptcy course in her final year and knew by the end of the first class that she had found her specialty. "In that first class, she explained really beautifully how bankruptcy is a crucial backstop for capitalism," she said. "As we encourage people to make risks, the bankruptcy system is there for when things don't go well. It helps capitalism function. I was basically hooked right from there."[14] A glimpse at the law textbook that Elizabeth and Jay Westbrook released in 2001, the year of Katie's final semester, offers a hint of the way Elizabeth approached the course. The thousand-page casebook titled *The Law of Debtors and Creditors* introduced bankruptcy as "a part of the law as filled with human drama as it is with intellectual complexity and social importance." While the circumstances that lead to bankruptcy are depressing, they wrote, "bankruptcy itself is the process of healing and restoration."[15]

On the somewhat rare days that Elizabeth asked students to sign their name for attendance, she had a rule that when they signed, they were saying that they had read and done the homework problems. Katie was always prepared and always signed, so one day, when Elizabeth asked what a particular statute was trying to do, she raised her hand and gave her answer. "I thought it was good, but it was wrong," she said.

"'Come on, Miss Porter, think, think!'" Katie recalled Elizabeth saying. "A little bit of me crumbled—I *was* thinking, and that's what I had come up with. Her point was keep thinking. If that's not right, keep going."[16]

Katie learned the benefits of this style of teaching and uses it herself:

> If you call on someone and they give a weak, tentative, incorrect answer, the most important thing you can do

is call on that person again, the same day if possible, if not the next day. If you don't call on them again, you're conveying to them that you've given up. If I call on someone and they give a bad answer, ten minutes later, it might be an easier question, but I'm coming back to them to get it right, to tell them I know you get this and I'm with you this entire time while you master this material. That is how Elizabeth thinks about these things.[17]

Back in the classroom, Katie remembered thinking, *What's going to happen now?* "She called on me again, and I answered that question right, and she said, 'Good, good!' She had that belief in her students' potential."

That same semester, Katie took an independent study to help conduct the research that went into the book that Elizabeth wrote with her daughter, Amelia, *The Two-Income Trap: Why Middle-Class Mothers & Fathers Are Going Broke.* She flew around the country and handed out questionnaires and surveys to families who were in bankruptcy, asking them to take the time to fill them out while they were in the courthouse. "I remember getting back and Elizabeth wanting to hear from me about what I'd seen," she said. "I told her that these people are coming into this and they're so stressed. They're people in wheelchairs, on oxygen, with small children, and it's really hard to ask these people for things." Elizabeth told her, "You have to ask them all, because they're all part of the system. Even though they're on oxygen or they have their hands full, we have to study, we have to see them all." Katie said Elizabeth taught her about the commitment to making sure that the research reflected everybody's voice, not just the people who were loud and easy to study, but everybody. "There is a whole collection of people around the country who are teaching, and teaching in a particular way, because of Elizabeth," Katie said.

Elizabeth and Katie stayed in touch after Katie graduated and became a practicing lawyer. When she decided that she really wanted to become a law professor, knowing how competitive that was, especially for women, she called Elizabeth for advice. "I told her I was ready," Katie said. "I was ready to do whatever it takes." Elizabeth said she needed to write and publish an article. Katie had been working on one but told her it was hard to do while working sixty hours a week as a lawyer. Elizabeth said she had to have more time to write—she couldn't do it when she was tired.

"How about this?" Elizabeth said. "How about you take a leave from your firm?"

"How will I live? My husband isn't working."

"Could you go live with your mom?"

They cooked up a scheme, and Katie took a gigantic leap of faith. Elizabeth told her that she would complete the article, it would be good and get published, and she would get a job. Katie quit her job at the firm and drove across the country with her husband and their dog to move into her mother's basement. She wrote every day while working part time at a nursery, got the article published in a law journal, and received an offer to be a visiting professor at the University of Nevada–Las Vegas. She kept writing and publishing and, after a series of visiting positions, was hired at the University of Iowa College of Law. She rose to full professor at Iowa and then moved on to the University of California–Irvine.

Elizabeth was committed to guiding her students through the

difficult paths of their early careers. When she went to Washington to chair the Congressional Oversight Panel and help watchdog the Treasury Department's Wall Street bailout in 2008, she asked Katie to take over mentoring several people she had helped usher into the pipeline to academia. Katie thought she wasn't ready, that she still needed mentoring herself, but Elizabeth said, "You're ready to mentor—now it's my time to mentor these people [on the oversight panel]."

Katie has collaborated on research with Elizabeth and Jay Westbrook, among others, on the Bankruptcy Project. She also coauthored a new edition of Elizabeth and Jay's bankruptcy law textbook, and along the way, she and her husband named their daughter Elizabeth. In 2016, when Elizabeth was visiting Amelia in California, Katie came by to talk to Elizabeth about her idea of running for Congress. Elizabeth said, "You will learn something every day that you're a candidate. You will learn something about an issue, about yourself, your strengths and weaknesses, and therefore you will constantly be learning. You will love this experience and see the value of it while you're running." Katie launched her campaign that year.

During that race, her nine-year-old son, Paul, met Elizabeth and said, "Senator, I have a question."

"What is it?"

"A few months ago, my mom says she has to raise a lot of monies and she said you raise millions of money, so how should my mom do that?"

"Well, first, Paul, you have to have something you believe in. And I know your mom believes in things."

"Oh, like Wells Fargo shouldn't break the rules?"

"Yes, people should follow the rules."

"My mom believes in stuff then, so now what?"

"Then, Paul, you have to have a lot of people's email addresses."

"Oh, I don't have any email addresses. I'm only nine."

Then he took off.[18]

Bruce and Elizabeth's new house in Cambridge stood on a small corner lot with a black wrought-iron fence surrounding the yard. Narrow-looking from the front, the three-story Victorian painted teal with ivory trim was about eight blocks north of Harvard Law School. They were a two-university academic couple again, with Bruce commuting back and forth every week from Philadelphia and his position at Penn Law.

Bruce worked out his teaching schedule to keep him in Philadelphia three days a week so that he could spend the rest of his time in Boston with Elizabeth. Kristie Blunt Welder, a lawyer in Kansas who took Bruce's property law class at Penn after Elizabeth had left for Harvard, described Bruce's teaching skills and personality that made him an award-winning professor. In the property law class, he challenged them to understand the historic significance of real estate as the story of who is important and who has legal rights in America. A law class that students feared would be horribly dry, Kristie said, turned out to be an enlightening experience about the machinations of power. Bruce was the quintessential law school professor, she said, "gruff, intimidating, and brilliant, but incredibly kid and warm underneath."

He wore bow ties and suspenders and "everyone absolutely

worshipped him," she said. "It was terrifying in class, waiting for him to call on you—he was a master of the Socratic method—but if you got called on and gave him a smart, well-thought-out answer, there was no better feeling on earth." The students made a game of guessing what color his suspenders were on any given day before he took off his jacket. "He was also so much fun," Kristie said. "At Penn, there's a tradition of first-year law students taking professors out to lunch in small groups, and he was always everyone's favorite, so much fun to hang out with outside class."[19]

While Bruce's and Elizabeth's careers were blazing, her mother's life was winding down. Pauline's doctors scheduled noninvasive cancer surgery for her in the summer of 1995, and Elizabeth and Bruce flew down to be with her and the family. The operation went fine, but the next day, she suffered a massive heart attack in her hospital bed and died. Elizabeth was in denial at first—how could her mother's sister Aunt Bee, ninety-three and ten years older than Pauline, still be lively and active but her mother gone in a blink of an eye? She drifted half-dazed through the week as relatives poured in, funeral arrangements were made, and neighbors brought over hot dishes and cake.[20]

As she sat with her father upstairs, they cried together, and it tore her apart to leave him after the funeral and gatherings were over. For the next few weeks, she pleaded with him to move in with her and Bruce up in Cambridge. There was plenty of room, with Aunt Bee settled in a senior residence in Oklahoma City, where she wanted to be. Donald wouldn't have it, so she settled for calling him every night and during weekend football games, when they'd stay on the phone and laugh or yell over the plays.

That year brought another life passage. It was only a matter of time before Elizabeth's stature as a bankruptcy expert would draw the attention of Washington, especially in the mid-1990s with bankruptcy filings skyrocketing. The government reached out in 1995 with a phone call from Michael Synar, a former congressman from Oklahoma. Mike was leading a new, nonpartisan commission to review the bankruptcy laws, and he was pulling together people to serve on it.[21] President Bill Clinton had selected Mike to chair the commission because of his active work in virtually every change in bankruptcy law since the 1978 overhaul. The Bankruptcy Review Commission, launched by Congress, was tasked with studying the issues and problems with the code, evaluating the fixes being proposed, collecting the views of everyone concerned with the bankruptcy system, and submitting a report to Congress, the chief justice of the Supreme Court, and the president.[22] The first meeting was scheduled for October, and their report was due in two years.

Elizabeth had met Mike, it turned out, about thirty years earlier at debate tournaments in high school—he was an Okie from Muskogee, literally.[23] Debaters from Muskogee had matched up with the Classen High School team from time to time, and Elizabeth recalled that she and Karl Johnson had beaten him in a tournament in their junior year. She had not spoken to him in all those years but knew who he was, a lawmaker who had served eight terms in Congress by the time he was forty-four and spent most of those years fighting for gun control, limits on tobacco advertising, campaign finance reform, higher grazing fees on public land—all missions of a self-proclaimed liberal maverick.[24]

Those battles had made Mike an outsider in generally conservative

Oklahoma, and the fight that wrangled his enemies most—and brought him the most renown—targeted the Gramm-Rudman federal deficit reduction plan, which President Ronald Reagan had signed into law in 1985. Initiated by Mike's lawsuit that argued that the automatic budget cuts in the plan were unconstitutional, the Supreme Court struck down the law. Special interests like the NRA and Big Tobacco fought him in the 1994 primary, where he lost to an unknown, seventy-one-year-old Democrat in a campaign season that saw billboards reading "Stalin, Hitler, Castro, Synar."

Elizabeth hesitated to join the commission, partly because she had checked out Mike before their first meeting with people who "suggested that during his time in Congress, Mike had a pretty friendly relationship with the banks," she wrote.[25] She knew that the banks were lobbying in the halls of Congress to weaken people's access to bankruptcy protection, and she couldn't help being skeptical about Mike's intentions. But when she went to Washington to hear him out, he convinced her that they were on the same side. "Here was a guy a lot of people thought would carry water for the industry," she wrote, "and instead he was trying to figure out how to expand bankruptcy protection for families who needed it. Wow." They agreed that if she would deliver him three positive changes that would improve the bankruptcy safety net, he would put all his legislative muscle into writing those three goals into law.

By joining the commission as a senior adviser, Elizabeth took the first turn in her career path, creating a fork in the road that split into "academia" and "politics." It is a rare move for scholars, and the two prongs would crisscross when her research needed politics and her politics needed her research.

The commission work was part time, allowing her to stay at Harvard, and she began by hiring researchers and laying out an efficient process for the work.[26] By the time of the first meeting in October 1995, however, Mike had been diagnosed with brain cancer. His treatments were making him too sick to work, and in December, he resigned from the commission. He died the next month at age forty-five.[27]

Elizabeth planned to resign after the funeral, figuring that since Mike was the sole reason she'd signed on, she was done. But a couple of months later, the new chairman, Brady Williamson, met with her to explain the tough road the project faced and urged her to stay on. The commission was stacked with both pro- and antibankruptcy members, and the banking industry was lobbying hard to cut back the laws. But if they could get enough people on the commission to vote for a few family-friendly changes to recommend in the report, they could stave off the lobbyists' impact on Congress, at least for a time.[28] Elizabeth knew that this would mean facing off point by point with commission member Judge Edith Jones, a high-powered conservative whom George W. Bush had dubbed "Auntie Edith" and put on his short list of Supreme Court nominees.[29] When it came to bankruptcy, Edith was vocal about what she called the "widespread gaming of the system" and the fact that "nobody is holding a gun to consumers' heads and forcing them to send in credit card applications." Since her beliefs contradicted Elizabeth and her team's findings in the Bankruptcy Project, the journey ahead looked rough. But Brady's view of the struggle made sense and sounded like a worthy fight. "As Brady pointed out," Elizabeth wrote, "every day the current bankruptcy protections stayed strong was a day that another five thousand families would get the fresh start they so desperately needed."[30]

Elizabeth traveled to public hearings in cities across the country to hear people share their bankruptcy stories, but the commission had a hard time finding people willing to talk to a room of strangers about what they figured was the biggest, most humiliating failure in their lives.[31] But the work went on, and in the second year, the group had drawn up a list of recommendations for updating the law that included allowing more credit card debt to be written off, creating a financial education program for debtors, and designing a national filing system that would make it easier to access information.[32] While these suggestions would strengthen the code, others, particularly those of Judge Jones, focused on new rules that increased the amount of debt filers still had to pay. One pro-creditor suggestion, for example, called for an income-based formula to decide who would be eligible for Chapter 13, the repayment option, or Chapter 7, which wiped out most debts. When the banking industry realized that Judge Jones's recommendations might not pass the final vote, it made a full-blown offensive play. "Instead of waiting for the commission's report, the industry wrote its own version of a bankruptcy bill and then shopped it around to some friendly members of Congress," Elizabeth wrote. "By beating us to the battlefield, the banking industry had more success at defining the terms of the fight."[33] Those terms tried to throw out all the facts and research and instead narrow the conversation to one question about debtors: Do they pay their bills, or don't they?

In a five to four vote, the commission approved a list of recommendations that would make bankruptcy more efficient and fair, such as preventing wealthy debtors from keeping their luxury homes. By that time, though, the bank-written bill had been in Congress's hands for a month. The bankruptcy wars were on.[34]

Soon after the commission filed its report in October 1997, Elizabeth's father took a turn for the worse in his failing health. He had been diagnosed with prostate cancer after Pauline died, and by the end of November, Elizabeth and her brothers were gathered around his bedside. "I couldn't remember that he had ever asked me for anything," Elizabeth wrote, "but he asked for this: Let me die at home." On December 3, he grasped Elizabeth's hand. "[He] told me how much he loved me and that I was strong and I was going to be fine. The last thing he said to me was, 'It's time for me to be with your mother.'"[35] At eighty-six, with his four children surrounding him, Elizabeth's daddy passed away.

With her Washington advising over, Elizabeth could have made a happy retreat to her former pace of research and teaching, but the debt crisis lay too deep beneath her skin. The staggering number of bankruptcy filings, now up to more than one million per year, was a colossal red flag flapping over the nation's entire economy.

When the banks and other credit card lenders were freed of interest caps and other rules, they mailed out more than four billion preapproved credit card offers each year and reached out to potential customers in college campuses, in malls, at sporting events, and on the phone.[36] Business columns reported enormous increases in credit card profits—25 percent one year at Citigroup, 27 percent at Bank of America, 27 percent at Bank One. These profits kept climbing even as bankruptcies rose right alongside them.[37] Credit card lending had become twice as profitable as any other lending banks offered.[38]

As groups like the American Association of Retired Persons (AARP), Consumer Federation of America, the American Federation of Labor and Congress of Industrial Organizations (AFL-CIO), and National Association for the Advancement of Colored People (NAACP) joined forces to rally against the bank-written bill, Elizabeth leapt back into the fight.[39] Her big win those first months came in a meeting with Senator Ted Kennedy in which she made the facts of the battle as clear as the office's towering view of Boston Harbor. With the help of Melissa Jacoby, who had been Elizabeth's chief counsel at the commission, and Melody Barnes, Senator Kennedy's chief counsel, she convinced Ted Kennedy to lead the fight against the bill in the Senate.[40]

They pulled in more leaders—Senators Dick Durbin, Chuck Schumer, Russ Feingold, and Paul Wellstone, who became one of her rocks.[41] Elizabeth and Paul shared the same energy and dogged determination to see a good fight through. With a PhD in political science, Paul, a five-foot-five college wrestling champion, had spent twenty years as a political science professor at Carlton College in Minnesota before going into politics. Through his teaching years, he'd kept his fiery civil rights era and antiwar movement activism on high and urged his students to seek out social justice careers. He was known as the "happy warrior" and "conscience of the Senate" for his unapologetic progressive values that played out in his focus on issues like veterans' homelessness and domestic violence, and by the time Elizabeth met him, he was an icon of liberal firebrand politics.[42] "Politics is not about money or power games," he famously wrote in *The Conscience of a Liberal*, "or winning for the sake of winning. Politics is about the improvement of people's lives."[43]

As they worked together to fight the bankruptcy bill, Elizabeth and Paul formed a friendship that included regular nighttime phone calls. She told the story at the University of Minnesota during an event honoring the late senator's legacy:

> I was teaching at Harvard, and my husband Bruce was teaching at Penn in Philadelphia, and so we commuted back and forth, but on a lot of weeknights…it was just the dog and me, and I'd stay up at the school and work until eleven o'clock or twelve o'clock… I'd be sitting there at my desk, and my office phone would ring at about eleven fifteen, and the voice on the other end would say, "Professor, what are *you* doing working at this hour?" And I would say, "Senator, what are *you* doing working at this hour?" and then we would both laugh hysterically, and it became a running joke. It might not have been very funny, but it was our version of an Abbott and Costello routine.[44]

They talked about bankruptcy and the economics around it, "totally nerdy conversations," as she put it, and about the stories on the back of the survey forms from her research that gave the real picture. "Paul took this stuff so personally," she said. "He saw students and farmers and veterans and blue-collar working men and women who were being overlooked because they didn't have the money or the power to influence Congress, so he fought to make their voices heard in Washington."[45]

Perry Lange, Paul's legislative assistant on banking and consumer finance issues at the time, recalled that Paul first got involved in the issue primarily because of Howard Metzenbaum. Howard, the Democratic senator from Ohio who worked on consumer protection issues and became the head of the Consumer Federation of America after he left the Senate in 1995, was Paul's personal hero. "Paul's role in resisting the bankruptcy legislation was that he was willing to use his powers as an individual senator to lie down on the tracks and obstruct the bill." Even though the Republicans had a supermajority in the Senate who were willing to vote for the thing, Perry explained, there were a lot of things one could do in the Senate to slow down the process. "Paul was willing to say, 'I'm going to spend the political capital on this and not allow it to happen.'"[46]

Paul's speeches on the bankruptcy issue were influenced by Elizabeth's research, Perry said, centering around the key theme "that bankruptcy is an important safety net—in America we don't punish failures. We give people a way to get back up, and that's an important part of the economy." Her research introduced Paul to a view of bankruptcy they considered radical and powerful, Perry said. Her data "particularly showed that the increases in bankruptcy were arguably related to the loosening of credit standards, the democratization of debt—pushing that down the income ladder, and we can debate whether doing that is a good or bad thing, but it's sort of ridiculous to turn around and accuse these lower-income middle-class families or regular middle-class families and say 'This is your problem because you took on more debt.' And there was somebody on the other side, the lender, who was also making the conscious decision to make riskier and riskier bets. To me, that was a radical and powerful thing."[47]

When the industry-friendly bankruptcy bill came up for a vote in 1998, Paul was the only senator who voted no.[48] The bill passed, but in meetings with First Lady Hillary Clinton, Elizabeth had convinced her that it was a bad bill, and Hillary vowed to help fight it. "Now the president was under enormous pressure from the banks to sign the bill," Elizabeth wrote, "but in the last days of his presidency, urged on by his wife, President Clinton…vetoed the industry's bill."[49] Elizabeth's discussion with Hillary about the bill had taken place in 1998, when the First Lady's White House staff asked her to come to a Boston hotel where Hillary was giving a speech. They engaged in a rushed, intense conversation after Hillary's talk, in which Elizabeth gave an impassioned presentation about the bill as a travesty for people in financial crisis, particularly women and children who were staring down a cliff due to divorce, a medical emergency, or job loss. "I mean this in the nicest possible way: She didn't know this stuff," Elizabeth told a reporter. "But [she was] one of the smartest people I ever sat down with." Hillary flung questions at Elizabeth and, after about a half hour of discussion, concluded, "We need to stop that awful bill!"[50]

The pressure returned as soon as George W. Bush was sworn into office and stated he would sign the bill. After Hillary became a senator and the bill came up for a vote again, she changed her position. Elizabeth described Hillary's 2001 turnaround as a switch from fighting for her beliefs to appeasing her banking industry campaign contributors. "Big banks were now part of Senator Clinton's constituency," she wrote in *The Two-Income Trap*. "She wanted their support, and they wanted hers—including a vote in favor of 'that awful bill.'"[51] Hillary responded that her decision had nothing to do with money, but with putting through changes for women and children that she had fought to insert into the bill. As it stood, the law would not have prioritized childcare payments and other issues, which would have been badly damaging for women and children, she explained in an ABC News interview. Her fellow senators said that in turn for making those changes at the last minute, she would have to commit to voting for the bill. Hillary chose to vote to help the groups that she had served for thirty years and who had desperately come to her for help. "I swallowed hard," she said. "I faced a choice... That's what you have to do." She voted for the bill, but it did not pass.[52] The lobbyists continued to push, however, and Congress would bring it up again.

In 2002, the fight lost one of its champions and Elizabeth lost her friend when Paul Wellstone was killed in a plane crash in northern Minnesota. Everyone on the plane, including his wife, Sheila, daughter, Marcia, three campaign staffers, and both pilots, were killed. The tragedy left Washington and Minnesota numb, and in the weeks to come, one of the tributes to Paul as a moral and ethical compass appeared throughout Minnesota on bumper stickers that read, "What Would Wellstone Do?"[53]

Two years before Paul's death, Elizabeth had sent him a letter[54] on her Harvard stationery that summed up her feelings about him and his work:

I cannot adequately express my admiration for you. This is, of course, a terrible confession for someone whose business is words. I can only say that your work on behalf of working families who will be hurt by the proposed bankruptcy bill is inspirational. In the face of overwhelming lobbying efforts to create a windfall for the banks, car lenders, landlords, pawn shops, and everyone else who does business with families in financial trouble, you have stood firm. Your efforts will not result in PAC contributions or newspaper headlines. Instead, you have simply done what you know is right. I can think of no higher compliment.[55]

Writing in *The Nation*, John Nichols recalled that Paul introduced him to Elizabeth in those days and "cherished her as an ally in a lonely struggle."[56] When he joked about his political isolation, he told John that he "could use ten more progressive senators—or, at the least, one Elizabeth Warren."[57]

"The bankruptcy wars changed me forever," Elizabeth wrote.[58]

In 2005, the lending-industry-friendly bankruptcy bill passed and was signed into law by President Bush. The new rules required more paperwork, which increased attorneys' fees and made the process of declaring bankruptcy more complicated; raised the cost of filing; changed who could be eligible; made it harder for single women to collect past-due child support; and included hundreds of other changes. As a result, the number of filings dropped significantly.[59]

In an appearance at the University of California, Berkeley two years after the bankruptcy bill passed, Elizabeth shared what she had learned about lobbyists' power and the deliberate false messaging created at the expense of people dealing with financial failure:

> It was senators themselves who said, "Professor, you don't understand. So-and-so over here has taken $300,000 from credit card companies and the financial services industry over the last so many years, and this is something that industry wants; they hire lobbyists. I see two lobbyists in here a day from the financial services industry to make this happen."
>
> And so, the reality of these families' lives had to be reshaped to tell a politically acceptable story about why "We need this legislation." All the arrows run the wrong way. Right? The credit card companies wanted a piece of legislation to cut their losses and boost their profits. And so, the story had to be told that this is the fault of these families who are in financial trouble. And you know, I wish that story were true, but the data are not just close on this question, the data are just overwhelming on this question, that that is just simply not the truth.[60]

Learning the political side of the research-to-policy pathway broadened Elizabeth's interests far beyond bankruptcy and into more questions about the problems of the middle class. As she pursued those questions, she felt her work take on more depth. "It enriched and in many ways transformed the work that interested me as a scholar—I was a scholar, but I moved from a one-dimensional scholar into a two-dimensional scholar."[61] Witnessing how powerful forces in Washington—forces silent and unseen to most Americans—could sway Congress and spread lies about millions of people in financial distress fired up her motivation to keep speaking the truth.

After ten more years of research, Elizabeth, Teresa Sullivan, and Jay Westbrook published the Bankruptcy Project's second book, *The Fragile Middle Class: Americans in Debt*, in 2000.

This study was based on twenty-four hundred bankruptcy cases—about a thousand more than in the first study—filed in 1991 across five states.[62] The filing information and personal stories that the debtors shared on the surveys revealed five major reasons that middle-class people fall into financial ruin. Layoffs and firings create gaps in income that put a family over the edge, and credit cards with high interest rates and fees create debt that escalates out of control. The medical bills and lost work time that come with illness and accidents also cause financial distress, and the financial instability in the wake of divorce means that a divorced person is twice as likely to go bankrupt. Finally, holding on to one's home when additional debt is piled on top of a mortgage creates a crisis that leads families into bankruptcy.[63]

Recalling the beginning of that research, when she began reading the bankruptcy filers' stories on their surveys, Elizabeth said that she was driven to tears. "These weren't just numbers anymore—these were personal stories about the death of a child, what it means to lose a job, a husband who disappeared." The filers came to life for her as "people filled with self-loathing at the mistakes they had made, and … filled with a sense of astonishment that they had ended up here."[64]

Elizabeth's study of the middle class, which overlapped with her work on the Bankruptcy Review Commission, led to a transformative decade in which she became a card-carrying Democrat. As she came to understand the convergence of events in the 1980s and 1990s that explained the uptick in bankruptcies, she could no longer affiliate herself with a political party committed to deregulation. Until then, her voting history had been all over the map, starting in 1972 when she voted for Democrat George McGovern in her first presidential election. In 1976 she voted for Republican Gerald Ford and in 1980 cast her ballot for Democrat Jimmy Carter in his reelection year. She was a registered Independent at the time, and only much later did she realize what a "pivotal historical moment" Ronald Reagan's election had been. When she moved to Pennsylvania in 1987, she registered as a Republican, but in 1988 voted for Democratic presidential candidate Michael Dukakis. In 1992 she voted for Democrat Bill Clinton and Pennsylvania's Republican Senator Arlen Specter.[65]

By the time her new awareness of the crushed and squeezed middle class came together in the mid-1990s, she was a Democrat, she said. In an interview on ABC's *This Week*, she explained to George Stephanopoulos why she dropped her Republican affiliation in 1996:

> I was with the GOP for a while because I really thought
> that it was a party that was principled in its conser-
> vative approach to economics and to markets. And
> I feel like the GOP party just left that. They moved

to a party that said, "No, it's not about a level playing field. It's now about a field that's gotten tilted." And they really stood up for the big financial institutions when the big financial institutions are just hammering middle class American families. I just feel like that's a party that moved way, way away.[66]

As the Bankruptcy Project team launched into another study following the publication of *The Fragile Middle Class*, Elizabeth became a grandmother and spent her 2001 summer break out in California with Amelia, her husband, and their baby daughter, Octavia.[67] Amelia had met her husband, Sushil Tyagi, at Wharton, where he was also working on his MBA.[68] Sushil had moved to the United States from India after finishing a bachelor's degree in civil engineering in Delhi, and before he arrived at Wharton, he had spent a lot of quality time in American universities.[69] At the University of Florida, he earned an MA in applied marine physics, and at the University of California at Berkeley he graduated with an MS in naval architecture engineering. When he and Amelia finished their degrees at Wharton, they moved to Los Angeles, where Sushil launched Tricolor Films and began producing international feature films and IMAX movies.

Elizabeth and Amelia spent afternoons talking about the new research and a startling discovery Elizabeth had recently made.[70] Between 1981 and 1999, the number of women filing for bankruptcy shot up 662 percent—from sixty-nine thousand filings to nearly five hundred thousand. Hundreds of thousands of married women were also going bankrupt with their husbands.[71] They wondered what a close look at the middle-class families of Amelia's generation and those of 1971, when Elizabeth was a young mother, would tell them. Elizabeth and Amelia decided to find out, and what they learned explained why so many couples with children today are struggling to keep afloat. "The middle class had turned upside down," Elizabeth wrote.[72] They decided to pursue the story and write a book together for the general public.

"The book was born over a zillion hours of chatting as one or the other of us rocked the baby," Amelia said. "A month or so later, Mom asked my help on some analysis—I'm something of a closet numbers geek—[and] it soon hatched into a giant book project." They spent the next year writing from their own desks; Elizabeth wrote in the mornings in Cambridge, and Amelia got to work in the afternoons after her babysitter arrived.[73]

The Two-Income Trap: Why Middle-Class Mothers and Fathers Are Going Broke, published in 2003, answered the question millions of Americans were asking: *If we're working so hard, why can't we make it?*

Elizabeth and Amelia discovered that most two-income families are worse off than the single-income families of a generation ago, when mothers stayed home to raise their families.[74] Even though today's two-income households earn seventy-five percent more income, they have less money left over after paying their basic expenses than their parents did. The culprit is the rising cost of those basics, such as housing, child care, and health care.

With every dollar stretched to pay the mortgage and bills every month, they found a job loss spells disaster. When Elizabeth's father lost months of work after his heart attack and later took on lower-paying work, her mom got a job at Sears and filled the gap. Today, mothers are already working, so there is no one to fall back on. Elizabeth and

Amelia explained that the competition for housing in neighborhoods where middle-class families want to live has driven up prices. "Average mortgage expenses have gone 70 times faster than the average father's income," Amelia told *Mother Jones*, "and the only way families are keeping up is by bringing in two incomes."[75] That's the trap.

The disturbing truth about middle-class America's shaky ground revealed that more people will go bankrupt than have a heart attack, be diagnosed with cancer, graduate from college, or get divorced. Parents and single women with children, they wrote, run the greatest risk of all. "Having a child is now the single best predictor that a woman will end up in financial collapse," they wrote.[76] At the end of the book, they gave advice for families in distress, including a staunch warning about the offers they may be bombarded with to refinance their homes:

> *Don't do it*. Refinancing their homes to pay down other bills is the single biggest mistake made by families in trouble... You will be jeopardizing the roof over your family's head. Take a moment to consider. Do you honestly believe those "low monthly payments" are a free gift? Not a chance. If the mortgage lender gives you a lower rate than the credit card company, it is because the mortgage lender gets something in return—the right to push you into the street, seize your home, and sell it.[77]

Elizabeth and Amelia also suggested policy solutions for lowering housing costs, such as an all-voucher school program that would allow parents to send their children to any school regardless of where they lived. They admitted that this long-range policy idea would be "a shock to the educational system," but argued that by reducing the competition for housing in neighborhoods with excellent schools, housing prices would fall, and parents would "take control over schools' tax dollars."[78] They also called for more regulation to curb subprime lending that put struggling people further into debt with credit cards as well as refinanced mortgages. On that point, they brought up Judge Edith Jones, Elizabeth's nemesis on the Bankruptcy Review Commission, quoting her statement that "overspending and an unwillingness to live within one's means 'causes' debt."[77] Would Judge Jones suggest that a mother move her kids into a shelter after her husband moved out instead of trying to hold on to her home, they questioned, or that she pay the credit card bills instead of feeding her children? "It is doubtlessly satisfying to point the long finger of blame at personal irresponsibility and overspending," they wrote. "But only the willfully ignorant refuse to acknowledge the real reasons behind all that debt."[80]

The shocking truths about the middle class in *The Two-Income Trap* struck a chord, and the book was the talk of the media. Praise came from *Time* magazine, which called it "a startling account of the elusiveness of the American Dream,"[81] and from the *New York Times*, in which Paul Krugman called it "revelatory" and "a wonderful book."[82] Another *New York Times* reviewer wrote that the authors, "more clearly than anyone else...have shown how little attention the nation and our government have paid to the way Americans really live."[83] CNN Money and CBS News wrote up pieces on their websites, NBC's *Today* show brought Elizabeth into the studio, and she did an interview with Michele Norris on National Public Radio's *Talk of the Nation*. If anything at all goes went wrong in a two-income family, she told Michele, the family becomes "like a race car that has just hit a huge rock in the road, and it can't get itself stabilized. It's headed for a crash."[84] She also learned that people, such as U.S. Senator John Kerry, were talking about the book in their own high-profile venues. Kerry was on the presidential campaign trail during the fall of 2003, and in one of his rallies, he called *The Two-Income Trap* "one of the best books that actually describes the transformation that has taken place in America."[85]

Their media tour also included the *Dr. Phil* show, and when they arrived at Paramount Studios in Hollywood, they learned, to their surprise, that it would not be a simple interview about the book. Instead, they would be advising two families in the front row who were in financial crisis. One couple had recently gone bankrupt, and the other had sold their home to pay off their debt. Knowing that she had an opportunity to reach millions of viewers about their options if they were in similar straits, Elizabeth told the second couple that she disagreed with their choice of putting credit card lenders before family. She used the analogy of Kmart, which had recently filed for bankruptcy, and asked, "Do you think that the CEO of Kmart stayed up at night worrying about the fact that all of the big banks weren't going to get paid? No, he did what was best for his shareholders. I think you need to do what is best for your children and yourselves. Your family is at least as important as those corporations."[86]

After the success of *The Two-Income Trap*, Elizabeth and Amelia decided to compile a program of financial advice and began writing their second book, *All Your Worth: The Ultimate Lifetime Money Plan*. While "money plan" may sound dry, the book's caring, one-on-one conversational tone and personal focus make it read more like a series of therapy sessions. Financial worksheets and self-inventories are interspersed with insights about personal behavior in chapters like "Love and Money," which delves into issues of money and marriage. The book was published in March 2005, and later that year, Amelia had her second child, a girl named Lavinia.

By 2005, Amelia had developed a wealth of management and health technology experience. She had spent her first three years in Los Angeles at McKinsey & Company, an international business consulting firm. As an engagement manager for health care and public education clients, she led projects from the initial stage of analyzing the problem to developing the solution and then implementing that solution on-site. Based on that experience, she cofounded and became vice president of a health tech business with other former McKinsey managers that focused on the health care industry. HealthAllies, launched in 1999, was the brainchild of Andy Slavitt, who saw a dire need for consumer information about health services after one of his friends came to him for help.* His friend, a woman who had lost her husband to cancer, was left with hundreds of medical bills from separate providers and didn't know how to start making sense of them. As he organized her bills, he began imagining a better way for uninsured or underinsured people to select and purchase their medical services.[87]

Andy, Amelia, and their team worked out of the guest cottage of Amelia's Los Angeles home to develop an online service that

---

* Health tech guru Andy Slavitt was part of UnitedHealth Group's team that fixed Healthcare .gov, the website for President Barack Obama's Affordable Care Act (known colloquially as Obamacare). The site was rife with technical problems when it originally went online in 2013. Slavitt and his team improved the website in time for the crucial enrollment deadline the next year. He later became the head of the Centers for Medicare and Medicaid Services in the Obama administration.

empowered these uninsured consumers to get discounted rates for medical care.[88] By negotiating directly with doctors to get more affordable rates, they were able to provide an easy-to-use, discounted program on their website. "The company was about getting people better rates—getting access to the care they want at the same rates that the insurance companies pay," Amelia said in a *Wharton Magazine* interview. "It was a thrill."[89] The website also provided prices for "bundles" of care, such as a discounted rate for a woman's entire maternity care, from doctor visits to the birth. In her book about consumer-driven health care, Regina Herzlinger used another illustration to show how HealthAllies' services worked:

> A woman who needs a hip replacement inquires about the charge at an academic medical center. She is quoted a price of $35,000. (In hotels, this kind of price is known as the *rack rate*, the rate quoted to individual customers who lack the bargaining power of a group.) She then logs onto the HealthAllies site to search for a better hip replacement price. In response to her specifications about the type of providers she wants (for example, a surgeon who performed more than 75 hip replacements last year and…is located within thirty miles of her home), she chooses a hospital that quotes a price of $25,000. Ironically, it is the same hospital that initially quoted the $35,000 price.[90]

After working as HealthAllies' vice president of corporate development for two years, Amelia struck out on her own as an independent management consultant. The successful health tech start-up was later sold to the health care giant UnitedHealth Group, where it is now called UnitedHealth Allies.[91]

Amelia's next career venture drew on her business management and consulting expertise and tapped into the exploding "gig economy," in which professionals work as freelancers rather than full-time employees. In 2007, she cofounded the Business Talent Group (BTG) with Jody Greenstone Miller, a lawyer who had worked as a venture capital partner, investment banker, digital television executive, and government adviser, including as a special assistant to President Bill Clinton.[92] Amelia was president, Jody the CEO, and together, they formed a cutting-edge firm that discovered project-based work for professional consultants and executives. Jody became a sought-after speaker about the future of work and established herself as the go-to expert in the field, appearing at conferences and in media interviews and being named one of *Fortune* magazine's ten most promising entrepreneurs in 2015. In an article she cowrote in the *Harvard Business Review*, Jody explained how the "supertemp" trend began:

> The forces driving this convergence are as impersonal as the Great Recession and as individual as a dream. For the talent, project-based work has simply become more attractive than the alternative. Today technology makes it easy to plug in, the corporate social contract guaranteeing job security and plush benefits is dead or dying, and 80-hour weeks are all too common in high-powered full-time jobs... Talented people are going

independent because they can choose what to work on
and with whom to work.[93]

Amelia and Jody's firm became the leading business of its kind
as freelance professional work hit the mainstream in virtually every
kind of business, from technology to pharmaceuticals and health
care to education. By 2018, BTG had opened offices in Los Angeles,
New York, Chicago, Austin, San Francisco, and Boston, and sent
more than seven thousand supertemps into projects for companies around the world.[94] According to the website, "the rise of the
independent high-end professional is dramatic and permanent"—
by taking the lead in linking those professionals to companies,
BTG has been successful.[95] The company's growth put it on *Inc.*
magazine's 5,000 list of fasting growing companies three years in
a row.[96]

Three years into BTG, in October 2010, Amelia gave birth to
her third child, a son named Atticus.[97] Throughout her years in
the company, she had been a member of the board of directors
of the progressive think tank, Demos, which had sought her out
following the release of *The Two-Income Trap*. Since 2010, she has
been the Demos chairman of the board and also serves as chairman
of the board of its affiliated magazine, *The American Prospect*.[98]

Amelia's birth father, Jim Warren, who had remarried, did not
live to see her latest career achievement or meet her second child.[99]
He passed away at age fifty-eight after being diagnosed with lung
cancer in 2003. "For Amelia and Alex," Elizabeth wrote in *A Fighting
Chance*, "the loss of their father hit hard."[100] Jim's death followed
the passing of Aunt Bee, who had died in her sleep in 1999 at age

ninety-eight. Elizabeth's kin from her parents' generation and older were gone, many of them now in the Wetumka cemetery where the Reed and Herring graves stood on opposite sides of her parents' plot like still-feuding clans.[101]

Eleven years after Elizabeth joined the Harvard faculty, she and Bruce became a full-time, same-city couple again at last. In 2006, Harvard hired Bruce as the Carl F. Schipper Jr. Professor of Law, and he left Philadelphia with their dog, Otis, whom he had brought home as a puppy the previous year. Although Elizabeth had vowed never to get another dog after Good Faith died in 2004 and broke her heart, she fell in love with the sweet new golden retriever. [102]

At Harvard, Bruce would teach courses on American legal history, property, and trusts and estates. During his nineteen years at Penn Law, he had won four teaching awards, including the Christian R. and Mary F. Lindback Foundation Award for Distinguished Teaching, an honor given to one professor chosen from the faculty of the entire university.[103] His 2002 book, *Republic of Debtors: Bankruptcy in the Age of American Independence*, was partly inspired by a question Elizabeth once asked him. As he notes in the acknowledgments, "Elizabeth Warren doubtless rues the day she asked the question that lengthened this project—an innocent inquiry about why Congress took so long to enact a bankruptcy law."[104]

The book chronicled how eighteenth-century debtors, creditors, and others struggled with "the place of failure in the new republic" and revealed the clashing attitudes about people in financial failure.[105]

While some labeled them as villains, others said, "A Man might be a Bankrupt, and yet be a Man of Honour and Fidelity."[106] It seems the bankruptcy wars were nothing new after all. The critical acclaim for the book included the SHEAR Prize from the Society for Historians of the Early American Republic, the Littleton-Griswold Prize from the American Historical Association, and the J. Willard Hurst Prize from the Law and Society Association.[107]

6

THE SHERIFF OF WALL STREET

"You won't win a fight if you don't pick a fight."
—PAUL WELLSTONE[1]

In writing books for general audiences and appearing on *Dr. Phil* and *The Daily Show*, Elizabeth transformed herself into a public intellectual, a scholar who brought her work into the public square to promote change. Her appearance on *Dr. Phil* was a defining moment—she realized that while she had been doing scholarly work for more than two decades, she may have accomplished more good in only a few minutes of a television appearance than in any of her writing. "I began to think that instead of writing one more thing to impress other academics or to reassure myself that I'm a serious scholar, I should [focus] on the question of change, of real impact, of how to be helpful," she said.[2] She started a blog and spread the message about Americans in financial peril in newspaper articles under titles such as "Digging Out of Debt," "Hung Out to Dry," "Who Speaks for a Struggling Middle Class," and "Sick and Broke."[3] All she needed was a television series to become the Carl Sagan of middle-class economics.

To some, that's a very good thing. To others, it violates the insular culture of scholarly work. To be pure, a specialty like astrophysics—or bankruptcy law—can't mingle with the culture without making itself vulnerable to influences that may pull it out of focus. It's a leap of faith to turn away from the sheltering walls of a university, and Elizabeth thought long and hard before jumping into the political chaos of the Bankruptcy Review Commission. "It was a hard decision for me," she said, "because I really felt like I was jumping into a different pool; I was losing this protection of the ivory tower."[4] But Carl Sagan believed that an informed public was an essential part of democracy and that people needed to understand the technology their leaders controlled. Elizabeth's drive to educate the public about the forces crushing the middle class came from that same place. Full-time working people couldn't solve their financial problems until they understood the forces that created them.

By the time she began appearing on national television, Elizabeth had secured a strong foundation as one of the nation's top experts in bankruptcy and commercial law, with all the publications, awards, and honors to back it up. *National Law Journal* had twice named her among the Fifty Most Influential Women Attorneys; *SmartMoney* magazine put her in the list of thirty people who influence the nation's money trends; and organizations such as the Federal Judicial Center, Commercial Law League of America, American Bar Association, and National Conference of Bankruptcy Judges had bestowed honors and awards on her. Elizabeth's activism in opposing the bankruptcy bill reinforced her fledgling public intellectual persona, and that role survived her next political post. When she became the chair of the Congressional Oversight Panel that watchdogged the government bailout of the Wall Street banks, she was "in" the establishment as part of the legislative branch of the federal government, but she had an outsider's job.

Congress had authorized $700 billion to stabilize the economy through the Troubled Asset Relief Program, or TARP, in October 2008 as the bottom was falling out of the banking industry.

Elizabeth had warned about subprime mortgages and the fragile state of the middle class five years earlier in *The Two-Income Trap*, just as the heat was building up for a perfect storm of risk, deception, and failure in the financial markets. It started with the low-interest mortgage rates, set at a fifty-year low in 2003, that brought on a home-buying frenzy.[5] With all the demand, prices kept rising, and the real estate industry and others believed there was no end in sight.[6] Decades of bank deregulations, including the repeal of what was left of the Glass-Steagall Act (the 1933 law that separated commercial banks from investment banks after the stock market crash of 1929), had erased the line between Main Street and Wall Street banks, drawing in more players to the mortgage market. Investment banks got creative in order to meet the demands of investors eager for higher returns and invented securities backed by high-interest mortgages (which meant high returns). With relaxed requirements, people with high amounts of debt and low incomes qualified for these subprime loans.

Lenders enticed customers with low initial rates that jumped up after the grace period—Elizabeth called these mortgages hand grenades with the pin pulled off—and borrowers could not afford the higher payments.[7] Without cash coming in, the securities backed by subprime mortgages lost their value, and the banks that underwrote them failed. Elizabeth had sent warning signals to members of Congress and others in Washington about the explosive risk of Wall Street's mortgage bundles, but no one wanted to hear it. All she got in response, as she told *Esquire* writer Charles Pierce, was *La, la, la—I can't hear you!*[8]

As the crisis escalated, she used the events as real-time case studies in her class at Harvard.[9] The day after the investment bank Lehman Brothers failed, for example, when her students showed up "freaked out" over the bankruptcy of the fourth biggest bank in the country, she went to the chalkboard and lined up each piece of the bank's downfall. The government let Lehman fail on September 30, 2008, to send "the message that the markets have to discipline themselves," she told them, and that they would not be bailed out. The next day, however, the government bailed out failing AIG, the company that sold insurance for the toxic, mortgage-backed securities. In class that day, she set aside everything else she had planned to discuss and asked the class to imagine they were the CEO of a giant bank:

> And I said, "So your job, CEO, is to make sure that your financial institution is going to be standing on the other side once the economy settles back down. Some are going to die. So how do you make sure yours

is going to survive?" And hands go up. And so I call on the first kid. He says, "Well, I sell off as many things as I can. Narrow down. Keep only high-quality assets and hold on to cash." And I'm, "*Mmm.* Anybody else?" And all the hands go down because that is the classic answer, right? You keep yourself safe. Kind of the bunker mentality.

And finally, one kid gasps. Almost like he'd been shot. And the hand goes up. And I just keep standing in the front waiting. And then another hand goes up. And another. And another. And another. And you watch kids, with this jolt, some of them laugh out loud when they get it. And I...call on someone. And the kid says, "You grow as fast as you can. You buy as much as you can with borrowed money. And you lend and borrow from as many other large institutions as possible. Because then the government can't afford to let you fail."[10]

Her students figured out the concept of too big to fail, Elizabeth said, "because it's not that hard." Firms that had bought out others, such as JPMorgan Chase's purchase of Bear Stearns in 2008, created such massive interconnections with other businesses throughout the country and around the world that the ripple effect of their failure would be catastrophic. As it turned out, the government let Lehman Brothers fail not so much to send a message (as AIG's bailout the next day proved) but because the bank was too far gone to legally bail out. The Treasury Department was "only allowed to lend against plausibly solid collateral," *Time* magazine reported, "and Lehman looked hopelessly insolvent."[11] Even with the bailouts that kept other banks alive, the impact crushed the economy and the financial lives of millions of Americans.

The recession destroyed nearly $20 trillion in financial assets owned by American households, and nine million people lost their jobs.[12] The median net worth of families—their wealth in the form of homes, cars, and stock, minus their debt—fell 39 percent by 2010.[13] While the brokers, bankers, insurers, and everyone else taking their cut in the free-for-all financial pipeline was getting rich, nearly two decades of family wealth was getting wiped out.

With less money, people quit spending, and businesses shrank, bringing on massive unemployment. Businesses were also hit by the lack of available credit to meet their payroll and inventory as the recession bore on.

The subprime loan crisis was especially hard on blacks of all income levels, whom the banks aggressively targeted for subprime loans, even when the customers qualified for traditional mortgages.[14] Wells Fargo, for example, was sued by the City of Baltimore for these practices, which included offering cash incentives for loan officers to market subprime mortgages, which some officers called "ghetto loans," in minority neighborhoods. As the housing boom kept rising to its peak before 2006, 6.2 percent of white people with a credit score of 660 and higher received high-interest loans, while 21.4 percent of black people with the same credit score expensive mortgages.[15]

In *The Two-Income Trap*, Elizabeth minced no words about the banks' strategies to prey on people of color: "Subprime lending, payday loans, and the host of predatory, high-interest loan products that target minority neighborhoods should be called by their true names: legally sanctioned corporate plans to steal from minorities."[16] She also devoted entire articles to the economics of race, explaining how subprime lending reduced the financial security of middle-class blacks and Hispanics. Targeting by class was the larger strategy, however, something she knew from her research but learned face-to-face during a meeting at Citibank. Executives wanted to hear her ideas for helping them cut their bankruptcy losses, and after her presentation, she advised them to stop lending to people who couldn't afford it. An older man at the table spoke up:

> He had been quiet, watching the discussion with a faintly bemused smile.
>
> "Professor Warren," he said firmly.
>
> The room went immediately silent, signaling that the Head Honcho was now speaking.
>
> "We appreciate your presentation. We really do. But we have no interest in cutting back on our lending to these people. They are the ones who provide most of our profits."[17]

Elizabeth's invitation to join the oversight committee tasked with keeping checks on the TARP bailout came from Senate majority leader Harry Reid, who called her at dinnertime one evening in November 2008. They had never met, but Harry had read *The Two-Income Trap*, and he liked her background. "She was surprised, to say the least, about the call," he said, "and she came down to DC and met me with her daughter, and we did the deal."[18]

As the chair of the five-person committee, she would hire staff and hit the ground running to make the deadline for the first report.[19] They wrote up questions to Treasury Department Secretary Henry Paulson to learn the current state of the regulators and the impact and effectiveness of the payouts, and the public waited for news about the billions being spent. To ramp up transparency, the committee created a website on which people could share their stories, and Elizabeth introduced each posted report in a video, seated in a room with French doors, a U.S. flag, and a green plant.[20] In the reports and the media, she did not hide her frustration about the administration's progress with TARP programs. After the committee released its second report, she went on CNN and other shows to talk about the weak response she'd received from the Treasury Department.[21] When a *Washington Journal* host asked her to sum up her emotions about the process of getting answers from the Treasury Department, Elizabeth said that she alternated between furious and astounded. The Treasury had a long history of operating in secret, she said, but these were not ordinary times. "When they turn to the American people and say, 'give us seven hundred billion dollars of your money to spend however we want to spend it'—to get that kind of discretion means they have to be willing to be completely open about how they're spending the money," she said. [22]

In January 2009, newly elected President Barack Obama appointed Tim Geithner to be secretary of the treasury and therefore in charge of the bailout. The president continued the same TARP strategy, and in March, the country learned that AIG, a too-big-to-fail player that received an $85 billion bailout, had treated the employees responsible for the near failure of the company to $168 million in bonuses.[23] Americans were outraged. The president and Tim Geithner explained that they were powerless to overturn AIG's bonus contracts with their executives, and the sparring began. "I teach contract law," Elizabeth said on CNN. "I want to see the contract that someone thinks doesn't have a place in it with ambiguity, room for negotiation, room for change when the circumstances change."[24] She argued that if Treasury had had a clear strategy from the beginning for dealing with AIG and had put clear terms in place, "we would not be here today." She put Tim on the hot seat about the AIG payments in oversight hearings, and as those broadcasts played on cable TV, lines were drawn.[25] Some felt she represented their fury over the bonuses and the bailout in general and admired her for grilling Tim for answers. Others were riled that she was going after answers from the Obama administration as forcefully as she had done with President George W. Bush's camp. "I wasn't going to stop and worry about that," she wrote.[26] The divide between Elizabeth and Tim widened as she kept her bite in her role as watchdog and he drew on his expertise in finance as a regulator of Wall Street banks to prevent the complete collapse of the U.S. economy. Many saw it as the people versus a government too cozy with Wall Street.

The next month, Elizabeth had dinner with Larry Summers, one of President Obama's economic advisers, and received some advice about working in Washington. "I had a choice," she wrote.

> I could be an insider or I could be an outsider. Outsiders can say whatever they want. But people on the inside don't listen to them. Insiders, however, get lots of access

and a chance to push their ideas. People—powerful people—listen to what they have to say. But insiders also understand one unbreakable rule: *They don't criticize other insiders.*[27]

In a May 2010 cover story, *Time* magazine portrayed Elizabeth as one of three women overseeing the country's financial industry. In "The New Sheriffs of Wall Street," Sheila Bair, the chair of the U.S. Federal Deposit Insurance Corporation (FDIC); Mary Schapiro, chair of the U.S. Securities and Exchange Commission (SEC); and Elizabeth, chair of the Congressional Oversight Panel for TARP, made up the trio. "It is their willingness to break ranks and challenge the status quo that makes these increasingly powerful women different from their predecessors," Michael Scherer wrote.[28]

All three women had faced run-ins with insiders in the agencies and organizations with whom they worked. Shortly after being appointed FDIC chair by President George W. Bush in 2006, Sheila learned that banks like Washington Mutual (WaMu), the biggest savings and loan in the country, were selling large amounts of subprime mortgages with "explosive adjustable rates."[29] The FDIC did not have first-in-line regulatory supervision of WaMu—that was the job of the Office of Thrift Supervision (OTS). The OTS cut off the FDIC's access to documents and on-site workspace at the bank, which hindered Sheila's ability to check out why the OTS gave WaMu a higher quality rating than the FDIC had given. When the OTS learned that Sheila called WaMu's CEO to alert him to the disagreement over these ratings, the head of the OTS emailed a colleague to complain, writing "I cannot believe the continuing audacity of this woman."[30] Sheila's concerns about WaMu were borne out when the bank failed in 2008—the biggest savings and loan bank collapse in U.S. history.[31]

As head of the Commodities Futures Trading Commission (CFTC), wrote *Time*, one of Mary Schapiro's first actions as leader of the agency ignited a hefty backlash from the head of the Chicago Board of Trade, who had requested that the board be exempt from federal regulations. When Mary rejected the request, the Chicago Board's Tom Donovan said that he would not be "intimidated by some blond, 5-ft. 2-in. girl." As *Time* wrote, "Schapiro responded by telling a reporter, 'I'm 5 ft. 5.'"[32]

Time described the third sheriff, Elizabeth Warren, as the TARP watchdog who has "wielded her clout like a cudgel, releasing monthly reports demanding more information…and greater efforts to help borrowers."[33] The article noted that Elizabeth had strained relationships with Treasury officials and quoted her exchange with someone on Capitol Hill who told her, "point-blank, 'That's not what reports are supposed to look like.' She asked, 'Why not?' The reply: 'The language is far too direct.'" Elizabeth remarked that she, Mary, and Sheila shared a common experience: "Let's face it, women in the financial-services industry are outsiders. You see the world from a different point of view." Sheila agreed, saying, "There is a tendency—with some, not all—to value us less, whether it's our opinion or our work product."

The oversight rolled on as the TARP programs unfolded, and the committee focused many of its concerns on the slow progress of foreclosure relief. From the start, Elizabeth framed the Home Affordable Modification Program (HAMP) as poorly designed, which explained why the Treasury Department's response was so slow.[34] In 2009, three million foreclosures hit the country, and as Elizabeth saw it, HAMP was bringing relief "with all the urgency of putting out a forest fire with an eyedropper." Tim Geithner's response was that, for the sake of economic recovery, banks couldn't afford to be overwhelmed with a flood of foreclosures to absorb. During that meeting, Elizabeth felt the gulf widen between her and the administration's perception of the crisis. "I felt as if one of us was standing on a snow-covered mountaintop and the other was crawling through Death Valley. Our views of the world—and the problems we saw—were that different."[35] Years later, a spokeswoman for Tim told the *New York Times*, "The financial rescue was effective in preventing a second Great Depression but could not prevent all damage from the crisis, and we are still living with those scars."

As the voice of TARP oversight, Elizabeth felt a responsibility to bring the bailout issues to the widest public possible, and on April 15, 2009, she appeared on Jon Stewart's *The Daily Show* for the first time.[36] Her nerves got the best of her, and she threw up in the backstage bathroom a couple of minutes before stepping onto the set.[37] In the first half, Jon grasped his head in his hands every time she made a point about what they didn't yet actually know about the billions of dollars flowing to the banks. "They're not telling you anything!" he said.[38]

After the commercial break, Jon's big question became, *What does the road look like going forward?* In her classic straightforward style, Elizabeth gave an economics lesson that explained the financial meltdown in a concise, breathless nutshell.

The boom-and-bust economic cycle that started in George Washington's era, she explained, was a constant until we put in banking regulations after the Great Depression. We went fifty years without a financial panic, but when we began turning back those regulations, we returned to crisis after crisis.[39]

She then told Jon that the government was going to make one of two choices over the next six months. They would decide that they didn't need to regulate, which she said would keep up the boom and bust cycle—"and good luck with your 401k"—or put in some rules that adapted to the new products in the markets.[40] With that choice, we would move forward with "some stability and some real prosperity for ordinary folks," she said. The audience burst into applause, and Jon said she had made him feel better than he had in a year. "I don't know what it is that you just did right there," he said, "but that was like financial chicken soup for me."[41]

During one of her future appearances, Jon looked at her admiringly after she had smoothly explained another heady nugget and said, "When you say it like that, when you look at me like that—and I know your husband is backstage—but I still want to make out with you." Bruce was indeed backstage, and he fell out of his chair laughing. "How could I be mad at him?" Mann asked a *Vogue* writer. "When I listen to her, I have the same response."[42]

When the government wrapped up TARP, the United States was in the black on the deal with a $15.3 billion profit.[43] Tim Geithner's plan was a huge success in terms of making a fair deal with taxpayers that would return them exactly what they put in. Over the two-year program, the government invested in stabilizing banks and AIG, saving the auto industry (specifically General Motors and

Chrysler), preventing foreclosures, and increasing available credit in the marketplace. Of the $426.4 billion invested, the program recovered $441.7 billion. Elizabeth was honored in Massachusetts for her oversight work in 2009 when the *Boston Globe* named her Bostonian of the Year, and her recognition went global when *Time* magazine included her among the 100 Most Influential People in the World in 2009, 2010, and 2017.[44] Her popularity gained another boost with her appearance in Michael Moore's documentary film, *Capitalism: A Love Story*, which debuted in theaters across the country in 2009, a year into her work as oversight chief of the TARP bailouts. Two years later, her home state recognized her achievements with its highest honor, inducting her into the Oklahoma Hall of Fame.

In 2007, Elizabeth planted the seed for her greatest achievement by talking about toasters.

In an article with a title that echoed the piece that launched Ralph Nader's crusade for car safety standards, "Unsafe at Any Rate" made the argument that credit cards and mortgages should meet the same safety standards as appliances.[45]

It just made sense, she argued, that credit card agreements and mortgages should be as transparent and safe for consumers as the safety-tested appliances they buy. "It is impossible to buy a toaster that has a one-in-five chance of bursting into flames and burning down your house," she wrote. "But it is possible to refinance an existing home with a mortgage that has the same one-in-five chance of putting the family out on the street—and the mortgage won't even carry a disclosure of that fact to the homeowner."[46] Families were paying a high cost to get tangled up in overpriced credit cards and loans, risky subprime mortgages, and misleading insurance plans, she said. The price came in the form of wiped-out savings, lost homes, higher car insurance rates, stress on marriages, and "broken lives."

The article offered some startling numbers showing that consumers spent $89 billion in fees, interest payments, and other credit card costs in 2006 alone, and she also explained what went on inside the payday loan offices in strip malls across the country. Buried in the small print were interest rate amounts of 485.45 percent and higher, meaning that customers were paying thousands of dollars for a $400 or $500 loan. Interest payments were coming into the payday loan companies at the rate of $4.2 billion a year, and cash-strapped veterans were particularly vulnerable to them. The trap of making high interest payments every two weeks put so many veterans in distress that the Defense Department said the situation undermined the country's military readiness. In response, Congress passed a law banning any company from charging more than 36 percent interest to military personnel.

These practices and others called for new regulations that focused on the rights of consumers, she argued, and since the financial services industry is "routinely one of the top three contributors to national political campaigns," the likelihood of churning out new laws one by one was "vanishingly slim." Her answer was a new agency that would subject financial products to the same routine safety screening that toasters, washing machines, and children's car seats must pass before hitting the market. The agency could be patterned after the U.S. Consumer Product Safety Commission (CPSC), she suggested, which protected the public from unsafe products used at home and in school by setting standards and having the power to order recalls.

By setting up rules for lenders that would demand clarity and fairness, the free market would provide the full information customers needed—and reverse the ways of the current destructive system, she said. "When a lender can bury a sentence at the bottom of 47 lines of text saying it can change any term at any time for any reason," she wrote, "the market is broken." An agency like the one she proposed would replace those hidden terms with open competition and get rid of the worst "tricks and traps."[47]

Two years later, with the financial crisis on the edge and TARP in gear, organizations like the AFL-CIO, the largest union in the country, and many others were coming together to talk about the impact they could have on building new regulations for the finance industry. "Everyone knew that Congress would soon start working on a law that would overhaul banking regulation," Elizabeth said, and she was invited to a meeting at the AFL-CIO offices in Washington to talk about a consumer protection agency.[48] The meeting was held in February 2009, while she was working part-time on the TARP oversight committee and teaching at Harvard. In addition to describing the banking and credit card tricks and traps from which consumers needed protection, she emphasized that they needed a smart political strategy to get something done. If they came to Congress with a hundred good ideas that lawmakers whittled down to a dozen, those "would be like fence posts on the prairie—the giant banks could see them from a mile off and run right around them," she wrote.[49] But if they presented one long-term solution that could become the foundation of reform over time, she explained, that structure "might give us a fighting chance to create an effective counterweight to the big banks."[50]

The eighty or so people in the room launched into a lively discussion, and knowing full well the size of the giants they were trying to rein in, they endorsed the idea.[51] The first members of a coalition devoted to an agency that would protect consumers' rights in the finance world, they made fast progress finding allies in the Senate.[52] Senators Dick Durbin and Chuck Schumer joined with Ted Kennedy to draw up a bill to create the agency. In spite of his battle with a brain tumor, Ted Kennedy was keeping up a strong pace and cheerfully reminded Elizabeth how much the bankers were going to hate the whole thing.[53]

In addition to introducing the bill in the Senate, the three senators went through the standard process of holding a press conference to announce the proposed agency to the public. While the media didn't jump on the idea like Elizabeth had hoped, concerns sprang up from other agencies that held watchdog powers over the industry.[54] "The Consumer Financial Protection Agency posed clear threats to the turf of what may be called the status-quo regulators of U.S. consumer finance," wrote Daniel Carpenter in *Reaching for a New Deal: Ambitious Governance, Economic Meltdown, and Polarized Politics in Obama's First Two Years*. The Federal Reserve had its own consumer protection department, and it shared concerns with other agencies that "significant parts of their governing authority, which one might call their policy turf, and in some cases their budgets and personnel would stand to be transferred to the new consumer agency," Carpenter wrote.[55]

A late-night TV surprise a few days after the press conference balanced out those early tensions. Elizabeth realized that President Obama had read or been briefed on her original article about the potential agency when he made an appearance on *The Tonight Show with Jay Leno* and used a familiar analogy. "When you buy a toaster," he began during his spot on the March 19, 2009, show, "if it explodes in your face, there's a law that says your toasters need to be safe."[56] He explained how consumers needed the same protections around financial products, and then they joked about Mr. Potter, the mean banker in *It's A Wonderful Life*.

Elizabeth learned that the best chance for the agency to become a reality was to make it part of the postcrisis financial reform bill originating in the House.[57] As chairman of the House Committee on Financial Services, Representative Barney Frank of Massachusetts was at the center of writing sweeping new changes for banking regulation designed to prevent another catastrophe. Speaker of the House Nancy Pelosi called Barney "the quarterback" and an "enormously valuable intellectual resource" for the giant reform effort. "He's solution-oriented, respectful of different perspectives, and brilliant," she said. "And it's brilliance that saves time, because he simplifies the complex for us." Barney, who in 1987 came out to the press and became the first openly gay member of Congress, had also been voted the "brainiest, funniest, and most eloquent congressman" by staffers in 2006.[58]

Elizabeth visited him at his home in Newton one Saturday morning to make her case for the agency. In her pitch at Barney's kitchen table, she said that the agency would actually help build support for the reform bill because it spoke to people about issues they understood, like credit card fees hidden in pages of small print.

Barney heard her out and, believing they could actually get the votes to support it now that the Democrats had won a majority in the House, agreed to include the agency in the package. During that visit, Elizabeth met Barney's "surfer-dude-handsome" boyfriend, Jim Ready, whom Barney would marry in 2012.[59]

The proposed agency earned its official name during the White House event in which President Obama announced his administration's plans for creating financial reform. Elizabeth was with her three brothers in Oklahoma when she received a call inviting her to the announcement ceremony. "Holy cow—the White House!" she wrote in *A Fighting Chance*.[60] Her construction-worker brother John, whom she called "a President Obama man," was excited for her, as were Don Reed and David, despite being "dyed-in-the-wool Republicans," she wrote.[61]

Since she had heard rumblings in the press that the consumer agency would be included in the White House announcement along with other initiatives the president supported, she dove into the handout as soon as she arrived at the event.[62] Dick Trumka, who was soon to rise from secretary-treasurer to president of the AFL-CIO, recalled seeing her at that event. "There was an empty seat in front of me, and she came from behind me and sat down," he said. "She was fighting to get the consumer bureau done and people were attacking her. She doesn't see me, and I lean up and I say to her, 'Don't worry, Elizabeth, I have your back,' and she turned around and smiled and said, 'Yes, you do, and I'll always have the back of the workers.'"[63]

Spotting the section about the agency in the document, Elizabeth read its official name for the first time: the Consumer Financial

Protection Bureau (CFPB). In the statement, the administration said that it proposed the formation of an agency with the authority "to make sure that consumer protection regulations are written fairly and enforced vigorously."[64] The agency had found its biggest champion, but the fight to keep the agency intact in the final bill—the Dodd–Frank Wall Street Reform and Consumer Protection Act—was heating up.

Antireform forces amassed an army of lobbyists to fight reform in Congress, and the CFPB became the banks' public enemy number one. The country's most powerful business lobby, the Chamber of Commerce, drew a major battle line in early 2009 when it announced it would "spend whatever it takes" to take down the CFPB.[65] The Goliath in this battle looked like a sculpture made of wadded-up lobbyist contracts as tall as the Empire State Building. Interest groups spent $1.3 billion lobbying against reform over fifteen months in 2009 and early 2010, according to the Center for Public Integrity.[66] This army of more than 850 banks, companies, hedge funds, and other organizations hired the equivalent of five lobbyists for every member of Congress—the squads at the front lines.

During the fight for the agency, Elizabeth said in an interview:

> I'd heard of lobbyists, but I didn't know it was going to be like this… They make sure they're in every senator and every congressman's office morning noon and night, handing them every piece of paper and dollar they can. I've never seen anything like it… A few weeks ago a memo leaked…that laid out in 17 pages how you can vote with the banks but use language that indicates

you really do hate them because you're on this side of the people… It's a level of flat-out lying that leaves me feeling spiritually depleted. Is there just nothing here that we hold on to?[67]

One of the fights to chip away at the agency's power came from the nation's car dealers, who did not want the agency to regulate how dealerships wrote up their auto loans. The National Automobile Dealers Association fiercely lobbied to strike the potential regulation in order to preserve the fees that dealerships make as middlemen between customers and their car loans from banks and other big financers. "Those dealers tack on unnecessary fees and steer customers into higher-cost loans, splitting the difference with lenders," reported Paul Kiel in *Mother Jones*. Customers with low incomes and minorities are more at risk to be steered toward those more expensive loans, Kiel wrote. Dozens of groups, including the National Consumer Law Center, Consumers Union, and NAACP lobbied to keep the regulation intact, but Republican and Democratic lawmakers did not want to irritate the dealers who had a strong local presence in their communities, and the auto dealership lobbyists won.[68] To keep the bill alive, Barney deleted that section of regulations in the document. The bill's name, the Dodd–Frank Wall Street Reform and Consumer Protection Act, was based on the names of its sponsors, Senators Christopher Dodd and Barney Frank, and also based on the prominent role of consumer protection in reforming the country's financial system.

In the midst of the fight to create financial reform, Ted Kennedy lost his yearlong battle with brain cancer and passed away on August

25, 2009. The country looked back on the career of the liberal lion of the Senate who had transformed the social landscape with his work on the Civil Rights Act, his introduction of the Americans with Disabilities Act, and his latest efforts for financial reform in the Great Recession. During the funeral Mass, held at the Basilica of Our Lady of Perpetual Help just outside Boston, President Obama said:

> Ted Kennedy's life's work was not to champion the causes of those with wealth or power or special connections. It was to give a voice to those who were not heard; to add a rung to the ladder of opportunity; to make real the dream of our founding. He was given the gift of time that his brothers were not, and he used that gift to touch as many lives and right as many wrongs as the years would allow.[69]

In her speeches and opinion pieces and interviews about the bureau, Elizabeth always emphasized that the mission of the CFPB was to strengthen markets by making them more transparent. "I am committed to building a consumer credit market that works—a market that works for American families, works for the financial services industry, and works for our economy," she told the Credit Union National Association.[70] As James Surowiecki wrote in the *New Yorker*, "Warren is far from the anti-capitalist radical that her critics (and some of her supporters) suppose... The core principle of Warren's work is also a cornerstone of economic theory: well-informed consumers make for vigorous competition and efficient markets."[71]

As the battle for Dodd–Frank advanced, Americans who viewed Wall Street banks as gangsters who got away with annihilating the economy, putting millions out of their homes, and committing fraud, made their outrage public. On Thursday, April 29, 2010, for example, six thousand people marched from New York City Hall to Wall Street holding signs that read MAKE WALL STREET PAY and RECLAIM AMERICA.[72] Organized by the AFL-CIO, the protest (which came a year and a half before the launch of Occupy Wall Street) voiced the anger of those who expected the bailed-out Wall Street banks to stop more foreclosures and bring jobs to "Main Street" instead of dole out billions in bonuses to their executives. The union's president at the time, Richard Trumka, echoed that sentiment as he addressed the protest, asking, "How long will we allow the spirit of greed to continue to drive us into economic holes?"

The next month, about one thousand demonstrators gathered on K Street in Washington, DC, the home of many lobbyist offices, to protest the $1.3 million spent per day to lobby against the Dodd–Frank bill. Days earlier, about six hundred people from that group had targeted two high-ranking figures, Peter Scher, a lobbyist for JPMorgan Chase, and Gregory Baer, a lobbyist for Bank of America, by gathering in front of their homes in Chevy Chase, Maryland.[73] Carrying signs and megaphones, they shouted phrases like "Bank of America, Bad for America" and "People First Economy" as they swarmed Baer's and Scher's lawns.

Congress could not ignore the public backlash heard in Washington and in cities across the country, and they ultimately voted to pass Dodd–Frank, which became law on July 21, 2010. With the new law came the creation of the new agency that Elizabeth had first promoted in an article three years earlier.

The fight was far from over—antiregulation members of Congress kept up their efforts and tried to weaken and eliminate the agency. Republican congressman Spencer Bachus of Alabama, a vocal opponent of Elizabeth and the CFPB, was now the chairman of the House Committee on Financial Services. He made it clear where he stood when he remarked to the press, "In Washington, the view is that the banks are to be regulated, and my view is that Washington and the regulators are there to serve the banks."[74] He later clarified his comment to say that regulators should not micromanage the banks.

As a lightning rod for antiregulation members of Congress, Elizabeth did not have much of a chance of winning Senate approval to become the director of the CFPB. She and President Obama discussed what her role could be over the next few weeks, while her supporters rallied for the president to nominate her as the head of the agency. After forty-four Republican senators announced they would block any nominee unless the administration weakened the power of the CFPB, Democratic senator Al Franken of Minnesota called on the president to make a recess appointment. Naming Elizabeth as the director in this way would be within the president's constitutional powers while Congress was out of session over the Memorial Day and Fourth of July holidays. The Senate prevented that by technically staying in session over those breaks, and at the same time, the president seemed resolved that Elizabeth's nomination would be too contentious to bring forward.[75] Instead of nominating her as the director, he gave her two temporary roles, both of which gave her the responsibility of setting up the agency. She became special adviser to the secretary of the treasury on the CFPB and assistant to the president, the latter a high-profile advisory role that closely aligned her work at the agency with the White House.[76]

With her new position established, she resigned from the Congressional Oversight Panel and took a leave from Harvard.[77] Up to that time, her work in Washington had not detracted from her teaching; in fact, in 2009, the graduating class honored her with the prestigious Sacks-Freund Award for Teaching Excellence.[78] During the ruckus over the directorship of the CFPB, her students pitched in to urge the president appoint her to head up the agency she spearheaded. In August 2010, sixty-seven of her current Harvard students signed a letter stating:

> No one could wear the 'expert' hat better than Professor Warren... We learned to question our assumptions, and when necessary, she persuaded skeptics with evidence instead of rhetoric... We learned from her that the best solutions emerge only after considering all the viewpoints of the legal and non-legal players in a system. Professor Warren would expect nothing less than such fairness and careful decision-making from herself and the CFPB staff.[79]

She had received the same award from the graduating class of 1997, and her reputation as a scholar was still at its peak. A study of professors with the most "scholarly impact," based on the number of times their work was cited in other published work between 2005 and 2009, put her at number three in the nation in the commercial law and bankruptcy category.[80] She actually shared that spot with Douglas Baird of the University of Chicago, with whom she had sparred over styles of bankruptcy research in her point-counterpoint article in the mid-1980s. Recognition from her peers included a passage in a 2004 article by Professor David Skeel Jr. of Penn Law that read: "I think there would be something like unanimous agreement that Elizabeth Warren has been the nation's leading consumer bankruptcy scholar over the last ten or twenty years. By whatever yardstick we might choose—scholarly productivity, institutional leadership, prominence in the media—Professor Warren stands alone at the top of the list."[81]

In mid-September 2010, she and Bruce moved into an apartment near the Treasury Building, where the agency would be housed, and almost became permanent Washingtonians. Since he was still at Harvard, Bruce became a commuter husband once again, driving back and forth to Cambridge every week.

Three years after offering her ideas for a consumer agency in "Unsafe at Any Rate," Elizabeth was at the temporary helm of a $550-million agency created to enforce the rules on the books for banks, credit unions, payday lenders, collection agencies, brokerage firms, and other financial institutions—and more.[82] The CFPB would also take consumer complaints, provide financial education, research consumers' experiences with financial products, and monitor the financial markets for new risks to consumers.

One of the CFPB's strengths came from its funding source, the Federal Reserve, which made it more powerful and independent.

The government agencies that traditionally held consumer financial protection responsibilities were funded by banks, which, according to Georgetown University law professor Adam Leviton, "severely compromised" the strength of those regulators. The funding aspect of banking regulation, Adam said, "was a major reason we needed a CFPB."[83]

From the start, the bureau was set up as a tech-savvy, twenty-first-century enterprise that took advantage of all the ways people could communicate and interact on the internet. One of the first boxes on Elizabeth's checklist was introducing herself to the bankers on Wall Street, folks like Jamie Dimon, the chairman, CEO, and president of JPMorgan Chase, the biggest bank in the country. She gave Will Sealy, a staffer in the agency's Office for Students and Young Americans, his first assignment: "My very first role for Elizabeth Warren was collecting the cell phone number for every Wall Street CEO so she could introduce herself to them as their new regulator," he said. "It's September 2010, and I'm this twenty-two-year-old calling Jamie Dimon's office. I don't even know if they're real people; they're like caricatures."[84]

The next day, "Jamie Dimon received a call while at a conference in Russia from Elizabeth Warren, who introduced herself as his new regulator," Will said.

Will was recruited by Elizabeth during his internship with the White House Business Council, which met with American businesses to discuss ideas for economic development and job creation. As the intern for the council's executive director, Elizabeth Vale, Will was close to the action around supporting the Dodd–Frank bill. Elizabeth Warren made a passionate pitch to him, saying,

"Will, I need a bunch of people to create this agency with me. It's going to be twenty-first century, data driven, and for the people, and the country needs this." Will's first thought was that he didn't want to be a government bureaucrat, and she somehow picked up on it. "Her emotional IQ is through the roof," he said. She kept going. "Look," she told him, "this is probably one of the most exciting things of your or my lifetime; this is historic. I want you to be part of it." He was in.

As he worked at the agency, Will was struck by how widely Elizabeth was misunderstood. Her opponents had framed her as a radical, hysterical leftist who wanted to destroy the markets, when she was actually a fervent capitalist who believed in safety nets. Will's job was to make sure the people who were the most vocal about that got to hear her own words so they couldn't just believe what other people said about her. He and his team were out to combat the stereotypes. "We put her in rooms with people from all segments of society, and she would talk for no more than ten minutes about how unbridled capitalism could undo its greatest rewards, but capitalism in balance never led to the ten-year boom-and-bust cycles." People were blown away by her, he said, and told her that she was not the person they imagined. "In these conversations, I got to see her run circles around people, unbelievably wealthy, successful people who had it in their heads they understood everything they came across."

The early work was heavily involved in combining seven different agencies with consumer protective units under one roof and working out the enforcement of nineteen consumer protection laws. "Her whole point was streamlining," Will said, "and from the get-go,

Have Been Sold Here
For Over Thirty Years

2 3-4 Size $200.00
3 inch size   205.00
Fall Terms

Herring Hardware Company
THE *WINCHESTER* STORE

Elizabeth (Herring) Warren's great-grandfather, J. H. Herring, opened Herring Hardware in Wetumka, Oklahoma, in 1910, and later opened a second store in Sallisaw. Elizabeth's father, Donald Herring, worked in the Wetumka store during his summer school breaks.

After the Oklahoma City Oil Field opened within city limits in 1930, oil derricks sprang up all over the city, including around the state capitol grounds. Elizabeth Warren's great-grandfather, J. H. Herring, owned land in another part of the city upon which Mid-Texas Petroleum, Inc. built and dug an oil and gas well named Mid-Texas No. 1.

Norman, Oklahoma, Elizabeth Warren's hometown,
in 1956, when she was seven years old.

Donald Herring, Elizabeth's father,
was a flight instructor in Muskogee,
Oklahoma, during World War II.

"Betsy" Herring with her
mother, Pauline.

Elizabeth's beloved Aunt Bee.

Elizabeth's debate team in her sophomore year at Northwest Classen High School in Oklahoma City, 1964. She is first on the left in the second row, and her debate partner, Karl Johnson, is fourth in the same row. Jim Warren is fifth from the right in the top row, and their friend Joe Pryor is third from the right in the same row.

Jim Warren, Elizabeth's high school
sweetheart, as a senior in 1964.

Elizabeth as a high school senior, 1966.

Elizabeth and her debate partner, Karl Johnson, with their
trophies. They won a national tournament their senior year.

The Betty Crocker Homemaker of Tomorrow hearth pin. Elizabeth won the award in her senior year by scoring highest in her high school on the exam designed by General Mills.

Elizabeth in her freshman year at George Washington University, 1966.

The George Washington University debate team. Elizabeth's debate partner, Gregory Millard, was the only black member of the team, and he went on to work for New York City Mayor Ed Koch.

Elizabeth as a sophomore at
George Washington University.

From the Rutgers Law
School student directory.

Amelia Louise
arrived in 1971.
Elizabeth's son, Alex,
was born five years
later, shortly after
Elizabeth graduated
from law school.

Father and daughter at Elizabeth's graduation from Rutgers Law School in New Jersey, 1976.

Elizabeth's father, Donald, worked as a maintenance man in the apartment building in which he and Pauline lived.

Brothers Don Reed, John, and David in 1980.

Elizabeth and fellow law professor Bruce Mann were married in July 1980, in Hartford, Connecticut.

Teaching at Harvard Law.

On the campaign trail on July 1, 2012, with granddaughter Lavinia, daughter Amelia Warren Tyagi, granddaughter Octavia, and husband Bruce Mann.

Elizabeth in her professor's regalia delivering the commencement address at the Framingham State University Commencement, May 19, 2013.

President Barack Obama with Treasury Secretary Timothy Geithner and Elizabeth Warren, whom he named assistant to the president and special advisor to the secretary of the treasury on the Consumer Financial Protection Bureau.

On stage with James Taylor at a fund-raising concert in the Colonial Theater in Norwich, New York, October 24, 2012.

Visiting her childhood home in Norman with *Boston Globe* journalists two months after she launched her Senate campaign in November 2011.

With U.S. Representative John Lewis at the famous civil rights site, the Edmund Pettus Bridge connecting Selma to Montgomery, Alabama, March 2015.

Elizabeth serving as the Caribbean Carnival Grand Matron in Boston during her Senate campaign, August 25, 2012.

The start of Elizabeth's first debate with U.S. Senator Scott Brown at the WBZ-TV studio in Boston, September 20, 2012, with moderator Jon Keller.

Victory night, November 6, 2012, with husband Bruce Mann.

Senator Joseph Biden swearing in Elizabeth on January 3, 2013, as Bruce holds Elizabeth's Bible for the oath.

she said she didn't want to create more government, but smarter and better government."

Will's team set up down the hall from Elizabeth's office and worked late, excited to be part of her mission and to take on the challenge of getting the agency up and running in six months. When Elizabeth left at eight, she told them all to go home, but they stayed until eleven and came in early the next day. The atmosphere buzzed with the level of talent and expertise Elizabeth brought in from industry, academia, policy, and government, Will said. As a ground-floor member of the agency, he saw how Elizabeth approached the challenge of providing consumers with better information to help them make financial decisions. She went to the top, recruiting a leading behavioral economist, Harvard's Sendhil Mullainathan, as the bureau's assistant director for research. "I was in the car with her on the way to Treasury where she still had an office, and she was trying to get Sendhil to join the CFPB," Will said. "She was saying, 'We need you. We need behavioral economics as the DNA of this agency, because part of the mess that created this financial crisis was that every policy maker was not thinking about the consequences.'"

She had a way with people, Will said, that made it impossible for them to say no. Soon, Elizabeth was announcing that under Sendhil, the Office of Research would "promote evidence-based policy making," and Will recalled how everyone learned about Sendhil's cutting-edge research on how poverty affects people's decision making. Elizabeth also brought in the University of Chicago's behavioral economist Richard Thaler, who would win the Nobel Prize a few years later. "I felt like I was at consumer protection university," Will said. "She knew that a lot of that thinking is critical to making policy."

Elizabeth's high standards for the agency lived side by side with her down-to-earth, considerate style of interacting with everyone, Will recalled. "She's someone who remembers birthdays," he said, "and asks in meetings how your family is doing. She's a really good person."

Once the bureau was up and running, it began enforcing regulations, creating new rules to stop predatory lending, and giving the public practical advice that helped them make financial decisions. A few examples reported by Erika Eichelberger for *Mother Jones* reveal the scope of the bureau's protections.[85] One new rule shut down the practice of pushing borrowers to high-interest loans even if they qualified for less expensive mortgages, an action that thrived during the financial crisis. Another rule forced mortgage lenders to make good faith efforts to help homeowners who were still struggling to avoid foreclosure. In a credit card case, the bureau secured $85 million in refunds for customers of three companies that had illegally charged excessive late fees and created misleading credit card offerings. After finding that JPMorgan Chase had charged about two million customers for identity theft and fraud monitoring services they didn't ask for, the bureau forced the bank to refund the customers $309 million. When the bureau learned that U.S. Bank and its auto-loan partner, Dealers' Financial Services, failed to tell army and other service customers about fees in their military car loan program, it ordered them to refund $6.5 million to the service people. In another action for military men and women, the bureau ordered the payday loan company Cash America to refund $14 million for illegally overcharging these customers.

Testimonials on the CFPB website shed light on how the agency solved problems for people struggling with mortgage issues, student loan payments, car loans, and other challenges.[86] One woman who was looking for a mortgage lender remarked about the hassles she avoided by using the tool designed to weed out lenders that were not being up front about the costs of taking out a mortgage. The bureau solved disputes between customers and their mortgage lenders by writing letters that got action—in one case, a man whose loan was not approved got his deposit back within days of the bureau writing on his behalf, and his check came with an apology from the lender. Student loan customers also shared stories of clearing up threats of wage garnishment and other collection acts after filing complaints on the CFPB website, which brought about reasonable payment plans. Other testimonials described how the bureau's complaint process helped resolve harassment problems coming from payday loan collection agencies and other debt collectors who threatened customers with arrest and jail time.

Soldiers and veterans also shared their stories: One man learned that his car loan company was mistreating him and other service members. His father wrote to the CFPB, which already had a file on the company, and the bureau took action for all the soldiers who were being treated unfairly with their loans.

The bureau also created the Office for Older Americans, the only federal office specifically dedicated to the financial health of Americans aged sixty-two and older. Hubert H. "Skip" Humphrey, son of the late vice president Hubert Humphrey and former Minnesota attorney general and state senator, was appointed the assistant director of the office. In testimony before the Senate Special

Committee on Aging, Skip discussed a number of the ways the elderly experienced financial abuse. "Older Americans are victimized by a broad range of perpetrators," he said, "including scam artists, family members, caregivers, financial advisers, home repair contractors, and fiduciaries such as agents under power of attorney and court-appointed guardians." His department in the CFPB created strategies for dealing with these "bad actors." Older adults' diminished capacity made it even more difficult for them to detect fraud, he said.[87]

During his first year, Skip traveled the country, meeting with state and tribal officials to listen to experiences, setbacks, and insights in fighting financial abuse targeting Americans aged sixty-two and older. Among his department's initiatives was the creation of user-friendly guides for "lay fiduciaries"—people under powers of attorney, guardians, and trustees, for example—that help them spot financial exploitation and learn the "critical basics to manage a vulnerable adult's money," he said.

The CFPB punched a hole in the rigged system that Elizabeth had been studying and warning the country about for decades. As the new cop on the beat, her bureau took a stand against those who had damaged millions of lives during the Great Recession and ignited a crisis that sent economies across the world into a tailspin. The bureau offered real help, one consumer at a time, and sent a signal that regular Americans deserved some justice, fairness, and dignity.

The creation of the CFPB was Elizabeth's highest achievement, and being passed up to be its director became the greatest blow to her career. People close by in Washington, like Harry Reid, as well as Democratic power players in Massachusetts, wanted her to run for the Senate as the ultimate consolation prize.[88] So did the man who championed the bureau from the beginning but could not, in the end, hand over the keys.

7

"I WILL BE YOUR CHAMPION"

"Don't get mad; get elected."
—Retired U.S. Senator Barbara Mikulski[1]

President Obama opened the east door of the Oval Office to lead Elizabeth outside for a final chat on her last day with the Consumer Financial Protection Bureau. It was July, and the sound of car horns and a siren filtered over the thick hedge surrounding their little table. She handed him an envelope containing her resignation, and they talked about the trouble a lot of people were still in during that summer of 2011...underwater mortgages, foreclosures, jobs gone. When the conversation eventually turned to the upcoming Senate race in Massachusetts, where Republican Scott Brown had won Ted Kennedy's seat in a special election in 2010, the president chimed in to a larger conversation that had been percolating in the press for weeks.

If she ran and beat Scott Brown, she'd have a lot of opportunities to fight for the economic issues she cared about.[2]

Barney Frank had already suggested the idea early that year, and Elizabeth remarked that at the time, she "fluffed it off. It's just one of those things you smile at and move to the next topic."[3] But by July, the president had announced his nominee for the director of the CFPB, Richard Cordray, and Democrats leaped on the idea that Elizabeth was now free to capitalize on her popularity with a Senate run. The day Richard was named, a grassroots organization called the Progressive Change Campaign Committee called for Elizabeth to jump in and set up a fund-raising goal of ten thousand donations of five dollars in four days—they overreached that in a day.[4] Senators Harry Reid and Patty Murray, chair of the Democratic Senatorial Campaign Committee, championed the idea, and Elizabeth said that she and Patty had actually discussed the notion much earlier. "Patty reached out to me long before I thought seriously about running for the Senate," Elizabeth said. "She was gently encouraging, willing to offer candid advice and to talk about both the good and the bad of running for office."[5]

Elizabeth knew the president's pick well, since she had hired Richard Cordray to lead the CFPB's enforcement division. As attorney general of Ohio, Richard had launched aggressive investigations into subprime lenders and fraudulent mortgage servicing companies during the financial crisis. Like Elizabeth, he believed in markets—he earned his law degree from the University of Chicago—but only when they worked on an even playing field. "[He] carefully describes his allegiance to capitalism," the *New York Times* wrote in 2010, "although he says the financial crisis should explode forever the efficient-markets theory, popular with economists, that the best market is a self-correcting one."[6] In that pre-CFPB profile, Richard described the view from his state in the wake of the Great Recession: "We see what Washington doesn't: the houses lying vacant, the eyesore stripped for copper piping with mattresses out back. We bailed out irresponsible banks, but we forgot about everyone else."[7]

After the president announced Richard as his choice for director, Elizabeth praised the decision. "Rich has always had my strong support because he is tough and he is smart—and that's exactly the combination this new agency needs," she said. As one of the first senior leaders she recruited for the agency, she said, his work and commitment had made it clear that he would make a "stellar director."[8] The president installed Richard through a recess appointment—the same path that Al Franken and others had previously hoped would usher Elizabeth into the job. Since Republican senators had announced that they would not allow any nominee to be considered until significant changes were made to the bureau, the president felt he had no choice but to bypass Congress. In announcing his politically defiant action, the president said, "The only reason Republicans in the Senate have blocked Richard is because they don't agree with the law setting up the consumer watchdog in the first place." He then defended the agency, pointing out that since a lack of oversight got them into the "financial mess," they should strengthen, not weaken that oversight.[9] Among their complaints about the bureau, Republicans argued that the agency put too much power in the hands of a single director. They called for a five-person commission to replace that role and would continue demanding this change along with others in their ongoing opposition to the agency.

While announcing Richard's installment as director on January 4, 2012, President Obama also expressed his admiration for Elizabeth: "This agency was Elizabeth's idea, and through sheer force of will, intelligence, and a bottomless well of energy, she has made, and will continue to make, a profound and positive difference for our country," he said.[10]

Even without the full powers of his role at the agency, which would not come until the Senate confirmed him a year and a half later, Richard took the helm and continued to carry out the bureau's mission. By the time he was confirmed[11] on July 16, 2013, the bureau had already handled 175,000 complaints from consumers, made credit card statements easier to understand, given veterans and seniors better protection from predatory lenders and scam artists, and developed new rules for mortgage lenders, among other actions.[12] Richard's Senate confirmation put the agency on firm ground, but the opposition's fight to weaken the bureau would continue.

At sixty-two, Elizabeth had mixed feelings about running, and so did her family.[13] Alex and her brothers thought she should give up fighting and settle back into teaching—and enjoying her grandchildren—but she was excited to test the waters. She gave the public a hint by writing a blog-post snapshot of her life story, all the way up to her exit from the CFPB, and said she was thinking about her next role:

I left Washington, but I don't plan to stop fighting for middle class families. I spent years working against special interests and have the battle scars to show it—and I have no intention of stopping now. It is time for me to think hard about what role I can play next to help rebuild a middle class that has been hacked at, chipped at, and pulled at for more than a generation— and that is under greater strain every day.[14]

To get a sense of how it felt to bring her message to a live room, Elizabeth quietly met with groups of curious progressive and independent voters in towns around the state, starting at a supporter's home in Boston's Dorchester neighborhood.[15] Joyce Linehan, a well-known publicist for Boston arts organizations such as the Institute of Contemporary Art, had started her career as the promotions director and talent scout for the punk-rock record label Sub Pop. In the 1990s, her home was the legendary pad where hundreds of stars, such as Courtney Love and Eddie Vedder of Pearl Jam, would hang out while on the East Coast.[16] In the next decade, she wove politics into her expanding cultural network, and in August 2012, she invited a few dozen people to her house to meet Elizabeth. "I'm one of the loudmouths with a laptop and an internet connection who has been urging her from afar to run for a couple of months now," she wrote in her blog after the event.[17] She described the impression Elizabeth made to the sixty or so who showed up in her home:

What a night. It was my honor to host one of the first house parties for Elizabeth Warren, as she talks to

Democrats about whether she will run for the United States Senate. She came to my house in Dorchester, and stood in my living room talking to about 60 of my friends, who shared their stories and frustrations, and asked brilliant questions, which she fielded with charm, charisma, and thoughtful, plain-spoken answers. It was fantastic and inspiring...

Before, it was more about thinking that she, unlike the current Democratic field, could beat Scott Brown. Now, for me, and I think for most who came to my house tonight, it's about much more than that. It's about choosing the kind of America we want to live in, and then working for it.[18]

The questions and conversations that night gave Elizabeth the sense that a campaign could tackle serious issues in a deep, engaged way and be fun at the same time. She learned that with supporters like Joyce and others who had attended, they had the capacity to build a grassroots campaign that had a real chance against a strong incumbent like Scott Brown.

Another early stop was in New Bedford, a seaport city on Buzzards Bay where about fifty people climbed the stairs to the second floor of a building in the August heat to hear what she had to say.[19] She spoke about the tough breaks hitting the middle class and how the Republicans in Congress had ideas that would only make things worse. After her talk, as people drifted out, a woman in her fifties stepped over and told her story. She had done everything right, worked since she was seventeen, earned two master's degrees, learned computer programming, but had been out of a job for a year and a half. She walked to the meeting because her car didn't run. She came because she was running out of hope.

The fans buzzed as Elizabeth grasped both her hands.

"I've read about you for a long time," the woman said, "and I'm here to see you in person, to tell you that I need you, and I want you to fight for me. I don't care how hard it gets. I want to know that you are going to fight."[20]

Elizabeth held onto her hands and stared back at her. This wasn't a moment for crying and commiserating and just walking away. This was a chance to feel if her heart was really in it.

"Yes, I'll fight," Elizabeth said.

On September 18, 2011, a supporter posted a video from an August house gathering in Andover, Massachusetts, where Elizabeth had responded to a comment about the national talk about "class warfare."[21] Republicans were expressing their frustration over President Obama's proposal for higher taxes on the wealthy and framing it as a war against the rich. Answering a question about that current debate, Elizabeth said:

> There is nobody in this country who got rich on his own—nobody. You built a factory out there? Good for you. But I want to be clear. You moved your goods to market on the roads the rest of us paid for. You hired workers the rest of us paid to educate. You

were safe in your factory because of police forces and fire forces that the rest of us paid for. You didn't have to worry that marauding bands would come and seize everything at your factory—and hire someone to protect against this—because of the work the rest of us did.

Now look, you built a factory, and it turned into something terrific or a great idea. God bless—keep a big hunk of it. But part of the underlying social contract is, you take a hunk of that and pay it forward for the next kid who comes along.[22]

The video showed Elizabeth with her white sweater sleeves rolled up, pointing at her heart or making a circular gesture with each "the rest of us" and getting applause from the crowded living- and dining-room audience. Within four days, the video had gone viral with over one hundred thousand views, and eventually, it topped more than one million. In simple language, she spoke to the anger and confusion of Americans who had seen the social contract erode into a system that didn't work for them but worked extremely well for those on top.

As Josh Freedman and Michael Lind discussed in an essay for *The Atlantic*, in the New Deal era following the Great Depression, in which high wages, good benefits, and pensions benefited everyone and built the middle class, corporations considered these wages and pensions part of their mission. They assumed this responsibility as part of a social contract—where workers and institutions created an ecosystem in which companies could thrive.

That belief took an about-face in the 1980s, Freedman and Lind continued, when global competition raised the cost of doing business, and deregulation created a new era of "shareholder capitalism."[23] When companies with falling stock prices became vulnerable to hostile "Gordon Gekko" takeovers, unhappy shareholders were willing to sell. Managers focused on share prices and speedy profits to lure investors and peeled away the social-contract reluctance to cut wages, lay off workers, close plants, and outsource. The interests of corporate shareholders took precedence and ushered in the "low-wage social contract," in which low pay is supposed to be balanced by cheap goods and tax credits for workers.[24] The formula may have worked if the cost of living had not shot up for other things people needed to buy, like health care (no longer subsidized by good jobs), child care, and college tuition, which was saddling Americans in debt.

By shaking her fist to demand that companies "pay it forward" at the gathering in Andover the day the viral video was recorded, Elizabeth plugged into the angst of Americans who felt cut off from the business world and workplace that used to be part of the same dream but were now caricatures of the villain. Laid-off workers were being escorted out of their offices by uniformed security personnel like criminals. They were bitter about companies that laid them off or kept them on to work two or three jobs at once with no increase in pay. And now the wealthy business leaders and their friends in Washington were complaining about possible tax increases. Elizabeth felt it, understood it, and knew how to articulate the injustice behind the failed social contract.

The small tryouts in gatherings around the state brought Elizabeth closer to her decision, but as she continued to weigh the pros and cons, she balked at how much she didn't know. "I didn't have a clue about how to run for the Senate in 2011," she later wrote on her Facebook page. "I knew what I wanted to fight for, but I had no experience with press scrums, fund-raising, or grassroots organizing."[25] Besides, she said, a lot of people told her she just couldn't win. Scott Brown had a 73 percent approval rating, $10 million in the bank, "and a cool truck." Another strike against her was that Massachusetts had never elected a woman as senator or governor, "a point many people drove home both publicly and privately," she wrote.

The clincher came with a call from her friend Senator Patty Murray. Out of the gate, her advice was simply "Run." It was just the shove Elizabeth needed:

> She knew what issues I cared about, and she talked about how I could fight for those things in the Senate. I heard her out, then I started listing the reasons why I might not be good enough for the job. She listened quietly for a couple of minutes, then cut me off with a voice as sharp as a knife: "Oh, please." She told me that women always think of reasons they aren't good enough. Men never ask if they're good enough to hold public office, Patty said. They just ask if they can raise enough money to win.
>
> "Of course you can do this," Patty told her. "And I'll help."[26]

On Wednesday, September 14, 2011, Elizabeth made her official announcement, which ran as an online video on the website

Blue Mass Group. "I'm going to do this," she began. "I'm going to run." She described the middle class as "chipped at, hacked at, squeezed, and hammered" and called Washington "rigged" for big corporations and lobbyists. "Rigged" would become the catchword of her campaign, the motto of an almost-insider who had worked in the system long enough to know where the real power seemed to lie.[27]

Her opponent, Scott Brown, had shaken the democratic establishment as a Republican winning the seat that Ted Kennedy had held for forty-seven years. Ted's brother, John F. Kennedy, had held the same seat until he was elected president in 1960. Before it became clear that Elizabeth was serious about running, Scott and his team thought they were in for an easy ride to his reelection.

Running against an incumbent as popular as Scott Brown set the tone for the campaign from the start. Since Scott was one of Wall Street's favorite senators, as Michael Tomasky wrote in *Foreign Affairs*, "the race was a perfect setup" for Elizabeth that gave her "ample opportunity to draw a stark contrast between them."[28] Scott had earned the love of many in his state with his personal story of rising from a troubled childhood, in which he was abused by his father and stepfathers, to a career in politics, all while staying a regular guy.[29] His trademark green GMC pickup, which he drove everywhere, symbolized his connection with working-class voters. Scott had gone to college as a basketball player and, after hitting fame as *Cosmo*'s Sexiest Man, spent two years as a professional model. After earning a law degree from Boston College Law School, he set up his own practice and ultimately ran successfully for the Massachusetts House of Representatives and state senate.

As a Massachusetts state senator, he ran in the special election for Ted Kennedy's open seat.

There is a saying among people who know campaigns: "When women run, women win."

Elizabeth began her campaign with the attitude that she was in it to win and to win by staying true to who she was. She had spent years in Washington fighting for the issues she believed in and saw those fights as natural extensions of her academic career. Becoming a candidate would not challenge her to find a new political identity. "This is not change for me," she said. "This is what I've worked on all my life."[30] Her service in Washington had given her glimpses of what she was headed for, but she wasn't intimidated; instead, she vowed to be as outspoken and action-oriented in the Senate as she had been in her other roles. "I'm not running for Senate so I can be the 100th-in-seniority, be-polite-and-make-no-difference senator from Massachusetts," she said.[31]

Her first TV ad offered a one-minute sweep of her life story:

> I'm Elizabeth Warren. I'm running for the United States Senate, and before you hear a bunch of ridiculous attack ads, I want to tell you who I am. Like a lot of you, I came up the hard way; my dad sold carpet, and when he had a heart attack, my mom went to work so we could keep our house. We all worked—my three brothers joined the military. I got married at nineteen

and had two kids, worked my way through college, taught elementary school, and then I went to law school. For years, I worked to expose how Wall Street and the big banks are crushing middle-class families. It just isn't right—I stood up to the big banks and their army of Washington lobbyists. I worked to hold them accountable. I led the fight for a new agency to protect consumers, and we got it, but Washington is still rigged for the big guys, and that's gotta change. I'm Elizabeth Warren, and I approve this message, because I want Massachusetts families to have a level playing field.[32]

The other Democrats vying for the candidacy were well-known local figures, including Alan Khazei, a social entrepreneur who cofounded Be the Change, a nonprofit group that built national coalitions to promote policies on poverty, education, and other issues. Newton mayor Setti Warren, an Iraq war veteran who had experience in Washington as an aide to Senator John Kerry, was the first black mayor elected in the state.[33] Another popular candidate, Bob Massie, was a lifelong social activist, executive director of the Coalition for Environmentally Responsible Economies, business scholar with a doctorate from Harvard Business School, and ordained Episcopal priest.[34] Warren's national prominence, however, put her at the top of this group when she entered the race.

Early on, a poll showed her nine points behind Scott Brown, closer than any of the others.[35] The road ahead would cut through a hot-button political climate and personal attacks about her family heritage that would find new ways to resonate in years to come. She taught her last classes at Harvard in the fall semester of 2011 so that by January 2012, she could devote all her time to the campaign.[36]

That campaign season, the culture wars flared up over a handful of issues such as Missouri congressman Todd Akin's statement that women don't get pregnant from "legitimate rape,"[37] and a couple of months later, Indiana treasurer Richard Mourdock's remark that pregnancies from rape were "something that God intended to happen."[38] In the spring of 2012, Missouri senator Roy Blunt proposed the Respect for Rights of Conscience Act, commonly called the Blunt amendment, which set off a national debate about religious freedom.[39] The combination of women's issue stories from the extreme right marked those months as a war on women, and the more details revealed in each case, the more incensed the debate.

When Roy Blunt tried to attach the amendment to a highway bill, he and his cosponsor, Scott Brown, argued that any employer should be able to opt out of providing insurance coverage for contraception or anything that ran contrary to the "religious beliefs or moral convictions" of the employer.[40] This "complicity claim" is based on the idea that allowing someone to act in a way that goes against one's religious beliefs makes one complicit in the sinful conduct. Christians who believe that contraception is a form of abortion supported Blunt's proposed change in the Affordable Care Act and his premise that forcing employers to cover contraception in their plans blocked the employers' religious freedom. Those who fought the amendment pointed out that religious freedom is already granted in the Constitution, and the amendment would simply be giving employers the right to discriminate against women.

That same year, in another response to the Affordable Care Act, the owners of Hobby Lobby won their suit to opt out of covering some types of contraception in their health plans. In its lawsuit, the Green family said that their religious beliefs "forbid them from participating in, providing access to, paying for, training others to engage in, or otherwise supporting abortion-causing drugs and devices."[41] The Supreme Court found that this would do no "harm" to female employees because the federal government would provide them with free contraception coverage.

One of Elizabeth's students from Penn Law, Professor Marci Hamilton, the church-state scholar at the University of Pennsylvania, brought clarity to the "war on women" issues that raged during the campaign season. She described the women at Hobby Lobby as "discriminated against because they don't believe what their employers believe."[42] Her legal work opposes the idea that religious believers and institutions should have a right to take actions that harm others and sees this as a core issue of the current balance of church and state in the United States. "We've created a culture of…religious believers who believe sincerely that their rights should trump anybody else's rights—that they're right and everybody else is wrong," she said in a speech. "They seem to believe they have a right to own the public square… This talk of the public square is an attempt to own the public square rather than share it."[43]

In that hotbed cultural environment, Elizabeth routinely spoke to girls throughout her campaign, taking them aside in the spirit of her second-grade teacher, Mrs. Lee. Whenever she met a little girl on the campaign trail, she bent down, took her hand, and told her quietly, "I'm Elizabeth, and I'm running for Senate, because that's what girls do."[44]

In January, ads funded by the fat, mostly anonymous super PACs hit the airwaves in Massachusetts. Karl Rove's super PAC, American Crossroads, targeted Warren, and the League of Conservation Voters struck at Scott's voting record.* Both Elizabeth and Scott were anxious to stop this influx of outside warfare, so they came up with a strategy that they hoped would shut down the process. Their solution was a model for how to keep these big-money forces out of elections.

Elizabeth and Scott made a deal that if a super PAC ran an ad against one of them, the other would have to donate 50 percent of the ad's cost to a charity of the opposition candidate's choice.[45] In other words, the next time American Crossroads ran an ad against Elizabeth, Scott would have to pull half of that ad's cost out of his campaign coffers and donate it to a charity of Elizabeth's choice. If the super PACS saw this as too harmful to their chosen candidate, it had a chance of working. They called their agreement the People's Pledge, and after they announced their pact on January 23, 2012, the super PAC ads disappeared for the rest of the campaign.

According to Thomas Barry, a college freshman who worked on her campaign staff and later interned in her Senate office, shifting into the life of a Senate candidate was a lot of work for Elizabeth. "It wasn't a natural transition," he said. "It was work, and she took classes on it."[46] He witnessed her makeover from what Elizabeth called her frumpy Harvard professor look to a more public-ready style. "She couldn't figure out what clothes to wear," he said, "but

---

* Super PACS, or Super Political Action Committees, the groups that can accept unlimited political donations, were born after the Supreme Court banned all caps on donations from individuals, corporations, and unions in its 2010 *Citizens United* ruling.

then a donor gave her a jacket that she loved. She thought it looked good on her profile, so she went out and bought more in different colors. Now you see her wear the same thing all the time. It's her version of a power suit." The campaign atmosphere was fast-paced, exciting, and glitzy with all the media attention. Whenever Elizabeth walked into a room, her energy lit everyone up, Thomas said. When working the phone banks, he got calls from across the country. "One woman called in from California and she gave twenty-five dollars, but she wanted me to know that it was really hard for her to give this twenty-five dollars," he said. "She would have to make a sacrifice somewhere else in her life. She was really passionate, telling me, 'You guys keep fighting—we need her in the Senate.'" Every time Thomas told someone he was working for Elizabeth, they asked if she was going to run for president. "I don't know if she wants it," he said. "She kept her family sacred, and I don't know if her family is ready for that kind of life."

Door-knocking in the communities of Massachusetts's North Shore, campaign staffer Jennifer Migliore found people excited to talk about Elizabeth. "They thought she was a fresh face and that she was willing to say things that most people weren't willing to say," she said. "They were excited about how passionate she was about helping the middle class and that everybody got a shot."[47] Working inside the campaign headquarters in a sprawling office building in Somerville, the town bordering Cambridge, Jennifer met people who showed up to volunteer who had never engaged in politics before, she said. After the campaign, she became one of Elizabeth's college interns, and two years after graduating from college, her campaign and Senate office work for Elizabeth motivated her to run for the Massachusetts House of Representatives. "That experience really inspired me to go into public service to try to be a voice for hardworking blue collar families," she said. "I grew up in a blue collar family, and I learned from the senator how short-changed the middle class is." Jennifer didn't win her election, but she took a job in politics at the Blue Lab in Boston, a campaign development group for first-time progressive candidates.

Elizabeth's progressive platform called for raising tax rates for the wealthy, ending special tax breaks for hedge fund managers and the oil and gas industry, and investing in rebuilding bridges and other infrastructure projects. Her stump speeches addressed reducing health care costs, streamlining small-business regulations, preserving clean air and water laws, and advancing clean energy. She promised to fight to protect Medicare and social security as well as access to birth control, and she identified herself as pro-choice and a supporter of equal pay for equal work. The last item targeted her in-depth knowledge of American women's finances—equal pay was critical, "especially now, when women are the sole breadwinners in many families struggling to make ends meet," a campaign piece stated.[48]

She also campaigned for LGBTQ rights and remarked that LGBTQ teenagers across Massachusetts told her, "I'm gay, and I'm counting on you."[49] She used every chance she could along the campaign trail to "tell those kids that I have their backs," she said. As Congressman John Lewis of Georgia stated at a rally, "She will vote so that you can marry the one that you love, and she will make certain that it is a woman's choice what she can and cannot do with her own body."[50]

Those who had followed Elizabeth in the press from her days as the Wall Street bailout watchdog knew how she felt about the role of government. In 2009, when *Newsweek* asked her why people were so angry about the government's actions with the too-big-to-fail banks, she made it clear that she felt the government should put people first. "Many Americans want to know if the people in Washington are on their side or on the side of the powerful banks," she said. "There should never be a doubt about the point of any government action: it should always be to help families directly, or help markets in ways that help families."[51] Since she had worked at ground zero of the bailout, bringing Treasury Secretary Timothy Geithner into the spotlight in hearings in order to bring more transparency to the process, voters had witnessed her consistency. Her focus on the citizens' side of the issues was a constant that voters could expect she would retain as a senator.

Campaigns swerve from the satisfactions of connecting with people on the issues to the headaches of rolling out mistakes. One mishap involved divulging the amount she had been paid to serve on the Congressional Oversight Panel monitoring the TARP bailout. After first stating that she had earned $64,289, *Politico* reported that the figure was incorrect, and her office issued a correction. The figure Elizabeth had given was for one year instead of both years she served, her spokesperson said, calling it an honest mistake released by her campaign office and correcting the total amount she received to $192,722.[52]

Another flap arose around a statement Elizabeth made about Occupy Wall Street, the movement that sprang up in the fall of 2011. Elizabeth and Occupy voiced the same outrage for the same reasons at the same time. Describing itself as a gathering "to express a feeling of mass injustice," Occupy initially released a declaration to create solidarity among those frustrated that democracy was no longer powered by people, but corporations. "We come to you at a time when corporations, which place profit over people, self-interest over justice, and oppression over equality, run our governments," the declaration stated. The document listed examples of corporate behavior to back up this assertion, such as the banks' illegal foreclosures, using bailout money to give Wall Street executives bonuses, burdening college students with debt, outsourcing jobs, monopolizing the agricultural system, donating money to the politicians who are supposed to be regulating them, and influencing the courts to allow them "to achieve the same rights as people, with none of the culpability or responsibility."[53]

Within a month of that statement, Occupy had expanded beyond New York City's Zuccotti Park (two blocks from Wall Street) to cities across the country. In an interview with the *Daily Beast*, Elizabeth expressed her support for the movement that so obviously aligned with the "system is rigged" message of her campaign. "I created much of the intellectual foundation for what they do," she said. "I support what they do."[54] In response, Karl Rove's Crossroads Grassroots Policy Strategies super PAC ran an ad that portrayed Elizabeth as endorsing a violent movement, using footage of police attacks on protesters. The ad falsely claimed that the violence erupted from protesters attacking police, when the opposite was true (Occupy was founded on nonviolence, and police used pepper spray to clash with protesters). Media reporting on the protests tended to paint the same picture, covering "demonstrations as if they were crime scenes," Todd Gitlin pointed out in *Occupy Nation: The Roots, the*

Spirit, and the Promise of Occupy Wall Street.[55] Elizabeth stood by her statement, appearing on a local Boston television program to take questions about the ad. "I've been fighting Wall Street for a very long time," she said. "I am glad to see lots of people start to really push on this issue."[56] Those words contrasted with portrayals of Occupy protesters as violent extremists and instead focused on the First Amendment right of "people peaceably to assemble, and to petition the Government for a redress of grievances."

While she defended her stance, she regretted her statement in the *Daily Beast*. In saying that she had "created much of the intellectual foundation" of the movement, she was trying to say that she had worked on those issues for a long time, but in retrospect she called it "a stupid mistake." She was embarrassed by it, she wrote, and realized that her words "made it seem as if I were trying to take credit for a protest I wasn't even part of."[57] She never took on the Occupy banner in earnest, regardless of her sympathies with Occupy's grievances. As the *New Republic* reported, soon after the attack ads, she refused to sign a petition written by the Harvard branch of Occupy and in coming months did not make more comments about the movement.[58]

Todd Gitlin, the author mentioned above, is a journalism and sociology professor at Columbia University and was active in Occupy. He reflected that Elizabeth may have distanced herself from the populist movement out of a need to choose between being an outsider or an insider. Even though her criticisms of both Republican and Democratic figures in charge of the TARP bailout had made her an outsider, in this case she was running to become one of the insiders. "Warren had set out to be a reformer,"

Todd said. "She's a radical reformer, an egalitarian reformer, but the world she had set out to work in is the world of electoral politics. In her position I would have done the same thing. I might have felt a nag of conscience about it, but said 'I've made a decision that I want to be a power figure in Washington with a following that cuts across all kinds of lines.'" Todd writes about the distinction between movement activity and political power activity, and how figures (like Elizabeth) feel compelled to choose between them. "My hypothesis," he said, "is that when people were urging her to support Occupy, she thought, 'For now I'm not doing outsider politics, I'm doing insider politics.'"[59]*

Regarding Elizabeth's campaign gaffes, from fumbles with numbers to a contested choice of words, retired Senator Barbara Mikulski said, "She was a new candidate, and you make mistakes."[60]

The fiercest attack from Scott's campaign targeted Elizabeth's claim to Native American ancestry, and the attack came in three parts. First, he accused her of claiming to be something she was not. In the candidates' first debate, Scott started off with, "Professor Warren claimed that she was a Native American, a person of color, and as you can see, she's not."[61] The second accusation stated that she had used her fake claim to "check the box" to gain minority status and improve her chances of getting hired as a professor.[62] Finally, he pointed to her parents as liars who deliberately made up the stories about their Native American ancestry.

Scott's assumption in his first attack appears to be that all Native

---

* Occupy, which went global before dissipating as a large-scale movement, spurred activism on the local level with splinter movements like Minnesota's Occupy Homes that helped homeowners contest foreclosure.

Americans share a distinct set of physical traits, which is common in a culture that is largely ignorant of the complexities of Native American identity. Many Americans choose to cling to myths and stereotypes, even when challenged to rethink these assumptions when, for example, Native Americans protest the use of Native American images as sports mascots. The late Vine Deloria Jr., a Standing Rock Sioux, lawyer, history professor, and author, approached this issue with mocking humor. In his most famous book, *Custer Died for Your Sins: An Indian Manifesto*, he wrote, "The American public feels most comfortable with the mythical Indians of stereotype-land who were always THERE. These Indians are fierce, they wear feathers and grunt. Most of us don't fit this idealized figure since we grunt only when overeating, which is seldom."[63]

Scott's attack ads set off biased reflexes among whites who fixated on the idea that Elizabeth was obviously 100 percent Anglo-Saxon. Native writers and scholars give us a closer look at the real nature of identity. Circe Sturm, a professor of anthropology and Native American studies at the University of Oklahoma, defines the variations of Cherokee identity. According to her descriptions, Elizabeth could best be labeled a Cherokee wannabe, a white person who self-identifies as Cherokee but does not possess a Certificate of Degree of Indian Blood (CDIB), issued by the Bureau of Indian Affairs, and "not politically recognized by the tribe."[64] The largest of the three federally recognized Cherokee tribes, the Cherokee Nation, does not require a specific degree of blood, while the United Keetoowah Band and Eastern Band have specific degree requirements. "Most Cherokees," Circe writes, "are well aware that many wannabes have some degree of Cherokee blood but cannot become tribal citizens because they lack the necessary documentation to procure a CDIB, to become card-carrying."[65] The wannabe term fits Elizabeth's case, since she has admitted that she has no documentation of her heritage, only family stories.

As Vine Deloria, Circe Sturm, and others explain, however, Native American identity is much more complex than degrees of blood: labeling strictly by blood equates identity with race. Kim Tallbear, on the Native Studies faculty at the University of Alberta, and member of a tribe that is part of the Santee Dakota people in South Dakota, described the limitations of this view. She and many of her relatives have nonnative fathers yet possess a strong sense of being Dakota because they were "raised within an extended Dakota kin group," she said. "We have a particular cultural identity based in a land that we hold to be sacred. That's what gives our lives meaning. It's what makes us who we are."[66]

Deloria believed that as more non-Native Americans identified as Native American, starting from the counterculture days of the 1960s, the ambiguity this created in the Native American community took a toll on traditional loyalties to family, clan, and tribe. He called for Native American leadership that expressed "an unqualified endorsement of traditions and values which have always been associated with the respective tribes and communities," emphasizing "the old codes of proper conduct and concern which once characterized Indians as a distinct group." Regaining a strong sense of community would, he wrote, call Native Americans "back to a confidence in themselves which can begin to address the areas that demand attention." Deloria's ideas reveal why some Native Americans are critical of white claims to their ancestry that are not connected to that person's living experience within the Native American community.

Tom Holm, a retired Creek/Cherokee professor of political science and American Indian studies at the University of Arizona, commented on the very different ways Native Americans and whites look at "culture." The TV ads for DNA ancestry tests really crack him up, he said. "One guy thinks he's German and is wearing lederhosen, and then he finds out he's Scot, so he goes out and buys a kilt," he said. The ad may be tongue in cheek, but it taps into the American sense that ethnicity is the same as culture, and wearing the trappings of ethnicity creates a cultural identity. Culture means something else to Native Americans. "You have to grow up in the culture to know and understand it," he said. "There is a notion of being a people. It has to do with language, it has to do with having a particular history that you understand and a ceremonial cycle that is hooked up with a place that you know."[67]

Therefore, when a white politician points at a white woman and says anyone can plainly see she's not Native American, he is saying that Native American identity is nothing more than skin color or a set of features. Native Americans take offense at this narrow view and the lack of understanding behind it.

Elizabeth's defense of her family stories of Cherokee and Delaware background led to a flurry of investigations into her family tree, including one by the New England Historic Genealogical Society. This group found a family newsletter stating that one of her relatives identified his mother as part Cherokee on his marriage license application. Since no one could track down the actual application or marriage license, there was no proof that

Elizabeth's great-great-great grandmother O. C. Sarah Smith was actually part Cherokee.

The second type of attack on Elizabeth's claims of Native American ancestry was the accusation that she had lied about her minority status to advance her career. This controversy erupted when the *Boston Herald* reported that she had listed herself as Native American in the American Association of Law Schools directory from 1986 to 1995. Elizabeth said that she had done so to try to connect with minorities like herself. "I listed myself in the directory in the hopes that it might mean that I would be invited to a luncheon, a group [or] something that might happen with people who are like I am," Warren said. "Nothing like that ever happened. That was absolutely not the use for it, and so I stopped checking it off."[68]

The officials who hired her at the laws schools at the University of Houston, University of Texas at Austin, University of Pennsylvania, and Harvard all confirmed that she was hired on her teaching and scholarly merits alone.[69] The Associated Press reported that Harvard Law School professor Charles Fried, who served as U.S. solicitor general under President Reagan, said that Warren was recruited to be a tenured professor because of her preeminent status as a scholar of bankruptcy and commercial law.[70] He added that he had been a member of the appointments committee that reviewed Warren and said the subject of her Native American ancestry was never mentioned. The idea that Elizabeth "attained her position and maintains her reputation on anything other than her evident merit is complete nonsense," he said. In another round of press stories about the controversy, Elizabeth's campaign released a statement that she had told the University of Pennsylvania and Harvard about her Native American heritage after she was hired, because she had been proud of it and open about it.[71]

In spite of the university officials' statements and other records, Scott repeated the accusation that she lied to get her jobs. "When you're checking a box," Scott said, "and you're getting benefits that are entitled to people who need them and who historically have been discriminated upon, and you have others relying on those representations, it is a problem," he said. Despite the fact that no "minority" boxes were checked in relation to her hiring (or her applications to college or law school), the idea had been out for weeks, and Elizabeth's opponents continued to arm themselves with it.[72]

The third form of the heritage attack came when Scott questioned the honesty of Elizabeth's parents. "My mom and dad have told me a lot of things too, but it's not accurate," he said.[73] Elizabeth fired back with a statement issued by her campaign in which she demanded an apology. "Scott Brown's comments about my parents are totally out of line," she said. "I resent him questioning their honesty... Don and Pauline Herring are not fair game and Scott Brown should apologize."[74] He didn't, and the wrangling endured.

The ancestry controversy could have been an opportunity to go deeper into the biases and stereotypes whites held about Native Americans, but this was a high-profile national race, and the media was in the business of sound-bite drama, not social analysis. The campaign did not ignite a national conversation in which Native Americans could weigh in about the many dimensions of Native identity. It didn't provide a space for them to explain the deep cultural reasoning behind the frustration of many over white claims of ancestry. Instead, the attack ads riled up certain Scott Brown supporters enough to taunt with tomahawk gestures before the cameras, the public learned nothing, and Elizabeth moved on.

Television ads reached a lot of voters in Massachusetts, but nothing in the campaign compared to the visibility Elizabeth received at the Democratic National Convention in Charlotte, North Carolina, on Wednesday night, September 5, 2012. President Obama, who would become the official Democratic presidential candidate at the convention, invited her to speak in the prime spot just before Bill Clinton. Her fifteen-minute speech reached twenty-five million viewers plus the crowd at the Time Warner Cable Arena whose wild cheers as she strode across the stage left no question that she was the rock star of the party and, in *Politico*'s words, a "hero of the left."[75]

Standing at the podium in a royal-blue jacket that matched the floor of the stage, she warmed up with her own story of growing up in a family "on the ragged edge of the middle class." Then came a salute to the opportunities that built the middle class, followed by straight talk about how that middle class had been "chipped, squeezed, and hammered."[76] Using key words that defined her position, her campaign, and her understanding of the national angst, she continued:

> People feel like the system is rigged against them.
> And here's the painful part: they're right. The system
> is rigged. Look around. Oil companies guzzle down

billions in subsidies. Billionaires pay lower tax rates than their secretaries. Wall Street CEOs—the same ones who wrecked our economy and destroyed millions of jobs—still strut around Congress, no shame, demanding favors, and acting like we should thank them.[77]

Stretching out her arm, she asked, "Does anyone here have a problem with that?" And the crowd roared.

She portrayed America as a place where we both celebrated financial success and "fought to level the playing field" back in the progressive era so that the game wasn't rigged. She followed that with a one-punch description of the other side: "The Republican vision is clear: 'I've got mine, the rest of you are on your own.'" What followed next raised a drawn-out clamor that nearly drowned out the next twenty seconds of the speech: "Republicans say they don't believe in government. Sure they do. They believe in government to help themselves and their powerful friends. After all, Mitt Romney's the guy who said *corporations are people*."

She ended with an inspirational call, complete with a biblical passage from Matthew, to act together to fight for a level playing field that will build a better country. "Barack Obama is ready," she said. "I'm ready. You're ready. America's ready. Thank you! And God bless America!"[78]

———

When the campaign got rough, her favorite Bible verse, Matthew 25:50, steered her back to her core, reminding her why she believed politics could be a force for good, a way for people to serve each other: "Verily I say unto you, inasmuch as ye have done it unto one of the least of these My brethren, ye have done it unto Me." Although she was born and raised a Methodist, she was seen many Sundays during the campaign in black churches, such as Pleasant Hill Baptist in Boston's Dorchester neighborhood. Pleasant Hill's pastor, Rev. Miniard Culpepper, became a spiritual companion to her and Bruce, joining them in prayer before her debates with Scott Brown and backstage before her speech at the Democratic National Convention. While very private about her religious life, Elizabeth has spent so much time at churches like Twelfth Baptist Church in Boston that the church's associate pastor, Rev. Jeffrey Brown, said "we sort of consider her a member."

When *Boston Globe* reporter Victoria McGrane interviewed religious leaders about Elizabeth in 2017, they said that they found her faith deep and authentic, a "constant, if quiet, presence in her life" that informed her work as a senator. The pastors who spoke to McGrane unanimously observed that Elizabeth's religious activities were genuine, not the actions of a political opportunist. The worn, heavily underlined Bible that she has carried with her since the fourth grade is the most visible symbol of the role that her faith has played throughout her life, and Reverend Brown believes she attends his and other black churches because she finds being present with the community helpful to her. Reverend Culpepper views Elizabeth as the type of person who doesn't wear her religion on her sleeve, but lives it instead. And as Elizabeth revealed in her remarks at the Martin Luther King Jr. Center's Beloved Community Talks in 2017, she is an inclusive Christian. "There's

God in every one of us," she said. "Inside, there's something holy in every single person."

Throughout the campaign, fund-raising totals kept climbing at a stunning rate, which showed the nonstop momentum of the race. Elizabeth's financial team, led by Michael Pratt, raised a total of $42 million, the largest amount of any campaign in the country.[79] Eighty percent of the donations were fifty dollars or less, Elizabeth noted in *A Fighting Chance*.[80] Even with that staggering amount, the account ended up in the red by $400,000, or 1 percent of the total money raised, after paying for a staff of 130, TV ads, feeding thousands of volunteers, and all the other costs of running the race. "It is not unusual for campaigns—even strong, well-funded campaigns—to end in the red," wrote Michael Levenson in the *Boston Globe*. Democratic strategist Mo Elleithee added that the "barely over budget" number actually spoke to some "pretty good management."[81]

The weeks leading up to Election Day held some roller coaster moments for the family. The big news was Alex's upcoming marriage to girlfriend Elise, a web designer from Los Angeles, which would take place after the election later in November.[82] They were buying a house in a suburb south of the city, which would put them about thirty-five miles from Amelia and Sushil's home. Back in Cambridge, the thrill of the upcoming wedding was dampened for a time when Elizabeth and Bruce's beloved Otis, now seven years old, passed away on November 1. He had been "a virtually inseparable companion" to Elizabeth and Bruce, wrote a *Boston Globe* columnist, "a serene, noble presence in their offices at Harvard University, on errands, and on the kitchen floor, where Warren would always run her fingers absently through his fur as she spoke on the phone."[83] It was a heartbreak that still brought Elizabeth to tears when she spoke to the columnist about it a month later. There would be no more walks around nearby Fresh Pond or evenings with Otis's big head resting on her leg as he took his spot with her on the couch.

On the morning of Election Day, November 6, 2012, Elizabeth slipped on an orange quilted overcoat and walked with Bruce to vote at the Graham and Parks School just two and a half blocks from their house in Cambridge.[84] The polls had been close throughout the fifteen months of the campaign, and the nation had its eye on Massachusetts as the votes came in.

That evening, Elizabeth and her supporters gathered at the Fairmont Copley Plaza hotel in Back Bay to watch the results, which kept looking better and better throughout the night. Around ten o'clock, the TV networks called the race—Elizabeth had defeated Scott by ten points, 54 percent to 46 percent. On the national stage, President Obama won his reelection decisively with 332 electoral votes to Mitt Romney's 206.

Standing before the cheering crowd in the hotel ballroom, Elizabeth stated her pride in a campaign that had raised more money from small donors than any Senate campaign in the history of the country. She promised the women of the state, "who are working your tails off," that she would fight for equal pay for equal work. And to everyone behind the victory, including the record thousands of volunteers who had knocked on doors, she said, "You did what everyone thought was impossible; you taught a scrappy, first-time candidate how to get in the ring and win." The win put Elizabeth in the record books as the first woman elected to the Senate from Massachussetts.

The next day, Warren pledged to take up Ted Kennedy's commitment to fighting for the working class, stating, "I won't just be your senator. I will also be your champion."[85] Later, for her swearing-in ceremony, she carried her maternal grandmother's diamond ring in her pocket. Hannie Crawford Reed had given Elizabeth, her youngest granddaughter, the ring when she was in her nineties. Elizabeth kept the ring with her that day, she wrote, because her grandmother was "tough. Strong. Persistent. I wanted a little piece of her with me when I was sworn in."

At the beginning of her term, Elizabeth attended Barbara Mikulski's "power workshop" for incoming women senators. Barbara, the Democrat from Maryland who served in Congress longer than any other woman in U.S. history, had first met Elizabeth years before Elizabeth's election when Senator Ted Kennedy introduced her to the Senate Democratic Caucus.* Senator Kennedy told Barbara and other senators that Elizabeth Warren had a lot to offer them as they discussed how health care issues impacted American families. "We were planning for one of our Democratic retreats where we would listen to people and discuss the desirability, feasibility, and achievability of health care proposals," Barbara said. "Kennedy said, 'You've

* As the main Democratic organization in the Senate, the Senate Democratic Caucus consists of all the Democratic Senators and meets to set the Senate agenda and make committee assignments.

got to meet this professor from Boston—Elizabeth Warren—she's just fantastic. She worked on a bankruptcy commission and is also an expert on banking, and what's she's finding is that when people are filing for bankruptcy, it's usually related to a catastrophic event in their life—loss of a job, health issues, or both. This is something we've got to be talking about.'"[86]

Barbara and other Democratic senators had also seen Elizabeth in action as she got the Consumer Protection Financial Bureau up and running when it was created in 2010. "What a powerhouse," Barbara said, "Senator Warren and all she knew, going after the big boys and stepping on toes and being the champion for military families, protecting them from unscrupulous predatory lending. Can you see why we liked her? And why the other party didn't like her?" There was a lot of talk that Elizabeth would make a great senator, she said. "Kennedy had passed away and we wanted that seat and that kind of champion. Harry Reid and Chuck Schumer really reached out to her and spoke to her, as did others, and I also called her and said, 'When we have these awful setbacks, women in the Senate have a saying: Don't get mad; get elected.'"[87]

In addition to campaigning for Elizabeth in 2012, Barbara encouraged her all along the way—including when fellow Democrats were less than supportive. "As smart and gifted as she was, the Boston old guard said she would be an egghead who couldn't connect with people," she said. "One thing that I have observed is that she is always underestimated either by the old boys or the new boys."

When Elizabeth came to the Senate, Barbara brought her into the training workshop she had launched in 1992, a breakthrough year for women elected to Congress known as the Year of the Woman.[88]

That year, a record-breaking number of women ran for federal office, galvanized by the 1991 Senate Judiciary Committee hearings in which Anita Hill testified about the sexual harassment she endured while working for Supreme Court nominee Clarence Thomas. Although Clarence Thomas's appointment to the Supreme Court was approved, Anita Hill's televised hearings were a public forum on sexual harassment that impacted the next year's election. As the U.S. House of Representatives Office of the Historian wrote, "The spectacle of the all-male Judiciary Committee offering Hill little sympathy and at moments treating her with outright hostility reinforced the perception that women's perspectives received short shrift on Capitol Hill."[89] This national frustration over women's demeaning treatment motivated women to run for office in record numbers in 1992, and in addition to three women winning Senate seats, twenty-four women were elected to the U.S. House of Representatives.[90]

Women like Patty Murray, then a senator in the Washington state legislature, remarked that she ran for the U.S. Senate that year because she thought people like her should have participated in that hearing to defend Hill and question Thomas. "I just said, 'I am going to run for Senate,'" she told author Jay Newton-Small in *Broad Influence: How Women Are Changing the Way America Works*, "because they need somebody there who is going to say what I would say if I was there."[91] That election also ignited a new surge of women of color winning national elections: of the fifty-eight African American, Latina, and Asian American women who have served in Congress, forty-seven were elected between 1992 and 2016.[92]

"There is no operating manual on how to be a good senator," Barbara Mikulski said, but new women senators find practical

instruction in the guide she wrote herself to help them get started.[93]
She mentored them in her power workshop about how to set up
their offices and get on committees, and she also organized the now-
legendary bipartisan women senators' dinners. Senator Barbara
Boxer described those monthly gatherings, held in each other's
homes or occasionally in restaurants, as evenings in which "we
talk about our work, our families; we share our struggles and our
triumphs, and what is said there stays there."[94] A week or two after
each election, Barbara Mikulski would host a tea to welcome new
women senators-elect in her hideaway office in the Capitol—her
"second" office that worked as a retreat and saved hikes to the Hart
Senate Office Building. (The unmarked offices vary in size, with
the largest earned by seniority. While Barbara's on the third floor
included seating areas and a fireplace, Elizabeth's was a windowless
cubbyhole the size of a closet in the Capitol basement.[95]) Barbara
regularly checked in on the new senators to be a sounding board
for their questions and any obstacles they may be facing. "If I had
advice, I shared it," she said, "or if I knew someone who had better
advice, I would point them to a senator who had lived through that
experience." As a senior member of the Senate Democratic Caucus,
Barbara had a say in Elizabeth's committee assignments. "We made
sure Elizabeth Warren got on the Banking Committee," she said,
"and the Health, Education, Labor, and Pensions Committee, where
she was a tremendous advocate as we moved through the Affordable
Care Act."[96]

Barbara, who retired from the Senate in 2017, traded places with
Elizabeth to become a senator-turned-professor at Johns Hopkins
University in Baltimore, Maryland, where she teaches public policy

and women's leadership. Her students benefit from the wisdom of the once-dean of senate women, whose lifetime in public service gives her the scope to challenge their generational outlook. "These students have come from social media and the attitude of 'Let's go to marches.' I say, absolutely, but you have to know how to go from outcry to outcome, from protest to policy. Get off the benches and into the trenches."

In a recent overview of the experiences of America's congress-women, the Center for American Women and Politics (CAWP) at Rutgers interviewed 83 of the 108 women who served in the 114th Congress to delve into some of the challenges and opportunities these women have faced in a Congress dominated by men since its inception in 1789.[97]

Twenty women served as senators in the 114th Congress—fourteen Democrats and six Republicans—and eighty-four women were elected to the House—sixty-two Democrats and twenty-two Republicans. A record thirty-three women of color served in the House, making up 6 percent of the combined chambers; in the Senate, Hawaiian senator Mazie Hirono remained the only woman of color. With just 19 percent of Congress made up of women, the U.S. ranking of women in national legislatures was 33rd in a group of 49 in high-income countries and 75th in a larger global group of 137 countries. Despite being part of a small percentage, the report notes that "the women on both sides of the aisle in the 114th Congress very much believe that their presence and their voices mattered, and they provided considerable evidence of achievements despite the overall environment of gridlock and party polarization in which they operated."[98]

Women generally run for office to make a difference, as opposed to some of their counterparts, the researchers said, and many of them see themselves as a voice for the voiceless and fight to represent children, the disadvantaged, immigrants, people of color, and others who might not otherwise be represented.[99] Senator Tammy Baldwin, a Democrat from Wisconsin, said, "More women go into politics to get something done, to solve a problem, to fix something than men do. Very few of my female colleagues got into politics because they just wanted to be a U.S. Senator. They got in because there was something awry that they wanted to work on... We're not there for the power of politics."

The majority of women interviewed agreed that they reach goals because they are results oriented rather than emphasizing ego over achievement. They also worked across party lines and were more concerned about achieving policy outcomes than receiving publicity or credit. "Women's greater bipartisan proclivity was attributed to factors such as being a woman in a male-dominated institution, a distinctive work style on the part of women, and different pathways to Congress that give rise to differences in legislative style," the report stated. The Congressional Caucus for Women's Issues played a big role in this bipartisan spirit as well. This does not, however, mean they easily agree. The very passion they feel toward their issues leads them to advocate for different policy positions. The crucial point is that they bring perspectives and issues to the agenda that would otherwise go ignored.

Representative Maxine Waters said, "I'm saying that Democratic women have carried issues that men just didn't pay attention to or that were not [even] considered issues."

Congresswomen of color brought their own experiences, perspectives, and underrepresented issues to the table and took pride in being powerful actors to affect change. Representative Barbara Lee of California spoke about how being a single mother and living on food stamps and public assistance was "kind of normal for a lot of women living in this country" and said that she saw her work as "trying to knock down some of those [barriers] to make things better for everybody."

California representative Judy Chu said immigration reform was very important to the Congressional Asian Pacific American Caucus, since they made up 40 percent of the 4.3 million visa backlog. "We emphasize greatly the family visa program and how it has to be fixed," she said, in addition to "the racial profiling issue pertaining to South Asians and Muslims. Actually, four out of the five countries with the biggest Muslim populations are from Asia." Other women of color expressed concerns about not being heard and respected within their own party but also noted their effectiveness in claiming and exercising their power. "Sometimes some of the guys try to take on women of color when they wouldn't take on their own peers," said Barbara Lee. "I've seen that happen a few times. It was wrong, and we beat it back—within [the party], but we beat it back."

The interviews revealed that women in general face many challenges before and after entering Congress. Many said that the challenges of campaigning and getting into office are far greater than the challenges faced once elected. Representative Jan Schakowsky, a Democrat from Illinois, said, "I think women are more reluctant to have their lives examined up and down and in and out. Women are more inclined to say, 'Who needs it?!'" This public scrutiny of female candidates prevents many from running, and once elected, women have to work harder to prove that they belong. According to Republican senator Susan Collins of Maine, "My experience has been, and sadly, I think this is still true today, that when a woman is elected to the Senate, she still has to prove that she belongs there, whereas when a man is elected to the Senate, it's assumed that he belongs here. I will say once you pass that first test…then you're a member of the club. But I think there still is a barrier that men don't face, and I think that's true of Democratic women as well as Republican women."

Despite the challenges these women have faced before and after being elected, some of the most successful legislators in recent years happened to be women. As Senator Barbara Boxer of California explained, "If you look at the most successful legislators the last couple of years, they are women. It's Dianne Feinstein on cyber security, it's Debbie Stabenow on an [agriculture] bill, it's myself on a transportation bill and a water bill, it's Patty Murray on a budget deal, and I can go on. It is Maria Cantwell on passing legislation for the Export-Import Bank."

The overview from Rutgers revealed that women across party lines have worked together and fought for the issues that motivated them to run for office and used their gender and race to their advantage, participating in settings and debates in which their parties needed gender diversity and inclusion. They are also proactive in finding ways to bring more women into their ranks, including New York senator Kirsten Gillibrand, who launched Off the Sidelines to support female candidates.[100]

In a speech at the 2012 Democratic National Convention, Senator Barbara Mikulski highlighted the difference women leaders make: "When women are in the halls of power, our national debate reflects the needs and dreams of American families... We know that every issue is a woman's issue."[101] In her three decades in Congress, she observed what so many other powerful women have reflected upon—the fact that women are routinely criticized and held to a different standard. "We're either called too outspoken or too soft spoken, or too smart," she said, and added that women always had to work extra hard to establish their credibility and competency in the Senate. "We often had to be twice as good at what we were doing just show that we not only had the right to be there, but that we could do the job." She had also seen the different way women were treated during their campaigns. "If the candidate is a guy, it's 'Let me help you up, buck,' but when a woman makes a mistake, it's 'See, she's not really up for this.'"[102]

Elizabeth's decades in academia and politics had given her insights into the way women are perceived and treated in these professional worlds. Before her campaign, she recalled, when President Obama was considering who should run the new Consumer Financial Protection Bureau, a White House adviser remarked that Elizabeth could be the "cheerleader" for the agency while someone else acted as director. "I had to wonder: Cheerleader?" she wrote. "Would the same suggestion have been made to a man in my position?"[103]

A woman's distinctive worldview, she believes, gives her a

different approach to negotiating than that of men. She offered her take on women's negotiating styles to Jay Newton-Small, author of *Broad Influence*. "Women are often not very good at negotiating on their behalf, but they are damn good at negotiating on behalf of others," she said. She continued:

> They are good at negotiating on behalf of those who don't have a voice, who aren't privileged in the game, whether it's children, whether it's seniors, whether it's those who are economically disadvantaged. That tells me that women are often better at seeing the world from multiple perspectives—that they can see their own self-interest, but they can also see other people's points of view and take those into account.[104]

Speaking at an event at Harvard in 2015 with the other two "sheriffs of Wall Street," Sheila Bair and Mary Shapiro, Elizabeth described the male-dominated corporate world as "The Club." There is a shortage of women at the top, she said, because "the group who's there doesn't want disruption. And when you bring in people who aren't part of 'The Club,' it's very disruptive—or it can be."[105] As a female senator, she was one more target for those who assess women's leadership qualities by a different standard. In her 2017 memoir *What Happened*, Hillary Clinton explored this double standard and how it had been applied to Elizabeth. "Think how often you've heard these words used about women who lead," she wrote, "angry, strident, feisty, difficult, irritable, bossy, brassy, emotional, abrasive, high-maintenance, ambitious (a word that

I think of as neutral, even admirable, but clearly isn't for a lot of people)."[106] She then quoted cognitive scientist and linguist George Lakoff, whose work analyzes the different ways conservatives and liberals think: "'Elizabeth [Warren] has a problem. She is shrill, and there is a prejudice against shrill women.'" Hillary wrote that we should stop criticizing *how* Elizabeth speaks, "which is just fine, by the way," and instead listen to *what* she has to say "about families and the economy."[107]

Even pro-Elizabeth television cohost Mika Brzezinski, the liberal foil to Joe Scarborough on MSNBC's *Morning Joe,* could not resist labeling Elizabeth's direct, focused commentary as "shrill." The day before, Elizabeth had made remarks on the Senate floor about the need to fight the Trump administration on issues about treating every American with dignity. "The American people," Elizabeth had said, "didn't give Democrats majority support so we can come back to Washington and play dead. They didn't send us here to whimper, whine, or grovel."[108] Mika said she loved Elizabeth, but was tired of her tone, adding, "There's an anger there that was shrill, a step above what it needed to be, unmeasured and almost unhinged."[109] Billionaire Warren Buffett shot a similar barb on a cable news show, saying that Elizabeth would do better if she was "less angry."[110] That comment prompted Terry O'Neill, president of the National Organization for Women, to criticize Buffett's statement as sexist. "Calling a woman angry is often a way to shut her down when she is being assertive and powerful," she said.[111]

As Hillary wrote, women face these obstacles in greater degrees as they move up the ladders of power. "In my experience, the balancing act women in politics have to master is challenging at every level, but it gets worse the higher you rise. If we're too tough, we're unlikable. If we're too soft, we're not cut out for the big leagues."[112]*

In 2017, Elizabeth joined the powerful, high-profile Senate Armed Services Committee, which many saw as an attempt to develop her foreign policy credentials should she decide to launch a 2020 presidential campaign. "The liberal firebrand—who is best known for dressing down Wall Street CEOs and pushing for ways to bolster the economic health of the middle class—will now be getting elbows deep in debates about defense spending, Russian cyberattacks, and deployment of the nation's military around the world," her hometown *Boston Globe* announced.[113] She continued to sit on the three committees to which she had been assigned from the start of her term, the Committee on Banking, Housing, and Urban Affairs; the Committee on Health, Education, Labor, and Pensions; and the Special Committee on Aging. That year she also released a new book, *This Fight Is Our Fight*, highlighting her five years in the Senate. Her latest effort to educate the public about Wall Street and other moneyed interests in Washington, the book serves as a primer on the nation's economy, from George Washington's day to the Trump era.

---

* While Elizabeth did not immediately throw her hat in the ring for Hillary during the 2016 presidential race, the two met early in the campaign season when Hillary called upon Elizabeth to recommend experts in areas she knew best, such as financial reform. With the bankruptcy bill controversy behind them, Hillary thought that they were both "a little wary," but they "approached each other with good faith, good intentions, and open minds." Hillary's team worked with the people Elizabeth listed to make sure "our agenda was informed by the perspectives of people she trusted," Hillary wrote. In June, Elizabeth announced her endorsement of Hillary as the Democratic candidate (over Senator Bernie Sanders) and began doggedly campaigning for her. Hillary later put Elizabeth on her shortlist of potential running mates.

Elizabeth's greatest achievements in the Senate have not been scored through passing bills, but in serving on committees and wielding her influence. She made it clear during her campaign that she wasn't going to Washington to "be a cosponsor of some bland, little bill nobody cares about," yet she has cosponsored dozens of small resolutions and worked on a handful of more substantial bills.[114] Her first major legislative effort, the Bank on Students Act, sought to turn around the $1.2 trillion total student loan debt by lowering student loan interest rates, but it did not pass. Intern staffer Jennifer Migliore recalled the many conversations Elizabeth had with the staff while working on the bill. "We spent a lot of time talking about student loans," she said. "She valued us and really utilized the college students and interns as resources, asking us, 'How are you dealing with this?'"[115]

With the Smart Savings Act, which did become law, she improved the returns federal government workers received in their retirement accounts. Other bills that became law included the Over-the-Counter Hearing Aid Act, cowritten with Republican Chuck Grassley of Iowa, that tackled the longstanding issue of hearing aids being priced out of reach for most who need them. In most states, the devices were only available from certified audiologists and cost about $2,300 each, with most patients needing two. At that price, only about one in seven of the thirty million Americans suffering from hearing loss could purchase them. The new law allows certain types of hearing aids to be sold over the counter, which would spur competition and lower prices. The Over-the-Counter Hearing Aid Act was signed by President Trump as part of the FDA Reauthorization Act of 2017.

In another bill cosponsored with Republican Senator Mike Enzi of Wyoming, Elizabeth strengthened the confidentiality of biomedical information with the Genetic Research Privacy Protection Act. "To help to bring forward the next generation of precision medicine," she said, "researchers are collecting more and more genetic information. When that genetic information is stored at our nation's research institutions, families should have complete confidence that it will remain private."[116] The stronger protocols became law when the act was signed into law as part of the 21st Century Cures Act in 2016.

As a force of influence, Elizabeth's success includes behind-the-scenes work in 2017 and 2018 in persuading Federal Reserve Chair Janet Yellen to take action against Wells Fargo, where a fake accounts scandal broke in 2016. The fourth largest bank in the country, Wells Fargo admitted to padding their sales numbers by opening accounts in customers' names without notifying them, and in some cases charging fees and penalties on those accounts. Then-CEO John Stumpf estimated that 2 million fake accounts had been opened, but a year later that figure was revised to 3.5 million.[117] In addition to making a $185 million settlement with the Consumer Financial Protection Bureau, the bank had to explain itself to the Senate Banking Committee.

In those televised hearings, Elizabeth grilled Stumpf about protecting the executives responsible for managing the bank and putting the blame on the 5,300 workers fired over the scandal. "Your definition of accountability is to push this on your low-level employees," she said. "This is gutless leadership."[118] In another exchange she asked him if he knew how much he earned on his Wells Fargo shares during the three years the illegal practice was going on and driving up Wells Fargo stock prices. He answered that his earnings were in the public filings. "You're right, it is all in the public records," she said, "because I looked it up."[119] She revealed that he had personally earned $200 million from those share increases during the scandal.

Her preparation in working out how much an individual CEO benefitted from a bank's illegal practices put a face on the Wall Street banks for the public, who was still angered about the lack of Wall Street accountability following the financial crisis.

John Stumpf retired within the month, and a year later, the committee summoned the new CEO, Tim Sloan, to a hearing to answer why the bank's scandals had only gotten worse. The latest abuses included illegally repossessing the cars of active-duty military service members and charging half a million auto loan customers for insurance policies they didn't buy. "At best, you were incompetent," Elizabeth told Sloan. "At worst, you were complicit. Either way, you need to be fired."[120] Since the bank showed little action in changing its ways, Elizabeth sought tougher actions from the Federal Reserve's Janet Yellen. "In the era of Trump," journalist David Dayen wrote, "there weren't many regulators with the will to take this on, so Warren focused on Yellen, an Obama-era holdover."[121] Elizabeth and her staff had learned that federal law gave bank regulators the power to remove board members at banks if the bank or its directors committed certain violations or used "unsound practices." They prepared a detailed letter for Janet, urging her to enforce this rule and remove the bank's twelve board members who were in place while the fake accounts scandal was underway. Elizabeth also wrote that making the board members accountable in this way would "show the rest of the banking industry that poor risk-management practices will not be tolerated."[122] The letter, as well as Elizabeth's other persistent efforts, were successful.

In her last act before leaving the Federal Reserve, Janet punished Wells Fargo by demanding the replacement of board members and putting a clamp on the bank's growth to be sure that the bank would not expand until it had revamped its practices. Writing about Elizabeth's role in this rare action, Dayen stated, "The incident shows that you can't always measure political leadership and success through a legislative scorecard... This should be the minimum expectation of our political leaders... It takes wanting to do something in office beyond getting reelected. And if done right, it can nudge progress forward."[123]

In 2014, Senate minority leader Harry Reid called Elizabeth into the inner circle of Democratic leadership with a special post in the Senate Democratic Caucus.[124] As the strategic policy adviser to the Democratic Policy and Communications Committee, she took a prominent position in shaping Democratic policy and messaging. This appointment, which came in the wake of the election that had lost the Democrats' control of the Senate, showed the trust Senator Reid had in Elizabeth's ability to move the party's agenda forward.

In her first major speech after ascending to that new role, Elizabeth told the audience at an event organized by the Center for American Progress that the Democrats knew how to fix the problems that were crushing the middle class. "The American Dream is slipping out of reach," she said. "The game is rigged, but we know how to fix it. We know what to do. We tested the Republican ideas, and they failed. They failed spectacularly[...] There's no denying that fact... We must fight back with everything we have."[125]

This had been her message from the start of her Senate campaign in 2011, and it reflected not only her awareness of the financial aspect of the crumbling American Dream, but also the soulful loss that that dismantling seemed to carry in the mood of the country. The nation's ideas about the American Dream were shifting. The idea at the heart of the nation's identity seemed to be, as Elizabeth said, fading from the landscape.

Sociologist Mark Rank described the traditional perception of the American Dream as the hope and promise of a good life achieved through self-reliance, rugged individualism, and determination. From the settlers of the eighteenth century who took enormous risks to the post–World War II middle class struggle to achieve a higher standard of living, the dream has been about economic prosperity and financial security. It has also been about "the manner in which our lives unfold and the ability of the individual," he wrote in *Chasing the American Dream: Understanding What Shapes Our Fortunes*, "no matter where he or she comes from, to exert considerable control and freedom over how that process occurs."[126] In the land of opportunity, hard work may not always guarantee economic and personal success, but it has been strongly suggested from the country's earliest days to the present. He quotes historian James Adams, who first coined the term *American Dream* in *The Epic of America* in 1931:

[The American Dream] has lured tens of millions of all nations to our shores in the past century. [But it] has not been a dream of merely material plenty, though that has doubtless counted heavily. It has been much more than that. It has been a dream of being able to grow to fullest development as man and woman, unhampered by the barriers which had slowly been erected in older civilizations, unrepressed by social orders which had developed for the benefit of classes rather than for the simple human being of any and every class. And that dream has been realized more fully in actual life here than anywhere else, though very imperfectly even among ourselves.[127]

The imperfect side, Rank wrote, comes through as "millions of Americans have been excluded throughout history from meaningful participation in the American Dream." Race, class, and gender have contributed to who has access to viable opportunities, and that's evident "in the legacy of slavery, broken treaties, Jim Crow, glass ceilings, and lingering patterns of residential and educational segregation."[128]

Millennials, the generation born in 1982 that entered the "adult" world at age twenty-two in 2004, appear to have a different notion of work and success. Even though they may be burdened by student debt, living with their parents instead of buying homes, and delaying marriage, they are looking for job fulfillment and opportunities to grow. Courtney E. Martin, author of *The New Better Off: Reinventing the American Dream*, argues that millennials are redefining the American Dream to be less materialistic and more communal. They are rethinking "well off" to mean having time to spend with people they love and do work they love, regardless of how lucrative the work.[129]

While their parents and grandparents have prioritized consistent employment at large companies, millennials dream of seeking new opportunities, changing careers, and working flexibly.[130] The rise of the "shared economy" driven by technology, convenience, and flexibility is fueling the economic ideal for many young Americans. The ease in which one can reach a customer base through online platforms allows entrepreneurial millennials—including the supertemps working with Amelia's Business Talent Group—to market their businesses and succeed in a way that was not possible for earlier generations.

In terms of the financial aspect of the American Dream, researchers from Stanford, Harvard, and U.C. Berkeley who developed the Equality of Opportunity Project found that the American Dream of the past is fading and the odds of children out-earning their parents dropped by more than 40 percent, due to the concentration of wealth among the rich.[131] Nathaniel Hendren, a Harvard economist and coauthor of the study, said, "If you don't have that kind of widespread economic growth across the income distribution, it's tough to grow up and earn more than your parents."[132]

Elizabeth's life work studying the economics of working Americans gives her unique insight into the plight of the largest-growing segment of the working class that is aspiring to be middle class. Her writing, both as a scholar and as an author for the general public, exposes the discriminatory practices of banks and the impact that has had on black and Latinx households and their slow ascendancy to the middle class. As a senator, she has been able to use expertise on these issues to speak about the racial inequity that holds back the black and Latinx working class. These groups vote overwhelmingly Democratic—sixty-five percent of the Latinx and 88 percent of the black vote went to Hillary Clinton in 2016.[133] Working-class people of color, still at the civil rights stage on the path toward the middle class, are striving to be equal citizens versus the targets of police or deportation policies or the overt racism that brought Donald Trump to the White House. Socially conscious white Democrats and Democrats of color understand that inequity must be fixed before the fastest-growing community of the working class can be in a position to progress toward economic opportunity.

Elizabeth built her political reputation by condemning Wall Street's damaging behavior while also proving to her surprised colleagues that she is a staunch believer in markets, when they're designed to work for everyone. Her anti–Wall Street message tapped into the diverse cross section of Americans that manifested as the Occupy movement, including reform-minded middle-class Democrats of all races. She may have more in-depth knowledge of the plight of working-class blacks and Hispanics than any other populist to come out of the Democratic party, and she has shared it with the general public in the media and her middle-class-at-risk manifesto, *The Two-Income Trap: Why Middle-Class Mothers and Fathers Are Going Broke*. While the title may not express it, this book talks hard and fast about race:

- "Subprime lending, payday loans, and the host of predatory, high-interest loan products that target minority neighborhoods should be called by their true names: legally sanctioned corporate plans to steal from minorities."
- "African American borrowers are 450 percent more likely than whites to end up with a subprime instead of a prime mortgage."

- "If the market were working properly, how could Citibank sell 40 percent of its high-priced subprime mortgages to [mostly minority] families with good credit who would have qualified for low-cost mortgages?"
- "Hispanic homeowners are nearly three times more likely than white homeowners to file for bankruptcy, and black homeowners are more than six times more likely."[134]

Throughout her career, Elizabeth has also published research about the unique burden women bear in the new economy. Her bankruptcy studies reveal that the number of single-women filers has grown by more than 600 percent in the past two decades and that women who file are on the bottom rung of the economic ladder, in other words, the poorest of the poor.[135] While she has published a great deal of research about the financial straits of women in scholarly journals as well as the popular media, race, as far as this author has been able to determine, is not factored in to her data about women. That is not particularly surprising, since black feminist research has only been trickling into the disciplines.

When she writes about how bankruptcy reforms have hit poor women the hardest, she does not discuss the demographics of race behind that fact. But her research-driven expertise in the crushing challenges of American working- and middle-class women may explain why Warren the professor never took on the women's rights banner as a campus activist. Instead, she carved out her time to advise women on how to navigate their professional careers and published research about the realities of women's financial lives. Her now-famous addition to the #MeToo movement in a network television interview about her experience as a faculty member at the University of Texas School of Law made up for her less-than-dominant girl power rhetoric in her first campaign.

Just as Elizabeth's broader understanding of the political impacts of economic policies transformed her from "a one-dimensional scholar to a two-dimensional scholar," her scholarly expertise has come to bear on the issues she has taken up and supported in the Senate. The more she addresses the issues of race that are most important to the people of color who aspire to the middle class, the more the hard-hitting "sheriff of Wall Street" will bring this message to a country torn apart by these hard realities.

Since steadily turning away from the working class and embracing the white-collar professional class over the past fifty years, the Democratic party has lost sight of the mission that formed its roots. Elizabeth is an outsider on the inside, continuing to critique the Wall Street elites who are the companions of many leaders in the new Democratic party, and that fight about the influence of Wall Street is intimately tied to the financial well-being of the working and middle class. In a country that is growing more diverse every decade, reversing the causes of inequity that threaten social and economic progress is an even bigger fight, the fight that must be won before any others can stand a chance to win.

In early 2018, Elizabeth returned to her controversial Native American ancestry claim and the ongoing bullying from the president of the United States that surrounded it in a speech to a meeting of the National Congress of American Indians (NCAI) in Washington, DC. In her talk, she confronted the issue head-on. "I get why some people think there's hay to be made here," she said. "You won't find my family members on any rolls, and I'm not enrolled in a tribe." Her emphasis on select words in her next lines ignited enthusiastic applause. "And I want to make something clear. I *respect* that distinction. I *understand* that tribal membership is determined by *tribes*—and *only* by tribes."[136]

She explained that she never used her family tree to advance her career and then began to chronicle the history of abuse of Native Americans by the government. This litany built up to the recognition that "the majority of violent crimes experienced by Native Americans are perpetrated by non-Natives, and more than half—*half*—of Native women have experienced sexual violence. This must stop." Here again, the group broke into energetic applause. "And I promise I will fight to help write a different story," she said. She listed ways in which "we," apparently meaning the government, could build opportunity in Indian country, such as stopping "giant corporations from stealing your resources," expanding "federally protected land that is important to your tribes," protecting historic monuments, and taking steps to "stop violence against Native people."

Most of all, she said, "we can fight to empower tribal governments and Native communities so you can take your rightful seat at the table when it comes to determining your own future."

With these commitments, Elizabeth picked up where she had left off in 2012, using her position as a senior senator to draw awareness to Native Americans and their challenges and proposing actions that the government could take. It sounded like a promise; however, some felt that the timing seemed overdue. "If her stepping out like this in front of that audience leads to better legislation, then Native folk will benefit from it," said Professor David Wilkins of the University of Minnesota. "But Native academics and many others outside of politics, being more focused on other dimensions, want to know where she's been all these years and want to know how someone can claim to be 'part' Native. You're either Native or not, from our perspective."[137]

With her reelection campaign underway, the Valentine's Day appearance at the National Council of American Indians meeting could easily have been construed as an attempt to resolve a controversy that had plagued her first campaign rather than a newfound commitment to serve America's Native population.

Her speech was a strong statement that she, a powerful Washington figure, knew the history that society chose to ignore as well as some of the critical issues that faced Native American communities. Choosing to give a speech on these issues in 2018, however, begged the question of how much stronger her impact may have been had she presented this platform in her first year or two in the Senate. As a junior senator, she was not the typical "I'm just learning the ropes" newbie in 2013 but rather a star of her party and hit-the-ground-running, influential force with strong allies in and outside the Senate. As a new senator, she had an extraordinary opportunity to share her vision for addressing Native American issues with the same fortitude with which she had defended her family's stories.

Regardless of the timing, Elizabeth's vocal commitment to these issues gives them a hefty chance of being addressed.

She also found a way to support Native American issues through the unlikely route of President Trump's repeated reference to her as

"Pocahontas," his attempt to besmear her over her claims of Native ancestry. The president infamously repeated the racist slur during an event honoring Native American veterans at the White House in November 2017.[138] The veterans had served as code talkers in the U.S. Marine Corps during World War II, providing 100 percent secure battlefield communications through a complex code based on their native language. During the ceremony, Trump told the veterans: "You were here long before any of us were here. Although we have a representative in Congress who they say was here a long time ago. They call her Pocahontas." Native American spokespeople such as John Norwood, an official with the Alliance of Colonial Era Tribes, said, "The reference is using a historic American Indian figure as a derogatory insult and that's insulting to all American Indians…[He] should stop using our historical people of significance as a racial slur against one of his opponents." Jefferson Keel, the president of the NCAI, told the press that he regretted that the president's use of the name as a slur to insult an adversary overshadowed the true purpose of the event.[139]

In her speech to the NCAI, Elizabeth had vowed to raise awareness about Native Americans every time someone brought up the issue of her ancestry, and in subsequent jabs from the president, that's what she did. After the president used the slur at a political rally in March 2018, for example, Elizabeth reiterated her vow on CNN and talked about the government's lack of action on the fact that "more than half of Native women in this country have been victims of sexual violence, and more than half of them are attacked by nonnatives…we need to make some changes on this."[140]

Fighting back the racist name-calling of a president was not the

most disappointing reality in store for Elizabeth in the first quarter
of the Trump administration. First, the president installed a self-
proclaimed enemy of the Consumer Financial Protection Bureau as
its new interim director, assuring a radical scale-down of the agency.
After Director Richard Cordray resigned in November 2017 to run
for governor in Ohio, his assigned replacement, Deputy Director
Leandra English assumed the interim post. At the same time, Trump
appointed Mick Mulvaney for the role, and when a court ruled that
the president had the authority to name an interim director, the president's choice was in. Mulvaney, the administration's director of the
Office of Management and Budget, had cosponsored a bill to eliminate the bureau when he was serving as a Republican Congressman
from South Carolina, and publicly described the CFPB as a "sick,
sad kind of" joke. [141]

The sweeping changes at the bureau under Mulvaney's watch
included withdrawing a lawsuit against four online payday loan
companies, including Golden Valley and Silver Cloud Financial
that charged up to 950 percent interest rates and illegally withdrew
money from customers' bank accounts.[142] Mulvaney also halted the
bureau's investigation into the massive 2017 data breach at Equifax,
the credit-reporting agency company, in which hackers stole 145
million Americans' social security numbers, addresses, license
numbers, birthdays, and tax ID numbers.[143]

From the start, Mulvaney reset the agency's entire mission as
outlined in a memo to the 1,600 staff members:

> We are government employees. We don't just work
> for the government, we work for the people. And that

means everyone: those who use credit cards, and those who provide those cards; those who take loans, and those who make them; those who buy cars, and those who sell them. All of those people are part of what makes this country great. And all of them deserve to be treated fairly by their government. There is a reason that Lady Justice wears a blindfold and carries a balance, along with her sword.[144]

That befuddling memo, which contradicted the very name of the agency, slapped a bright red bull's-eye on the bureau. Elizabeth held out hope during the nightmare of Mulvaney's takeover with a focus on her faith in the staff. "The people who work at the CFPB are a pretty tough lot," she told the *Boston Globe*. "They didn't come to the CFPB because they thought the lenders that had cheated families were somehow going to lay down and die. They came to the CFPB knowing they would wade into one fight after another."[145]

The next disappointment came with legislation that eased up the regulations in the Dodd–Frank financial reform law that was designed to protect the economy from too-big-to-fail banks. While raising the bar that defines "too big" and eliminating stress tests (analyses of how well a bank could survive a financial emergency) for all but the nation's twelve biggest banks, the Economic Growth, Regulatory Relief, and Consumer Protection Act removed other protections Barney Frank and his allies had fought for. Sixteen Democrats joined Republicans to pass the bill with a 67 to 31 vote in the Senate.

Elizabeth denounced the bill throughout the media, but her

fellow Democratic Banking Committee member Heidi Heitkamp argued that Elizabeth's assertions were exaggerated at best. As Heidi explained, the legislation had been in the works for five years to help community banks and credit unions in the country's rural areas.[146] Many of those small lenders could not afford to comply with the regulations and were phasing out their mortgage lending, so the bill was designed to lighten up those restrictions. Elizabeth countered that if the bill were only about helping those smaller banks, she would fully support it, but she highlighted how the removal of stress-tests and other changes would once again make banks too risky. At the time of this writing, the Senate and House were working on a combined version of the bill.

As a senator in the twenty-first century, when the income gap is widening like a deep ocean rift, Elizabeth Warren is in the good fight. She works on the inside, but she's never considered herself an insider.

She was an outsider as a professor, an Okie with a law degree from a public law school who had no business making it to an endowed chair at Harvard. "There is nobody on the faculty of Texas Law or Harvard Law whose father was a maintenance man," said Calvin Johnson, Elizabeth's former colleague at Texas Law. "We don't have any working-class roots. She went to the top in spite of that."[147] She was an outsider on the inside, and one of their best.

In politics, years before she joined the Senate, she discovered another insider's realm, where elite alliances form the fabric of power. The stunning revelation of Washington—the conservative prime directive to serve the wealthiest—put her outsider status in high relief. But her Senate campaign connected her to the matrix of outsiders, people with pain, resilience, and hope. The game was rigged against them, and she wanted to be their voice.

Elizabeth's message about the "rigged" system echoed the work of sociologists who have described how our society's embedded discriminatory processes show up in policies and practices. Douglas S. Massey describes capitalism as an economic system that channels benefits, opportunities, and resources to favored groups (whites, the wealthy, those in power). When the laws and assumptions in a society are set up to disadvantage people according to their race, class, and gender, the mechanisms to create this movement of the most going to the top is already built in.[148] Others explore how the wealthiest Americans use their privilege to prevail on politicians to write tax law in their favor, rigging the system to place more of the tax burden on everyone else. Data about the teaching gap in public education, which has persisted for fifty years, shows that decade after decade, the majority of teachers and school leaders remains white, despite the fact that white children are now the minority in our public schools. The conscious and unconscious bias that impacts how teachers act in the classroom keeps revealing itself in the stubborn gaps between the achievements of different races, rigging the system in favor of white students.[149]

Elizabeth's career as a scholar, which evolved into her work in Washington and ultimately the Senate, awakened her to deeper issues of race, class, and gender that form the country's trifecta of inequality. As a senator with that background, she personifies the type of leader whose challenge in this century is, as Cornel West describes, "to help Americans determine whether a genuine multi-racial democracy can be created and sustained in an era of global economy and a moment of xenophobic frenzy."[150]

She would always be a teacher, but her party has never found the secret to penetrating the other side. The unsolved mystery, as economist Philip Kotler puts it, "is how it can be that so many Americans who are poor, working class, or even middle class identify their interests with the political party whose whole basis is to defend the interests of the super-rich."[151] Can a populist like Warren break that spell?

Outsider status, for someone who knows the inside well, brings clarity and opportunity, and that's how Elizabeth Warren likes it. "I'll always be an outsider," she said. "There's a real benefit to being clear about this. I know why I'm here."[152]

AFTERWORD

"We may have democracy, or we may have wealth concentrated in the hands of a few, but we cannot have both."

—Louis D. Brandeis,
Associate Supreme Court Justice, 1916–1939

In a 2014 speech at Netroots Nation, the country's largest annual conference for liberal writers and activists, Elizabeth Warren listed eleven tenets in response to the question, "What does it mean to be a progressive?" In style and substance, her chosen statements could be called the Progressive's Creed:

- "We believe that Wall Street needs stronger rules and tougher enforcement, and we're willing to fight for it."
- "We believe in science, and that means that we have a responsibility to protect this Earth."

- "We believe that the internet shouldn't be rigged to benefit big corporations, and that means real net neutrality."
- "We believe that no one should work full time and still live in poverty, and that means raising the minimum wage."
- "We believe that fast-food workers deserve a livable wage, and that means that when they take to the picket line, we are proud to fight alongside them."
- "We believe that students are entitled to get an education without being crushed by debt."
- "We believe that after a lifetime of work, people are entitled to retire with dignity, and that means protecting social security, Medicare, and pensions."
- "We believe—I can't believe I have to say this in 2014— we believe in equal pay for equal work."
- "We believe that equal means equal, and that's true in marriage, it's true in the workplace, it's true in all of America."
- "We believe that immigration has made this country strong and vibrant, and that means reform."
- "And we believe that corporations are not people, that women have a right to their bodies. We will overturn *Hobby Lobby* and we will fight for it. We will fight for it!"

APPENDIX 1

Elizabeth Warren "formally" introduced her idea for an agency to protect consumers from the tricks and traps of the financial industry three years before the Consumer Financial Protection Bureau was created as part of the Dodd–Frank Wall Street Reform and Consumer Protection Act.

Democracy: A Journal of Ideas, Summer 2007

UNSAFE AT ANY RATE

It is impossible to buy a toaster that has a one-in-five chance of bursting into flames and burning down your house. But it is possible to refinance an existing home with a mortgage that has the same one-in-five chance of putting the family out on the street—and the mortgage won't even carry a disclosure of that fact to the homeowner. Similarly, it's impossible to change the price on a toaster once it has been purchased. But long after the papers have been signed, it is possible to triple the price of the credit used to finance the purchase of that appliance, even if the customer meets all the credit terms, in full and on time. Why are consumers safe when they purchase tangible consumer products with cash, but when they sign up for routine financial products like mortgages and credit cards they are left at the mercy of their creditors?

The difference between the two markets is regulation. Although considered an epithet in Washington since Ronald Reagan swept into the White House, the "R-word" supports a booming market in tangible consumer goods. Nearly every product sold in America has passed basic safety regulations well in advance of reaching store shelves. Credit products, by comparison, are regulated by a tattered patchwork of federal and state laws that have failed to adapt to changing markets. Moreover, thanks to effective regulation, innovation in the market for physical products has led to more safety and cutting-edge features. By comparison, innovation in financial products has produced incomprehensible terms and sharp practices that have left families at the mercy of those who write the contracts.

Sometimes consumer trust in a creditor is well-placed. Indeed, credit has provided real value for millions of households, permitting the purchase of homes that can add to family wealth accumulation and cars that can expand job opportunities. Credit can also provide a critical safety net and a chance for a family to borrow against a better tomorrow when they hit job layoffs, medical problems, or family break-ups today. Other financial products, such as life insurance and annuities, also can greatly enhance a family's security. Consumers might not spend hours pouring over the details of their credit card terms or understand every paper they signed at a real estate closing, but many of those financial products are offered on fair terms that benefit both seller and customer.

But for a growing number of families who are steered into over-priced credit products, risky subprime mortgages, and misleading insurance plans, trust in a creditor turns out to be costly. And for families who get tangled up with truly dangerous financial products, the result can be wiped-out savings, lost homes, higher costs for car insurance, denial of jobs, troubled marriages, bleak retirements, and broken lives.

Consumers can enter the market to buy physical products confident that they won't be tricked into buying exploding toasters and other unreasonably dangerous products. They can concentrate their shopping efforts in other directions, helping to drive a competitive market that keeps costs low and encourages innovation in convenience, durability, and style. Consumers entering the market to buy financial products should enjoy the same protection. Just as the Consumer Product Safety Commission (CPSC) protects buyers of goods and supports a competitive market, we need the same for consumers of financial products—a new regulatory regime, and even a new regulatory body, to protect consumers who use credit cards, home mortgages, car loans, and a host of other products. The time has come to put scaremongering to rest and to recognize that regulation can often support and advance efficient and more dynamic markets.

DO YOU HAVE CREDIT PROBLEMS?

Americans are drowning in debt. One in four families say they are worried about how they will pay their credit card bills this month.

Nearly half of all credit card holders have missed payments in the past year, and an additional 2.1 million families missed at least one mortgage payment. Last year, 1.2 million families lost their homes in foreclosure, and another 1.5 million families are likely headed into mortgage foreclosure this year.

Families' troubles are compounded by substantial changes in the credit market that have made debt instruments far riskier for consumers than they were a generation ago. The effective deregulation of interest rates, coupled with innovations in credit charges (e.g., teaser rates, negative amortization, increased use of fees, cross-default clauses, penalty interest rates, and two-cycle billing), have turned ordinary credit transactions into devilishly complex financial undertakings. Aggressive marketing, almost nonexistent in the 1970s, compounds the difficulty, shaping consumer demand in unexpected and costly directions. And yet consumer capacity—measured both by available time and expertise—has not expanded to meet the demands of a changing credit marketplace. Instead, consumers sign on to credit products with only a vague understanding of the terms.

Credit cards offer a glimpse at the costs imposed by a rapidly growing credit industry. In 2006, for example, Americans turned over $89 billion in fees, interest payments, added costs on purchases, and other charges associated with their credit cards. That is $89 billion out of the pockets of ordinary middle-class families, people with jobs, kids in school, and groceries to buy. That is also $89 billion that didn't go to new cars, new shoes, or any other goods or services in the American economy. To be sure, the money kept plenty of bank employees working full-time, and it helped make "debt collector" one of the fastest-growing occupations in the economy. But debt repayment has become a growing part of the American family budget, so much so that now the typical family with credit card debt spends only slightly less on fees and interest each year than it does on clothing, shoes, laundry, and dry-cleaning for the whole family.

Nor are all costs associated with debt measured in dollars; not surprisingly, the effect on family life is considerable. Anxiety and shame have become constant companions for Americans struggling with debt. Since 2000, families have filed nearly 10 million petitions for bankruptcy. Today about one in every seven families in America is dealing with a debt collector. Mortgage foreclosures and credit defaults sweep in millions more families. How do they feel about their inability to pay their bills? The National Opinion Research Council asked families about negative life events, on a ranking of one thorough 100: Death of a child (94.3) and being forced to live on the street or in a shelter (86.7) topped the list, but filing for bankruptcy ranked close behind (83.5), more serious than death of a close friend (80.8) or separating from a spouse (82.1). About half won't tell a friend their credit card balances, and 85 percent of those who file for bankruptcy are struggling to hide that fact from families, friends, or neighbors.

Why do people get into debt trouble in the first place? People know that credit cards are dangerous, all the more so if the customer carries a balance. Mortgage financing is a serious undertaking, with reams of documents and papers; any consumer who signed papers without reading carefully or seeking legal assistance should not be surprised if terms come to light later that are unfavorable to the consumer. Payday lenders have a bad reputation for taking advantage of people; no one should expect to be treated well by them.

Car lenders, check-cashing outlets, overdraft protection—the point can be repeated again and again: Financial products are dangerous, and any consumer who is not careful is inviting trouble. And yet, dangerous or not, millions of Americans engage in billions of credit transactions, adding up to trillions of dollars every year.

Some Americans claim that their neighbors are drowning in debt because they are heedless of the risk or because they are so consumed by their appetites to purchase that they willingly ignore the risks. Surely, in such circumstances, it is not the responsibility of regulators to provide the self-discipline that customers lack. Indeed, there can be no doubt that some portion of the credit crisis in America is the result of foolishness and profligacy. Some people are in trouble with credit because they simply use too much of it. Others are in trouble because they use credit in dangerous ways. But that is not the whole story. Lenders have deliberately built tricks and traps into some credit products so they can ensnare families in a cycle of high-cost debt.

To be sure, creating safer marketplaces is not about protecting consumers from all possible bad decisions. Instead, it is about making certain that the products themselves don't become the source of the trouble. This means that terms hidden in the fine print or obscured with incomprehensible language, unexpected terms, reservation of all power to the seller with nothing left for the buyer, and similar tricks and traps have no place in a well-functioning market.

How did financial products get so dangerous? Part of the problem is that disclosure has become a way to obfuscate rather than to inform. According to the *Wall Street Journal*, in the early 1980s, the typical credit card contract was a page long; by the early 2000s, that contract had grown to more than 30 pages of incomprehensible text. The additional terms were not designed to make life easier for the customer. Rather, they were designed in large part to add unexpected—and unreadable— terms that favor the card companies. Mortgage-loan documents, payday-loan papers, car-loan terms, and other lending products are often equally incomprehensible. And this is not the subjective claim of the consumer advocacy movement. In a recent memo aimed at bank executives, the vice president of the business consulting firm Booz Allen Hamilton observed that most bank products are "too complex for the average consumer to understand."

Creditors sometimes explain away their long contracts with the claim that they need to protect themselves from litigation. This ignores the fact that creditors have found many other effective ways to insulate themselves for liability for their own wrongdoing. Arbitration clauses, for example, may look benign to the customer, but their point is often to permit the lender to escape the reach of class-action lawsuits. This means the lender can break the law, but if the amounts at stake are small—say, under $50 per customer—few customers would ever bother to sue.

Legal protection is only a small part of the proliferating verbiage. For those willing to wade through paragraph after paragraph replete with terms like "LIBOR" and "Cash Equivalent Transactions," lenders have built in enough surprises in some credit contracts that even successful efforts to understand and assess risk will be erased by the lender's own terms. So, for example, after 47 lines of text explaining how interest rates will be calculated, one prominent credit card company concludes, "We reserve the right to change the terms at any time for any reason." Evidently, all that convoluted language was there only to obscure the bottom line: The company will charge whatever it wants. In effect, such text is an effort for lenders to have it both ways. Lenders won't be bound by any term or price that becomes inconvenient for them, but they will expect their customers to be bound by whatever terms the lenders want to enforce—and to have the courts back them up in case of dispute.

Even worse, consumers wary of creditor tricks may look for help, only to rush headlong into the waiting arms of someone else who will fleece them—and then hand them over to the creditors for further fleecing. In the mortgage market, for example, consumers may respond to advertisements for "a friend to help you find the best possible mortgage," "someone on your side," and "access to thousands of mortgages with a single phone call—do all your comparison shopping here." When they call a mortgage broker, they may believe they will receive wise advice that will guide them through a dangerous thicket. Some mortgage brokers will do just that. But consumers are just as likely to encounter a broker who is working only for himself, taking what amounts to a bribe from a mortgage company to steer a family into a higher-priced mortgage than it could qualify for, all the while assuring the family that this is the best possible deal. For example, a family that might qualify for a 6.5 percent fixed-rate, 30-year mortgage could easily end up with a 9.5 percent mortgage because the broker can pocket a fee (what the industry calls a "yield service premium," or YSP) from the mortgage company to place the higher-priced loan. High YSPs helped drive the wild selling that led to the recent meltdown in the subprime mortgage market.

Despite the characterization of YSPs by one Fannie Mae vice

president as "lender kickbacks," the practice of taking these fees is legal. Under pressure from the mortgage-broker industry, Congress and the regulatory agencies have generally approved of YSPs. In fact, mortgage brokers face few regulatory restrictions. It is no surprise, then, that mortgage brokers originate more than half of all mortgage loans, particularly at the low-end of the credit market. YSPs are present in 85 to 90 percent of subprime mortgages, which implies that brokers are needlessly pushing clients into more expensive products. And the costs are staggering: Fannie Mae estimates that fully 50 percent of those who were sold ruinous subprime mortgages would have qualified for prime-rate loans. A study by the Department of Housing and Urban Development revealed that one in nine middle-income families (and one in 14 upper-income families) who refinanced a home mortgage ended up with a high-fee, high-interest subprime mortgage. Of course, YSPs are not confined to subprime mortgages. Pushing a family who qualifies for a 6.5 percent loan into a 9.5 percent loan and pocketing the difference will cost the family tens of thousands of dollars, but it will not show up in anyone's statistics on sub-prime lending.

Other creditors have their own techniques for fleecing borrowers. Payday lenders offer consumers a friendly hand when they are short of cash. But hidden in the tangle of disclosures is a staggering interest rate. For example, buried in a page of disclosures for one lender (rather than on the fee page, where the customer might expect to see it) was the note that the interest rate on the offered loan was 485.450 percent. For some families, the rates run even higher. In transactions recently documented by the Center on Responsible Lending, a $300 loan cost one family $2,700, while another borrowed $400, paid back

$3,000, and was being hounded by the payday lender for $1,200 per month when they gave up and filed for bankruptcy. In total, the cost to American families of payday lending is estimated to be $4.2 billion a year. The Department of Defense identified payday lending as such a serious problem for those in the military that it determined the industry "undermines military readiness." In fact, the practices were so outrageous that Congress banned all companies from charging military people more than 36 percent interest. This change in the law will protect military families from payday lenders, but it will leave all other families subject to the same predatory practices.

For some, Shakespeare's injunction that "neither a borrower nor a lender be" seems to be good policy. Just stay away from all debt and avoid the trouble. But no one takes that position with tangible consumer goods. No one advocates that people who don't want their homes burned down should stay away from toasters or that those who don't want their fingers and toes cut off should give up mowing the lawn. Instead, product safety standards set the floor for all consumer products, and an active, competitive market revolves around the features consumers can see, such as price or convenience or, in some cases, even greater safety. To say that credit markets should follow a caveat emptor model is to ignore the success of the consumer goods market—and the pain inflicted by dangerous credit products.

Indeed, the pain imposed by a dangerous credit product is even more insidious than that inflicted by a malfunctioning kitchen appliance. If toasters are dangerous, they may burn down the homes of rich people or poor people, college graduates or high-school dropouts. But credit products are not nearly so egalitarian. Wealthy families can ignore the tricks and traps associated with credit card debt, secure in the knowledge that they won't need to turn to credit to get through a rough patch. Their savings will protect them from medical expenses that exceed their insurance coverage or the effects of an unexpected car repair; credit cards are little more than a matter of convenience. Working- and middle-class families are far less insulated. For the family who lives closer to the economic margin, a credit card with an interest rate that unexpectedly escalates to 29.99 percent or misplaced trust in a broker who recommends a high-priced mortgage can push a family into a downward economic spiral from which it may never recover.

THE TRADITIONAL SOLUTIONS HAVE HIT THEIR LIMITS

The credit industry is not without regulation; credit transactions have been regulated by statute or common law since the founding of the Republic. Traditionally, states bore the primary responsibility for protecting their citizens from unscrupulous lenders, imposing usury caps and other credit regulations on all companies doing business locally. While states still play some role, particularly in the regulation of real-estate transactions, their primary tool—interest rate regulation—has been effectively destroyed by federal legislation. Today, any lender that gets a federal bank charter can locate its operations in a state with high usury rates (e.g., South Dakota or Delaware), then export that states' interest rate caps (or no caps at all) to customers located all over the country. As a result, and with no public debate, interest rates have been effectively deregulated across the country, leaving the states powerless to act. In April of this year, the Supreme Court took another step in the same direction in

Watters v. Wachovia, giving federal regulators the power to shut down state efforts to regulate mortgage lenders without providing effective federal regulation to replace it.

Local laws suffer from another problem. As lenders have consolidated and credit markets have gone national, a plethora of state regulations drives up costs for lenders, forcing them to include repetitive disclosures and meaningless exceptions in order to comply with differing local laws, even as it also leaves open regulatory gaps. The resulting patchwork of regulation is neither effective nor cost-effective. During the 1970s and early 1980s, for instance, Congress moved the regulation of some aspects of consumer credit from the state to the federal level through a series of landmark bills that included Truth-in-Lending (TIL), Fair Credit Reporting, and anti-discrimination regulations. These statutes tend to be highly specific. TIL, for example, specifies the information that must be revealed in a credit transaction, including the size of the typeface that must be used and how interest rates must be stated. But the specificity of these laws works against their effectiveness, trapping the regulations like a fly in amber. The statutes inhibit some beneficial innovations (e.g., new ways of informing consumers) while they fail to regulate dangerous innovations (e.g., no discussion of negative amortization). What's more, these generation-old regulations completely miss most of the new features of credit products, such as universal default, double-cycle billing, and other changes in credit.

Any effort to increase or reform statutory regulation of financial products is met by a powerful industry lobby on one side that is not balanced by an equally effective consumer lobby on the other.

As a result, even the most basic efforts are blocked from becoming law. A decade ago, for example, mortgage-lender abuses were rare. Today, experts estimate that fraud and deception have stripped $9.1 billion in equity from homeowners, particularly from elderly and working-class families. A few hearty souls have repeatedly introduced legislation to halt such practices, but those bills never make it out of committee.

Beyond Congress, some regulation of financial products occurs through the indirect mechanism of the Federal Reserve, the Office of the Comptroller of the Currency (OCC), and the Office of Thrift Supervision. Each agency, for example, has some power to control certain forms of predatory lending. But their main mission is to protect the financial stability of banks and other financial institutions, not to protect consumers. As a result, they focus intently on bank profitability and far less on the financial impact on customers of many of the products the banks sell.

The current regulatory jumble creates another problem: Consumer financial products are regulated based, principally, on the identity of the issuer, rather than the nature of the product. The subprime mortgage market provides a stunning example of the resulting fractured oversight. In 2005, for example, 23 percent of subprime mortgages were issued by regulated thrifts and banks. Another 25 percent were issued by bank holding companies, which were subject to different regulatory oversight through the federal system. But more than half—52 percent, to be exact—of all subprime mortgages originated with companies with no federal supervision at all, largely stand-alone mortgage brokers and finance companies. This division not only creates enormous loopholes, it also triggers a kind of regulatory arbitrage. Regulators are acutely aware that if they push financial institutions too hard, those institutions will simply reincorporate in another form under the umbrella of a different regulatory agency—or no regulatory agency at all. Indeed, in recent years a number of credit unions have dissolved and reincorporated as state or national banks, precisely to fit under a regulatory charter that would give them different options in developing and marketing financial products. If the regulated have the option to choose their regulators, then it should be no surprise when they game the rules in their own favor.

Unfortunately, in a world in which the financial services industry is routinely one of the top three contributors to national political campaigns, giving $133 million over the past five years, the likelihood of quick action to respond to specific problems and to engage in meaningful oversight is vanishingly slim. The resulting splintered regulatory framework has created regulatory loopholes and timid regulators. This leaves the American consumer effectively unprotected in a world in which a number of merchants of financial products have shown themselves very willing to take as much as they can by any means they can.

THE FINANCIAL PRODUCT SAFETY COMMISSION

Clearly, it is time for a new model of financial regulation, one focused primarily on consumer safety rather than corporate profitability. Financial products should be subject to the same routine safety screening that now governs the sale of every toaster, washing machine, and child's car seat sold on the American market.

The model for such safety regulation is the U.S. Consumer Product

Safety Commission (CPSC), an independent health and safety regulatory agency founded in 1972 by the Nixon Administration. The CPSC's mission is to protect the American public from risks of injury and death from products used in the home, school, and recreation. The agency has the authority to develop uniform safety standards, order the recall of unsafe products, and ban products that pose unreasonable risks. In establishing the Commission, Congress recognized that "the complexities of consumer products and the diverse nature and abilities of consumers using them frequently result in an inability of users to anticipate risks and to safeguard themselves adequately."

The evidence clearly shows that CPSC is a cost-effective agency. Since it was established, product-related death and injury rates in the United States have decreased substantially. The CPSC estimates that just three safety standards for three products alone—cigarette lighters, cribs, and baby walkers—save more than $2 billion annually. The annual estimated savings is more than CPSC's total cumulative budget since its inception.

So why not create a Financial Product Safety Commission (FPSC)? Like its counterpart for ordinary consumer products, this agency would be charged with responsibility to establish guidelines for consumer disclosure, collect and report data about the uses of different financial products, review new financial products for safety, and require modification of dangerous products before they can be marketed to the public. The agency could review mortgages, credit cards, car loans, and a number of other financial products, such as life insurance and annuity contracts. In effect, the FPSC would evaluate these products to eliminate the hidden tricks and traps that make some of them far more dangerous than others.

An FPSC would promote the benefits of free markets by assuring that consumers can enter credit markets with confidence that the products they purchase meet minimum safety standards. No one expects every customer to become an engineer to buy a toaster that doesn't burst into flames, or analyze complex diagrams to buy an infant car seat that doesn't collapse on impact. By the same reasoning, no customer should be forced to read the fine print in 30-plus-page credit card contracts to determine whether the company claims it can seize property paid for with the credit card or raise the interest rate by more than 20 points if the customer gets into a dispute with the water company.

Instead, an FPSC would develop precisely such expertise in consumer financial products. A commission would be able to collect data about which financial products are least understood, what kinds of disclosures are most effective, and which products are most likely to result in consumer default. Free of legislative micro-managing, it could develop nuanced regulatory responses; some terms might be banned altogether, while others might be permitted only with clearer disclosure. A Commission might promote uniform disclosures that make it easier to compare products from one issuer to another, and to discern conflicts of interest on the part of a mortgage broker or seller of a currently loosely regulated financial product. In the area of credit card regulation, for example, an FPSC might want to review the following terms that appear in some—but not all—credit card agreements: universal clauses; unlimited and unexplained fees; interest rate increases that exceed 10 percentage points; and an issuer's claim that it can change the terms of cards after money has been borrowed. It would also promote such market-enhancing practices as a simple, easy-to-read paragraph that explains all interest charges; clear explanations of when fees will be imposed; a requirement that the terms of a credit card remain the same until the card expires; no marketing targeted at college students or people under age 21; and a statement showing how long it will take to pay off the balance, as well as how much interest will be paid if the customer makes the minimum monthly payments on the outstanding balance on a credit card.

With every agency, the fear of regulatory capture is ever-present. But in a world in which there is little coherent, consumer-oriented regulation of any kind, an FPSC with power to act is far better than the available alternatives. Whether it is housed in a current agency like the CPSC or stands alone, the point is to concentrate the review of financial products in a single location, with a focus on the safety of the products as consumers use them. Companies that offer good products would have little to fear. Indeed, if they could conduct business without competing with companies whose business model involves misleading the customer, then the companies offering safer products would be more likely to flourish. Moreover, with an FPSC, consumer credit companies would be free to innovate on a level playing field within the boundaries of clearly disclosed terms and open competition—not hidden terms designed to mislead consumers.

The consumer financial services industry has grown to more than $3 trillion in annual business. Lenders employ thousands of lawyers, marketing agencies, statisticians, and business strategists to help them increase profits. In a rapidly changing market, customers need someone on their side to help make certain that the financial products they buy meet minimum safety standards. A Financial Product Safety Commission would be the consumers' ally.

A WELL-REGULATED MARKET

When markets work, they produce value for both buyers and sellers, both borrowers and lenders. But the basic premise of any free market is full information. When a lender can bury a sentence at the bottom of 47 lines of text saying it can change any term at any time for any reason, the market is broken.

Product safety standards will not fix every problem associated with consumer credit. It is possible to stuff a toaster with dirty socks and start a fire, and, even with safety standards, it will remain possible to get burned by credit products. Some people won't even have to try very hard. But safety standards can make a critical difference for millions of families. Families who are steered into higher-priced mortgages solely because the broker wanted a higher fee would have a greater chance of buying—and keeping—a home. A student who wanted a credit card with a firm credit limit—not an approval for thousands of dollars more of credit and higher fees and interest—could stay out of trouble. An older person who needed a little cash to make it until her Social Security check arrived would have a manageable loan, not one that would escalate into thousands of dollars in fees.

Industry practices would change as well. Corporate profit models based on marketing mortgages with a one-in-five chance of costing a family its home would stop. Credit card models that lure 18-year-olds with no income and no credit history into debt with promises of "no parental approval"—on the assumption that their parents will pay it off, rather than see their children begin their adult lives with ruined credit histories—would stop. Rollovers that can turn a simple loan into a mountain of debt would stop.

Personal responsibility will always play a critical role in dealing with credit cards, just as personal responsibility remains a central feature in the safe use of any other product. But a Financial Product Safety Commission could eliminate some of the most egregious tricks and traps in the credit industry. And for every family who avoids a trap or doesn't get caught by a trick, that's regulation that works.

APPENDIX 2

Time Warner Cable Arena, Charlotte, North Carolina, September 5, 2012

SPEECH AT THE DEMOCRATIC NATIONAL CONVENTION

Thank you! I'm Elizabeth Warren, and this is my first Democratic Convention. Never thought I'd run for senate. And I sure never dreamed that I'd get to be the warm-up act for President Bill Clinton—an amazing man, who had the good sense to marry one of the coolest women on the planet. I want to give a special shout out to the Massachusetts delegation. I'm counting on you to help me win and to help President Obama win.

I'm here tonight to talk about hard-working people: people who get up early, stay up late, cook dinner and help out with homework; people who can be counted on to help their kids, their parents, their neighbors, and the lady down the street whose car broke down; people who work their hearts out but are up against a hard truth— the game is rigged against them.

It wasn't always this way. Like a lot of you, I grew up in a family on the ragged edge of the middle class. My daddy sold carpeting and ended up as a maintenance man. After he had a heart attack, my mom worked the phones at Sears so we could hang on to our house. My three brothers all served in the military. One was career. The second worked a good union job in construction. The third started a small business.

Me, I was waiting tables at 13 and married at 19. I graduated from public schools and taught elementary school. I have a wonderful husband, two great children, and three beautiful grandchildren. And I'm grateful, down to my toes, for every opportunity that America gave me. This is a great country. I grew up in an America that invested in its kids and built a strong middle class; that allowed millions of children to rise from poverty and establish secure lives. An America that created Social Security and Medicare so that seniors could live with dignity; an America in which each generation built something solid so that the next generation could build something better.

But for many years now, our middle class has been chipped, squeezed, and hammered. Talk to the construction worker I met from Malden, Massachusetts, who went nine months without finding work. Talk to the head of a manufacturing company in Franklin trying to protect jobs but worried about rising costs. Talk to the student in Worcester who worked hard to finish his college degree, and now he's drowning in debt. Their fight is my fight, and it's Barack Obama's fight too.

People feel like the system is rigged against them. And here's the painful part: they're right. The system is rigged. Look around. Oil companies guzzle down billions in subsidies. Billionaires pay lower tax rates than their secretaries. Wall Street CEOs—the same ones who wrecked our economy and destroyed millions of jobs—still strut around Congress, no shame, demanding favors, and acting like we should thank them.

Anyone here have a problem with that? Well I do. I talk to small business owners all across Massachusetts. Not one of them—not one—made big bucks from the risky Wall Street bets that brought down our economy. I talk to nurses and programmers, salespeople and firefighters—people who bust their tails every day. Not one of them—not one—stashes their money in the Cayman Islands to avoid paying their fair share of taxes.

These folks don't resent that someone else makes more money. We're Americans. We celebrate success. We just don't want the game to be rigged. We've fought to level the playing field before. About a century ago, when corrosive greed threatened our economy and our way of life, the American people came together under the leadership of Teddy Roosevelt and other progressives, to bring our nation back from the brink.

We started to take children out of factories and put them in schools. We began to give meaning to the words "consumer protection" by making our food and medicine safe. And we gave the little guys a better chance to compete by preventing the big guys from rigging the markets. We turned adversity into progress because that's what we do.

Americans are fighters. We are tough, resourceful, and creative. If we have the chance to fight on a level playing field—where everyone pays a fair share and everyone has a real shot—then no one can stop us. President Obama gets it because he's spent his life fighting for the middle class. And now he's fighting to level that playing field—because we know that the economy doesn't grow from the top down, but from the middle class out and the bottom up. That's how we create jobs and reduce the debt.

And Mitt Romney? He wants to give tax cuts to millionaires and billionaires. But for middle-class families who are hanging on by their fingernails? His plans will hammer them with a new tax hike of up to 2,000 dollars. Mitt Romney wants to give billions in breaks to big corporations—but he and Paul Ryan would pulverize financial reform, voucher-ize Medicare, and vaporize Obamacare.

The Republican vision is clear: "I've got mine, the rest of you are on your own." Republicans say they don't believe in government. Sure they do. They believe in government to help themselves and their powerful friends. After all, Mitt Romney's the guy who said corporations are people.

No, Governor Romney, corporations are not people. People have hearts, they have kids, they get jobs, they get sick, they cry, they dance. They live, they love, and they die. And that matters. That matters because we don't run this country for corporations, we run it for people. And that's why we need Barack Obama.

After the financial crisis, President Obama knew that we had to clean up Wall Street. For years, families had been tricked by credit cards, fooled by student loans, and cheated on mortgages. I had an idea for a consumer financial protection agency to stop the rip-offs. The big banks sure didn't like it, and they marshaled one of the biggest lobbying forces on earth to destroy the agency before it ever saw the light of day. American families didn't have an army of lobby-ists on our side, but what we had was a president—President Obama leading the way. And when the lobbyists were closing in for the kill, Barack Obama squared his shoulders, planted his feet, and stood firm. And that's how we won.

By the way, just a few weeks ago, that little agency caught one of the biggest credit card companies cheating its customers and made it give people back every penny it took, plus millions of dollars in fines. That's what happens when you have a president on the side of the middle class.

President Obama believes in a level playing field. He believes in a country where nobody gets a free ride or a golden parachute. A country where anyone who has a great idea and rolls up their sleeves has a chance to build a business, and anyone who works hard can build some security and raise a family. President Obama believes in a country where billionaires pay their taxes just like their secretaries do, and—I can't believe I have to say this in 2012—a country where women get equal pay for equal work.

He believes in a country where everyone is held accountable. Where no one can steal your purse on Main Street or your pension on Wall Street. President Obama believes in a country where we invest in education, in roads and bridges, in science, and in the future, so we can create new opportunities, so the next kid can make it big, and the kid after that, and the kid after that. That's what President Obama believes. And that's how we build the economy of the future. An economy with more jobs and less debt. We root it in fairness. We grow it with opportunity. And we build it together.

I grew up in the Methodist Church and taught Sunday school.

One of my favorite passages of scripture is: "Inasmuch as ye have done it unto one of the least of these my brethren, ye have done it unto me." Matthew 25:40. The passage teaches about God in each of us, that we are bound to each other and called to act. Not to sit, not to wait, but to act—all of us together.

Senator Kennedy understood that call. Four years ago, he addressed our convention for the last time. He said, "We have never lost our belief that we are all called to a better country and a newer world." Generation after generation, Americans have answered that call. And now we are called again. We are called to restore opportunity for every American. We are called to give America's working families a fighting chance. We are called to build something solid so the next generation can build something better.

So let me ask you—let me ask you, America: are you ready to answer this call? Are you ready to fight for good jobs and a strong middle class? Are you ready to work for a level playing field? Are you ready to prove to another generation of Americans that we can build a better country and a newer world?

Joe Biden is ready. Barack Obama is ready. I'm ready. You're ready. America's ready. Thank you! And God bless America!

APPENDIX 3

March 19, 1986

The Honorable Strom Thurmond, Chairman
Committee on the Judiciary
United States Senate
Dirksen Senate Office Building
Washington, DC 20510

Re: Nomination of Jefferson B. Sessions
U.S. Judge, Southern District of
Alabama Hearing, March 13, 1986

Dear Senator Thurmond:

I write to express my sincere opposition to the confirmation of Jefferson B. Sessions as a federal district court judge for the Southern District of Alabama. My professional and personal roots in Alabama are deep and lasting. Anyone who has used the power of his office as United States Attorney to intimidate and chill the free exercise of the ballot by citizens should not be elevated to our courts. Mr. Sessions has used the awesome powers of his office in a shabby attempt to intimidate and frighten elderly black voters. For this reprehensible conduct, he should not be rewarded with a federal judgeship.

I regret that a long-standing commitment prevents me from appearing in person to testify against this nominee. However, I have attached a copy of my statement opposing Mr. Sessions's confirmation and I request that my statement as well as this letter be made a part of the hearing record.

I do sincerely urge you to oppose the confirmation of Mr. Sessions.

Sincerely,
Coretta Scott King

APPENDIX 4

Washington, DC, February 14, 2018

SPEECH AT THE NATIONAL CONGRESS OF AMERICAN INDIANS MEETING

Thank you for having me here today.

I want to start by thanking Chairwoman Andrews-Maltais for that introduction. It has been an honor to work with, to learn from, and to represent the tribes in my home state of Massachusetts, the Wampanoag Tribe of Gay Head—the Aquinnah—and the Mashpee Wampanoag.

I also want to thank President Jefferson Keel, and everyone at the National Congress of American Indians. For over seventy years, you've championed the rights and dignity of First Americans, and I am honored to be here with you today.

I've noticed that every time my name comes up, President Trump likes to talk about Pocahontas. So I figured, let's talk about Pocahontas.

Not Pocahontas, the fictional character most Americans know from the movies, but Pocahontas, the Native woman who really lived, and whose real story has been passed down to so many of you through the generations.

Pocahontas—whose original name wasn't even Pocahontas.

In the fairy tale, Pocahontas and John Smith meet and fall in love.

Except Smith was nearly thirty, and Pocahontas was about ten years old. Whatever happened between them, it was no love story.

In the fairy tale, Pocahontas saves John Smith from execution at the hands of her father.

Except that was probably made up too.

In the fable, her baptism as "Rebecca" and her marriage to a Jamestown settler are held up to show the moral righteousness of colonization.

In reality, the fable is used to bleach away the stain of genocide.

As you know, Pocahontas's real journey was far more remarkable—and far darker—than the myth admits.

As a child, she played a significant role in mediating relations between the tribes ruled by her father and the early settlers at Jamestown. Those efforts helped establish early trade relations between the two peoples. Without her help, the English settlers might well have perished.

But in her teens, Pocahontas was abducted, imprisoned, and held captive. Oral history of the Mattaponi tribe indicates that she was ripped away from her first husband and child and raped in captivity.

Eventually she married another John—John Rolfe. Her marriage led to an uneasy harmony between Jamestown and the tribes, a period that some historians call the Peace of Pocahontas.

But she was not around to enjoy it. John Rolfe paraded her around London to entertain the British and prop up financial investments in the Virginia Company. She never made it home. She was about twenty-one when she died, an ocean separating her from her people.

Indigenous people have been telling the story of Pocahontas—the real Pocahontas—for four centuries. A story of heroism. And bravery. And pain.

And, for almost as long, her story has been taken away by powerful people who twisted it to serve their own purposes.

Our country's disrespect of Native people didn't start with President Trump. It started long before President Washington ever took office.

But now we have a president who can't make it through a ceremony honoring Native American war heroes without reducing Native history, Native culture, Native people to the butt of a joke.

The joke, I guess, is supposed to be on me.

I get why some people think there's hay to be made here. You won't find my family members on any rolls, and I'm not enrolled in a tribe.

And I want to make something clear. I respect that distinction. I understand that tribal membership is determined by tribes—and only by tribes. I never used my family tree to get a break or get ahead. I never used it to advance my career.

But I want to make something else clear too: My parents were real people.

By all accounts, my mother was a beauty. She was born in eastern Oklahoma, on this exact day—Valentine's Day—February 14, 1912. She grew up in the little town of Wetumka, the kind of girl who would sit for hours by herself, playing the piano and singing. My daddy fell head over heels in love with her.

But my mother's family was part Native American. And my daddy's parents were bitterly opposed to their relationship. So, in 1932, when Mother was nineteen and Daddy had just turned twenty, they eloped.

Together, they survived the Dust Bowl and the Great Depression. They saved up to buy a home. They raised my three older brothers, and they watched as each one headed off to serve in the military. After Daddy had a heart attack and was out of work, after we lost the family station wagon and it looked like we would lose our house and everything would come crashing down, my mother put on her best dress and walked to the Sears and got a minimum-wage job. That minimum-wage job saved our house and saved our family.

My parents struggled. They sacrificed. They paid off medical debts for years. My daddy ended up as a janitor. They fought and they drank, but more than anything, they hung together. Sixty-three years—that's how long they were married. When my mother died, a part of my daddy slipped away too.

Two years later, I held his hand while cancer took him. The last thing he said was, "It's time for me to be with your mother." And he smiled.

They're gone, but the love they shared, the struggles they endured, the family they built, and the story they lived will always be a part of me. And no one—not even the president of the United States—will ever take that part of me away.

Our stories are deeply woven into the fabric of who we are. The stories of immigrants and slaves, of explorers and refugees, have shaped and reshaped our country right up to the present day. For far too long, your story has been pushed aside, to be trotted out only in cartoons and commercials.

So I'm here today to make a promise: Every time someone brings up my family's story, I'm going to use it to lift up the story of your families and your communities.

Your story is about contributions. The contributions you make to a country that took so much and keeps asking for more, contributions like serving in the military at rates higher than any other group in America.

It is a story about hope. The hope you create as more Native people go to college, go to graduate school, and grow local economies.

It is a story about resilience. The resilience you show as you reclaim your history and your traditions.

And it is a story about pride and the determination of people who refuse to let their languages fade away and their cultures die.

I honor that story.

But there's another story that also needs to be told. The story of our country's mistreatment of your communities. And this isn't just a story about casual racism—war whoops and tomahawk chops and insulting Facebook memes.

It's a story about discrimination and neglect—the unmet health care needs of Native children and families, the alarmingly high rate of suicide among Native teenagers, the growing opioid crisis and the broader epidemic of substance abuse that has ravaged so many Native communities.

It's a story about greed. For generations—Congress after Congress, president after president—the government robbed you of your land, suppressed your languages, put your children in boarding schools and gave your babies away for adoption. It has stolen your resources and, for many tribal governments, taken away the opportunity to grow and prosper for the good of your people.

Even today, politicians in Washington want to let their big oil buddies pad their profits by encroaching on your land and fouling your rivers and streams. Meanwhile, even as the economic future of your communities hangs in the balance, they want to cut nutrition assistance, cut Medicaid, and cut other programs that many Native families rely on to survive.

It's a story about violence. It is deeply offensive that this president keeps a portrait of Andrew Jackson hanging in the Oval Office, honoring a man who did his best to wipe out Native people. But the kind of violence President Jackson and his allies perpetrated isn't just an ugly chapter in a history book. Violence remains part of life today. The majority of violent crimes experienced by Native Americans are perpetrated by non-Natives, and more than half—*half*—of Native women have experienced sexual violence.

This must stop. And I promise I will fight to help write a different story.

Washington owes you respect. But this government owes you much more than that. This government owes you a fighting chance to build stronger communities and a brighter future—starting with a more prosperous economic future on tribal lands.

For example. Banking and credit are the lifeblood of economic development, but it's about twelve miles on average from the center of tribal reservations to the nearest bank branch. Meanwhile, Native business owners get less start-up funding than other business owners.

And when it comes to crucial infrastructure, Native communities are far behind the rest of the country. Rural broadband access on tribal lands is worse than anywhere else in America, and more than a third of those living on tribal lands don't have high-speed broadband at all. Without it, Native communities are simply shut out of a twenty-first-century economy.

It's time to make real investments in Indian country to build opportunity for generations to come.

And that's only part of the real change we can make.

We can stop giant corporations from stealing your resources.

We can expand federally protected land that is important to your tribes.

We can protect historic monuments like Bears Ears from companies that see it as just another place to drill.

We can take steps to stop violence against Native people—including passing Savanna's Act to fight the plague of missing Native women and girls.

Most of all, we can fight to empower tribal governments and Native communities so you can take your rightful seat at the table when it comes to determining your own future.

And we can fight to make sure that all Americans who have been left out in our economy, left out in our democracy, and left out in our history can take their rightful seat at that table.

At a time when children are still drinking bottled water in Flint, when families are still desperate for help in Puerto Rico, and when tribal governments are still asking Washington to live up to its promises, we must demand a federal government that works for all of us—because if we don't, we become a country that belongs to only a privileged few.

That's why, even when divide-and-conquer looks to some like smart politics, we must choose unity. We must be willing to join together in each other's fights. And at a time when bigotry threatens to overwhelm our discourse, we must amplify voices of basic human respect.

We must stand with everyone who has gotten the short end of the stick from Washington over and over and over. We must weave our voices together to make them strong. We must come together to write a new story, not just for Native Americans, but for all Americans.

A story of power and respect. A story in which everyone's voice can be heard.

A story worthy of those who came before us. A story our children and grandchildren will be proud to tell.

Thank you!

PHOTO CREDITS

page 1   Newspapers.com (top). Oklahoma Historical Society (bottom).

page 2   Cleveland County Historical Society (top). Elizabeth Warren Campaign (bottom left and bottom right).

page 3   Elizabeth Warren Campaign (top). Northwest Classen High School Yearbook, 1964 (bottom).

page 4   Northwest Classen High School Yearbook, 1964 (top left). Northwest Classen High School Yearbook, 1966 (top right and bottom).

page 5   General Mills Archives (top). *Cherry Tree* yearbook, 1967, p. 74, Special Collections Research Center, George Washington University Libraries (middle). *Cherry Tree* yearbook, 1967–1968, p. 76, Special Collections Research Center, George Washington University Libraries (bottom).

page 6   *Cherry Tree* yearbook, 1967–1968, p. 124, Special Collections Research Center, George Washington University Libraries (top left). Elizabeth Warren Campaign (top right and bottom).

page 7   Elizabeth Warren Campaign (all).

page 8   Elizabeth Warren Campaign (top left). Suzanne Kreiter/Boston Globe via Getty Images (bottom).

page 9   Elizabeth Warren Campaign (all).

page 10   Alex Wong/Getty Images (top). Elizabeth Warren Campaign (middle). Darren Durlach/Boston Globe via Getty Images (bottom).

page 11   Elizabeth Warren Campaign (all).

page 12   Rick Freidman/Corbis via Getty Images (top left). Elizabeth Warren Campaign (top right and bottom).

NOTES

Introduction

1   Paolo Freire, *Pedagogy of the Oppressed*, 30th anniversary ed. (New York: Bloomsbury, 2001), 91.

2   Elizabeth Warren, "Elizabeth Warren's Democratic Convention Speech," September 5, 2012, ABC News, transcript, http://abcnews.go.com/Politics/OTUS /transcript-elizabeth-warrens-democratic-convention-speech/story?id=17164726.

3   Sheryl Sandberg, *Lean In: Women, Work, and the Will to Lead* (New York: Knopf, 2013), 47–48.

4   Michael Sherer, Sam Frizell, and Zeke J. Miller, "Up with People," *Time* magazine, July 20, 2015.

5   "U.S. Senate Confirms Jeff Sessions, Takes Tom Price Nomination," C-SPAN, February 6, 2017, https://www.c-span.org/video/?423606-103/us -senate-confirms-jeff-sessions-takes-tom-price-nomination.

6   Barbara Mikulski, phone interview with the author, December 4, 2017.

7   Jordan Crook, "Sen. Elizabeth Warren gets 6M+ Facebook Live Views after Being Silenced by Republicans," Tech Crunch, February 8, 2017, https://techcrunch. com/2017/02/08/sen-elizabeth-warren-gets-6m-facebook-live-views-after-being -silenced-by-republicans/.

8   Cornel West, Race Matters (Boston: Beacon Press, 2001), 8.

9   Elizabeth Warren, "Elizabeth Warren's Speech to the NAACP", *Detroit News*, April 23, 2017, http://www.detroitnews.com/videos/news/local/detroit-city/2017/04/23 /elizabeth-warren's-speech-naacp/100831660/.

Chapter 1

1   Willa Cather, "Prairie Spring," Poets.org, https://www.poets.org/poetsorg/poem/prairie-spring.

2   Bob Hammock, interview with the author, October 25, 2017.

3   Northwest Classen High School Roundtable yearbooks (1963–1966).

4   Jahree Herzer, interview with the author, October 25, 2017.

5   Katrina Cochran, interview with the author, January 12, 2018.

6   Russell Berman, "The Red-State Revolt Spreads to Oklahoma," *The Atlantic*, November 27, 2017, https://www.theatlantic.com/politics/archive/2017/11/the-red-state-revolt-spreads-to-oklahoma/546671/.

7   Lynn Rostochil, "From Civil Rights to The Who: A Look at Wedgewood Village Amusement Park," OkieModSquad, July 10, 2014, http://okcmod.com/2014/07/in-celebration-of-wedgewood/.

8   Jim Reid, *Daily Oklahoman*, 24.

9   Judy Garrett, phone interview with the author, November 16, 2017.

10 Garrett, interview.

11 Garrett, interview.

12 Joe Pryor, interview with the author, October 27, 2017.

13 Elizabeth Warren, "Elizabeth Warren's Democratic Convention Speech."

14 Joe Mallonee, phone interview with the author, November 7, 2017.

15 Don Mecoy, "Elizabeth Warren: An Okie in Washington Riles Wall Street," *The Oklahoman*, August 1, 2010, http://newsok.com/article/3481388.

16 Mallonee, interview.

17 Karl Johnson, phone interview with the author, January 17, 2018.

18 Karl Johnson, interview.

19 Pryor, interview.

20 Pryor, interview.

21 Karl Johnson, interview.

22 Karl Johnson, interview.

23 Pryor, interview.

24 Pryor, interview.

25 Pryor, interview.

26 Karl Johnson, interview.

27 Karl Johnson, interview.

28 Pryor, interview.

29 Mallonee, interview.

30 Karl Johnson, interview.

31 Northwest Classen High School Roundtable yearbook (1963).

32 Cochran, interview.

33 Cochran, interview.

34 Elizabeth Warren, *A Fighting Chance* (New York: Metropolitan Books, 2014), 13.

35 Warren, *A Fighting Chance*, 11.

36 Warren, *A Fighting Chance*, 11.

37 Northwest Classen High School Roundtable yearbook (1966), 71.

38 Northwest Classen High School Roundtable yearbook (1966), 9.

39 B. J. Osborn, *Wetumka: A Centennial History* (Lincoln, NE Writers Club Press, 2002), 80.

40 Osborn, *Wetumka*, 138.

41 Osborn, *Wetumka*, 131–141.

42 Elizabeth Warren, *This Fight Is Our Fight: The Battle to Save America's Middle Class* (New York: Metropolitan Books, 2017), 63.

43 Warren, *This Fight Is Our Fight*, 64.

44 Advertisements, *Democrat-American* (Sallisaw, OK), 1919–1935.

45 *Wetumka Gazette*, March 23, 1932.

46 Osborn, *Wetumka*, 26.

47 Elizabeth Warren and Amelia Warren Tyagi, *The Two-Income Trap: Why Middle-Class Parents Are Going Broke* (New York: Basic Books, 2003): 137.

48 Warren and Tyagi, *The Two-Income Trap*, 138.

49 "Local Happenings" newsletter, 5.

50 "Father of Local Man in Oil Game," *Democrat-American* (Sallisaw, OK), June 13, 1930.

51 "Father of Local Man in Oil Game."

52 American Oil and Gas Historical Society, "This Week in Petroleum History, December 4 to December 10," accessed November 2, 2017, https://aoghs.org/this-week-in-petroleum-history/december-7/.

53 Barb Ziegenmeyer, "History of Richland County: Origin of the County," Richland County, Illinois, Genealogy and History, accessed May 1, 2018, http://genealogytrails.com/ill/richland/richlandhistory1.html; "Rev. Joseph Reed memorial," FindAGrave.com, accessed May 1, 2018, https://www.findagrave.com/memorial/44310864.

54 Illinois Election Returns, 1818–1848, ed. by Theodore Calvin Pease, 400.

55 Warren, *A Fighting Chance*, 239.

56 Warren, *A Fighting Chance*, 239.

57 Wetumka Gazette Staff, "Herring-Reed," 1.

58 Jeffrey Toobin, "The Professor," *The New Yorker*, September 17, 2012, https://www.newyorker.com/magazine/2012/09/17/the-professor-5.

59 Warren, *A Fighting Chance*, 239–240.

60 Laurence French, *Native American Justice* (Chicago: Burnham, Inc., Publishers: 2003), 11.

61 Caryl-Sue, "1889: Oklahoma Land Rush," National Geographic This Day in History, last modified April 11, 2014, https://www.nationalgeographic.org/thisday/apr22/oklahoma-land-rush/.

62   Richard Mize, "Sequoyah Convention," *The Encyclopedia of Oklahoma History and Culture*, accessed April 30, 2018, http://www.okhistory.org/publications/enc/entry.php?entry=SE021.

63   Mize, "Sequoyah Convention."

64   ICT Staff Writer, "Elizabeth Warren's Genealogical Challenge," *Indian Country Today*, May 15, 2012, https://indiancountrymedianetwork.com/news/elizabeth-warrens-genealogical-challenge.

65   Cherokee Nation, accessed April 30, 2018, http://www.cherokee.org/About-The-Nation.

66   ElizabethforMA, "Elizabeth Warren's Speech to the National Congress of American Indians," YouTube, published February 14, 2018, accessed May 1, 2018, https://www.youtube.com/watch?v=eAxHa92QmTc.

67   ICT Staff Writer, "Elizabeth Warren's Genealogical Challenge."

68   ICT Staff Writer, "Elizabeth Warren's Genealogical Challenge."

69   Garance Franke-Ruta, "Is Elizabeth Warren Native American or What?" *The Atlantic*, May 20, 2012, https://www.theatlantic.com/politics/archive/2012/05/is-elizabeth-warren-native-american-or-what/257415/.

70   Michael Fullilove, *Rendezvous with Destiny: How Franklin D. Roosevelt and Five Extraordinary Men Took America into the War and into the World* (New York: Penguin, 2013), 98.

71   Fullilove, *Rendezvous with Destiny*, 98.

72   Warren, *A Fighting Chance*, 9.

73   Wallace F. Waits Jr., "Hatbox Field," *The Encyclopedia of Oklahoma History and Culture*, accessed April 30, 2018, http://www.okhistory.org/publications/enc/entry.php?entryname=HATBOX%20FIELD.

74   Dianna Everett, "Camp Gruber," The Encyclopedia of Oklahoma History and Culture, accessed May 1, 2018, http://www.okhistory.org/publications/enc/entry.php?entry=CA022.

75   Warren, *A Fighting Chance*, 9.

76   Sue Schrems and Vernon Maddux, *Images of America: Norman: 1889–1949* (Charleston, SC: Arcadia Publishing, 2013), 43.

77   Noah Bierman, "A Girl Who Soared, But Longed to Belong," *The Boston Globe*, February 12, 2012, https://www.bostonglobe.com/metro/2012/02/12/for-warren-seeds-activism-forged-plains-oklahoma/rx59B8AcqsZokclyJXkg7I/story.html.

78   Warren, *This Fight Is Our Fight*, 109.

79   Bierman, "A Girl Who Soared."

80   Schrems and Maddux, *Images of America*, 22.

81   Bierman, "A Girl Who Soared."

82   Warren, This Fight Is Our Fight, 108.

83   National Weather Service, "Norman, Oklahoma Tornadoes 1890–Present," accessed April 30, 2018, https://www.weather.gov/oun/tornadodata-city-ok-norman.

84 National Weather Service, "Tornadoes in the Oklahoma City, Oklahoma Area Since 1890," last modified February 2017, accessed April 30, 2018, https://www.weather.gov/oun/tornadodata-okc.

85 Warren, *A Fighting Chance*, 1.

86 Warren, *This Fight Is Our Fight*, 109.

87 Warren, *A Fighting Chance*, 10.

88 Warren, *A Fighting Chance*, 6.

89 Warren, *This Fight Is Our Fight*, 10–11.

90 Maeve Reston, "Elizabeth Warren, in Spotlight, Hits 'Late Show with David Letterman,'" *Los Angeles Times*, September 4, 2014, http://www.latimes.com/nation/politics/politicsnow/la-pn-elizabeth-warren-late-show-david-letterman-20140904-story.html.

91 Warren, *This Fight Is Our Fight*, 14.

92 Warren, *This Fight Is Our Fight*, 11.

93 Press release, "Senator Warren Delivers Remarks on Devastating Impact of GOP Tax Plan on Small Businesses," Elizabeth Warren's website, remarks at Center for American Progress event, November 14, 2017, https://www.warren.senate.gov/newsroom/press-releases/senator-warren-delivers-remarks-on-devastating-impact-of-gop-tax-plan-on-small-businesses.

94 Cochran, interview.

95 Pryor, interview.

96 Warren, *A Fighting Chance*, 10.

97 Cochran, interview.

98 Warren, *A Fighting Chance*, 32.

99 Kara Baskin, "Elizabeth Warren Was 1966's 'Betty Crocker Homemaker of Tomorrow,'" Grub Street, June 20, 2012, http://www.grubstreet.com/2012/06/elizabeth-warren-betty-crocker.html.

100 General Mills, "Betty Crocker Homemaker of Tomorrow Test Review 1966," 1965.

101 Warren, *This Fight Is Our Fight*, 110.

102 Angela Davis, *Women, Race, and Class* (New Delhi: Navayana, 2011), 231.

103 Warren, *This Fight Is Our Fight*, 109.

104 General Mills, "Betty Crocker."

105 Mikulski, interview.

106 Warren, *This Fight Is Our Fight*, 109.

107 General Mills, "Betty Crocker."

108 Baskin, "Elizabeth Warren Was 1966's 'Betty Crocker Homemaker of Tomorrow.'"

109 Warren, *This Fight Is Our Fight*, 11.

110 Warren, *A Fighting Chance*, 11–12.

111 Warren, *A Fighting Chance*, 12.

112 Warren, *A Fighting Chance*, 13.

113 Warren and Tyagi, *The Two-Income Trap*, 61.

114 Mallonee, interview.

115 Northwest Classen High School Roundtable yearbook (1966), 233.

116 "Battlefield: Vietnam Timeline," PBS.org, accessed April 30, 2018, http://www
.pbs.org/battlefieldvietnam/timeline/index1.html.

Chapter 2

1   Elizabeth Warren, "The Market for Data: The Changing Role of Social Sciences
in Shaping the Law," Wisconsin Law Review, no. 1 (October 13, 2002).

2   Harry Kreisler, "Law, Politics, and the Coming Collapse of the Middle Class,"
Berkeley Globetrotter, accessed April 30, 2018, http://globetrotter.berkeley.edu
/people7/Warren/warren-con1.html.

3   Dennis Henigan, phone interview with the author, January 26, 2018.

4   Bill Toutant, phone interview with the author, January 10, 2018.

5   Henigan, interview.

6   Cherry Tree yearbook, George Washington University Cherry Tree yearbook
(1967–1968), 76, https://ia801302.us.archive.org/0/items/gwu_cherry_tree_1968
/gwu_cherry_tree_1968.pdf.

7   "Gregory B. Millard, 37, Arts Official with City," *New York Times*, October 7, 1984,
https://www.nytimes.com/1984/10/07/obituaries/gregory-b-millard-37-arts
-official-with-city.html.

8   American Forensic Association, National Debate Tournament Topics 1946–2012,
http://groups.wfu.edu/NDT/HistoricalLists/topics.html.

9   Toutant, interview.

10   Henigan, interview.

11   DiscoverGW, "Senator Elizabeth Warren Discusses Her Time at GW," YouTube,
published May 8, 2013, https://www.youtube.com/watch?v=4CBbiZYQ0mg.

12   George Washington University Cherry Tree yearbook (1967), 208, https
://ia601304.us.archive.org/18/items/gwu_cherry_tree_1967/gwu_cherry_tree
_1967.pdf.

13   DiscoverGW, "Senator Elizabeth Warren Discusses Her Time at GW."

14   DiscoverGW, "Senator Elizabeth Warren Discusses Her Time at GW."

15   George Washington University Cherry Tree yearbook (1967–1968), 76, https
://ia801302.us.archive.org/0/items/gwu_cherry_tree_1968/gwu_cherry_tree
_1968.pdf.

16   Clay Dillow and Brooks Rainwater, "Why Free Money for Everyone Is Silicon
Valley's Next Big Idea," Fortune, June 29, 2017, http://fortune.com/2017/06/29
/universal-basic-income-free-money-silicon-valley/.

17   Warren, *A Fighting Chance*, 13.

18   Warren, *This Fight Is Our Fight*, 104.

19   Warren, *This Fight Is Our Fight*, 110.

20   Warren, *A Fighting Chance*, 13.

21   Texas Divorce Index, November 3, 1968.

22   Warren, *This Fight Is Our Fight*, 111.

23   Jason Perlow,"IBM and UNIVAC in the Apollo Program," ZDNet.com, July 13, 2009, http://www.zdnet.com/pictures/ibm-and-univac-in-the-apollo-program/.

24   IBM, "The Apollo Missions," IBM 100, accessed May 1, 2018, http://www-03 .ibm.com/ibm/history/ibm100/us/en/icons/apollo/.

25   Warren, *This Fight Is Our Fight*, 104.

26   Warren, *This Fight Is Our Fight*, 111.

27   Warren, *This Fight Is Our Fight*, 111.

28   Kathleen O'Brien, "How Elizabeth Warren's Rutgers Roots Forged Her Future VP Prospects," NJ.com, last modified June 26, 2016, http://www.nj.com/news /index.ssf/2016/06/sen_elizabeth_warren_-_her_jersey_years.html.

29   Warren, *A Fighting Chance*, 14.

30   Warren, *This Fight Is Our Fight*, 111.

31   Warren, *A Fighting Chance*, 14.

32   O'Brien, "How Elizabeth Warren's Rutgers Roots Forged Her Future VP Prospects."

33   Kreisler, "Law, Politics, and the Coming Collapse of the Middle Class."

34   Warren, *A Fighting Chance*, 14.

35   Warren, *A Fighting Chance*, 14.

36   Warren, *A Fighting Chance*, 15.

37   Kreisler, "Law, Politics, and the Coming Collapse of the Middle Class."

38   Warren, *A Fighting Chance*, 14.

39   Warren, *A Fighting Chance*, 15.

40   Kreisler, "Law, Politics, and the Coming Collapse of the Middle Class."

41   Warren, *A Fighting Chance*, 15.

42   Warren, *This Fight Is Our Fight*, 111; Bob Braun, "Head of Congressional Oversight Panel Has New Jersey Roots,"NJ.com, last modified September 1, 2009, http://blog.nj.com/njv_bob_braun/2009/06/head_of_congressional_oversigh. html; Jocelyn K. Wilk, University Archivist, Columbia University Rare Book and Manuscript Library, email interview with the author, January 24, 2018.

43   Kreisler, "Law, Politics, and the Coming Collapse of the Middle Class."

44   Paul Tractenberg, *A Centennial History of Rutgers Law School in Newark: Opening a Thousand Doors* (Charleston, SC: The History Press, 2010), chapter 4.

45   Tractenberg, *A Centennial History of Rutgers Law School in Newark*, chapter 4.

46   Tractenberg, *A Centennial History of Rutgers Law School in Newark*, chapter 4.

47   Tractenberg, *A Centennial History of Rutgers Law School in Newark*, chapter 4.

48   O'Brien, "How Elizabeth Warren's Rutgers Roots Forged Her Future VP Prospects."

49   Warren, A Fighting Chance, 16.

50 Cynthia Grant Bowman, "Women in the Legal Profession from the 1920s to the 1970s: What Can We Learn from Their Experience about Law and Social Change?" Maine Law Review 61, no. 1 (2009): 1–25.

51 Bowman, "Women in the Legal Profession from the 1920s to the 1970s."

52 Elizabeth Warren, "Rutgers School of Law Commencement Address," May 26, 2011.

53 RutgersNewark, "Interview with RU-N Alumna Elizabeth Warren," YouTube, published November 9, 2011, https://www.youtube.com/watch?v=NItCGcV84GM&t=203s.

54 O'Brien, "How Elizabeth Warren's Rutgers Roots Forged Her Future VP Prospects."

55 O'Brien, "How Elizabeth Warren's Rutgers Roots Forged Her Future VP Prospects."

56 Calvin Johnson, phone interview with the author, January 23, 2018.

57 Ruth Bader Ginsburg, "In Memory of Allan Axelrod," Rutgers Law Review 61, no. 1 (2008): 14–15.

58 Stephanie Panico, "In Memory of Allan Axelrod," Rutgers Law Review 61, no. 1 (2008): 28.

59 Howard A. Latin, "In Memory of Allan Axelrod," Rutgers Law Review 61, no. 1 (2008): 27.

60 Ginsburg, "In Memory of Allan Axelrod," 14.

61 Calvin Johnson, interview.

62 RutgersNewark, "Interview with RU-N Alumna Elizabeth Warren."

63 RutgersNewark, "Interview with RU-N Alumna Elizabeth Warren."

64 RutgersNewark, "Interview with RU-N Alumna Elizabeth Warren."

65 Elizabeth Warren, "Busing: Supreme Court Restricts Equity Powers of District Courts to Order Interschool Busing," Rutgers Law Review 28 (1975).

66 Warren, A Fighting Chance, 16.

67 Michael Scherer, "The New Sheriffs of Wall Street," Time magazine, May 13, 2010, http://content.time.com/time/magazine/article/0,9171,1989144,00.html.

68 Warren, A Fighting Chance, 17.

69 Warren, A Fighting Chance, 17.

70 Kreisler, "Law, Politics, and the Coming Collapse of the Middle Class."

71 Warren, A Fighting Chance, 18.

72 Kreisler, "Law, Politics, and the Coming Collapse of the Middle Class."

73 Calvin Johnson, interview.

74 O'Brien, "How Elizabeth Warren's Rutgers Roots Forged Her Future VP Prospects."

75 Elizabeth Warren, "Regulated Industries' Automatic Cost of Service Adjustment Clauses: Do They Increase or Decrease Cost to the Consumer," Notre Dame Law Review 55, no. 3 (1980): 333–355.

76 Warren, A Fighting Chance, 18.

77 Warren, A Fighting Chance, 18–19.

78 Julius Getman, In the Company of Scholars: The Struggle for the Soul of Higher Education (Austin: University of Texas Press, 1992).

79 John Mixon, *Autobiography of a Law School: Stories, Memories, and Interpretations of My Sixty Years at the University of Houston Law Center* (Houston: University of Houston Law Foundation, 2012), 338.

80 Elizabeth Warren, "Rutgers School of Law Commencement Address."

Chapter 3

1   Bertolt Brecht, *The Rise and Fall of the City of Mahagonny*, trans. and ed. by Steve Gils (London: Methuen Drama, 2007).

2   Warren, *A Fighting Chance*, 20; "Irene Merker Rosenberg," University of Houston Law Center Faculty, accessed May 2, 2018, http://www.law.uh.edu/faculty/main.asp?PID=37.

3   Cynthia Fuchs Epstein, *Women in Law*, 2nd. ed. (Urbana: University of Illinois Press, 1993), 220–221.

4   Getman, *In the Company of Scholars*.

5   Mixon, *Autobiography of a Law School*, 321.

6   Mixon, *Autobiography of a Law School*, 339.

7   Julia Jacobs and Victoria McGrane, "This Isn't the First Time Warren Spoke about That Office Incident," *Boston Globe*, October 24, 2017, http://www.bostonglobe.com/news/politics/2017/10/23/warren-view-office-incident-evolved-along-with-society-changing-approach-harassment/qVgXJtPz4s8Imw7bJW034H/story.html?s_campaign=bdc:article:stub.

8   NBC News, "Women Senators Say #MeToo, Reveal Stories of Sexual Harassment," YouTube, published October 23, 2017, https://www.youtube.com/watch?v=Q5fhDShPCvA, corrected against NBC, Meet the Press transcript, https://www.nbcnews.com/meet-the-press/meet-press-october-22-2017-n813071.

9   Jacobs and McGrane, "This Isn't the First Time."

10 Joe Dwinell, "Advocates: Elizabeth Warren's Story Is 'Universal," *Boston Herald*, October 25, 2017, http://www.bostonherald.com/news/local_coverage/2017/10/advocates_elizabeth_warren_s_story_is_universal.

11 Mixon, *Autobiography of a Law School*, 339.

12 Jacobs and McGrane, "This Isn't the First Time."

13 Sarah Mirk, "These Letters about Sexual Harassment from the 1970s Could Be about Trump Today," BitchMedia, October 19, 2016, https://www.bitchmedia.org/article/these-letters-about-sexual-harassment-1970s-could-be-about-trump-today.

14 Eric Gerber, "Elizabeth Warren Looks Back at Her Cougar Roots," *University of Houston Magazine* (Spring 2003): 27.

15 Mixon, *Autobiography of a Law School*, 338

16 Gerber, "Elizabeth Warren Looks Back at Her Cougar Roots," 27.

17 Mixon, *Autobiography of a Law School*, 338.

18 Getman, *In the Company of Scholars*.

19 Warren, *A Fighting Chance*, 20.

20 Warren, *A Fighting Chance*, 21.

21   Warren, *A Fighting Chance*, 21.

22   Warren, *A Fighting Chance*, 21–22.

23   Warren, *A Fighting Chance*, 22–23.

24   Warren, *A Fighting Chance*, 23.

25   Warren, *A Fighting Chance*, 24.

26   Warren, *A Fighting Chance*, 23.

27   Warren, *A Fighting Chance*, 24.

28   John Mixon, phone interview with the author, January 3, 2018.

29   Investopedia Staff, "Economic Efficiency," Investopedia, accessed May 2, 2018, https://www.investopedia.com/terms/e/economic_efficiency.asp.

30   Investopedia Staff, "Rational Choice Theory," Investopedia, accessed May 2, 2018, https://www.investopedia.com/terms/r/rational-choice-theory.asp.

31   Calvin Johnson, interview.

32   Jason DeParle, "Goals Reached, Donor on Right Closes Up Shop," *New York Times*, May 29, 2005, http://www.nytimes.com/2005/05/29/politics/goals-reached -donor-on-right-closes-up-shop.html.

33   DeParle, "Goals Reached."

34   DeParle, "Goals Reached."

35   Jane Mayer, *Dark Money: The Hidden History of the Billionaires Behind the Rise of the Radical Right* (New York: Anchor Books, 2017), 132.

36   DeParle, "Goals Reached."

37   Mayer, *Dark Money*, 132.

38   University of Chicago Law School, "Henry G. Manne, '52, 1928–2015," accessed May 2, 2018, https://www.law.uchicago.edu/news/henry-g-manne-52-1928-2015.

39   Calvin Johnson, interview.

40   DeParle, "Goals Reached."

41   Mixon, interview.

42   Warren, *A Fighting Chance*, 25.

43   Liz Brunner, "At Home with Elizabeth Warren," WCVB, November 5, 2012, http://www.wcvb.com/article/at-home-with-elizabeth-warren/7863078.

44   Warren, *A Fighting Chance*, 26.

45   Elizabeth Warren, Facebook post, July 12, 2016, https://www.facebook.com /ElizabethWarren/posts/10153894305058687:0.

46   Warren, *A Fighting Chance*, 26.

47   Warren, Facebook post.

48   Warren, *A Fighting Chance*, 26–27.

49   Mixon, interview.

50   Warren, *A Fighting Chance*, 26.

51   Warren, *A Fighting Chance*, 26.

52   Glenn E. Pasvogel Jr., "The Bankruptcy Reform Act of 1978—A Review and Comments," *University of Arkansas at Little Rock Law Review* 13, no. 3 (1980): 13.

53 Warren, *A Fighting Chance*, 27.

54 Warren, *A Fighting Chance*, 28.

55 Warren, "The Market for Data," 7.

56 Warren, "The Market for Data," 7.

57 Warren, *A Fighting Chance*, 28.

58 Warren, *A Fighting Chance*, 29.

59 Patricia Cain, phone interview with the author, January 31, 2018.

60 Elizabeth Warren CV, Harvard Law School Faculty, accessed May 2, 2018, http ://www.law.harvard.edu/faculty/ewarren/Warren%20CV%20062508.pdf.

61 Calvin Johnson, interview.

62 Warren, *A Fighting Chance*, 30–31.

63 Warren, *A Fighting Chance*, 31.

64 Mark Gergen, phone interview with the author, January 26, 2018.

65 Cain, interview.

66 Cain, interview.

67 Cain, interview.

68 Warren, *A Fighting Chance*, 33.

69 Kreisler, "Law, Politics, and the Coming Collapse of the Middle Class."

70 Kreisler, "Law, Politics, and the Coming Collapse of the Middle Class."

71 Teresa A. Sullivan, Jay Lawrence Westbrook, and Elizabeth Warren, *As We Forgive Our Debtors: Bankruptcy and Consumer Credit in America* (Beard Books, 1999), 4.

72 Sullivan, Westbrook, and Warren, *As We Forgive Our Debtors*, 8.

73 Sullivan, Westbrook, and Warren, *As We Forgive Our Debtors*, 4.

74 Sullivan, Westbrook, and Warren, *As We Forgive Our Debtors*, 5.

75 Sullivan, Westbrook, and Warren, *As We Forgive Our Debtors*, xiii.

76 Mixon, interview.

77 Getman, *In the Company of Scholars*.

78 Gergen, interview.

79 John Mixon, "Neoclassical Economics and the Erosion of Middle-Class Values: An Explanation for Economic Collapse," *Notre Dame Journal of Law, Ethics & Public Policy* 24, no. 2 (2011): 355.

80 Mixon, "Neoclassical Economics," 369.

Chapter 4

1 Paul Krugman, *The Conscience of a Liberal* (New York: Norton, 2009), 18.

2 Warren, *A Fighting Chance*, 34.

3 Teresa A. Sullivan, Jay Lawrence Westbrook, and Elizabeth Warren, "Laws, Models, and Real People: Choice of Chapter in Personal Bankruptcy," *Law & Social Inquiry* 13, no. 4 (Autumn 1988): 668.

4 Sullivan, Westbrook, and Warren, "Laws, Models, and Real People," 662.

5 Sullivan, Westbrook, and Warren, "Laws, Models, and Real People," 662.

6   Calvin Johnson, interview.

7   Warren, "The Market for Data," 36.

8   Warren, *A Fighting Chance*, 36.

9   Bob Hammack, interview with the author, October 26, 2017.

10 Gergen, interview.

11 Isabelle Taft, "How a Decade in Texas Changed Elizabeth Warren," *The Texas Tribune*, July 13, 2016, https://www.texastribune.org/2016/07/13 /how-decade-texas-changed-elizabeth-warren/.

12 Warren, *A Fighting Chance*, 38.

13 Gergen, interview.

14 Warren, *A Fighting Chance*, 38–40.

15 Fox Butterfield, "Harvard Law Professor Quits Until Black Woman Is Named," *New York Times*, April 24, 1990, https://www.nytimes.com/1990/04/24/us /harvard-law-professor-quits-until-black-woman-is-named.html.

16 Butterfield, "Harvard Law Professor Quits."

17 "Regina Austin L'73," University of Pennsylvania Law School, accessed May 2, 2018, https://www.law.upenn.edu/cf/faculty/raustin/.

18 American Bar Association, "A Snapshot of Women in the Law in the Year 2000," accessed May 2, 2018, https://www.americanbar.org/content/dam/aba/marketing /women/snapshots.authcheckdam.pdf.

19 Alix James, phone interview with the author, January 12, 2018.

20 James, interview.

21 James, interview.

22 James, interview.

23 Elizabeth Warren, "Bankruptcy Policy," *University of Chicago Law Review*, no. 775 (1987): 776.

24 Warren, "Bankruptcy Policy," 778.

25 Warren, "Bankruptcy Policy," 812.

26 Warren, "Bankruptcy Policy," 814.

27 Sullivan, Westbrook, and Warren, *As We Forgive Our Debtors*, 10.

28 Sullivan, Westbrook, and Warren, *As We Forgive Our Debtors*, 91.

29 Sullivan, Westbrook, and Warren, *As We Forgive Our Debtors*, 188.

30 Sullivan, Westbrook, and Warren, *As We Forgive Our Debtors*, 158.

31 Sullivan, Westbrook, and Warren, *As We Forgive Our Debtors*, 77.

32 "Personal Bankruptcies Exceed 700,000, Survey Shows," United Press International, March 6, 1991, https://www.upi.com/Archives/1991/03/06/Personal -bankruptcies-exceed-700000-survey-shows/5045668235600/ph.

33 Bruce Mann, "Failure in the Land of the Free," *American Bankruptcy Law Journal* 77, no. 1 (Winter 2003): 1.

34 Mann, "Failure in the Land of the Free," 1.

35 Mann, "Failure in the Land of the Free," 2.

36   Bruce Mann, "Tales from the Crypt: Prison, Legal Authority, and the Debtors' Constitution in the Early Republic," *The William and Mary Quarterly* 51, no. 2 (1994): 183–202.

37   Mann, "Tales from the Crypt," 193.

38   "Appointments," *The Law Alumni Journal* 25, no. 3 (Spring 1990): 2, http://scholarship.law.upenn.edu/cgi/viewcontent.cgi?article=1060&context=plj.

39   Elizabeth Warren CV.

40   Warren, *A Fighting Chance*, 44.

41   Warren, *A Fighting Chance*, 44.

42   Warren, *A Fighting Chance*, 44–45.

43   Fox Butterfield, "First Black Elected to Head Harvard's Law Review," *New York Times*, February 6, 1990, https://www.nytimes.com/1990/02/06/us/first-black-elected-to-head-harvard-s-law-review.html.

44   Warren, *A Fighting Chance*, 45.

45   Warren, *A Fighting Chance*, 43–44.

46   Warren, *A Fighting Chance*, 46.

47   Warren, *A Fighting Chance*, 46.

48   Nancy Moffitt, "The Two-Income Trap," *Wharton Magazine*, accessed May 2, 2018, http://whartonmagazine.com/issues/fall-2003/the-two-income-trap/#sthash.nisAOOOP.dpbs.

49   Michael Levenson, "Warren and Brown Share July 12 Anniversary Date," *Boston Globe*, July 11, 2012, https://www.bostonglobe.com/metro/massachusetts/2012/07/11/warren-and-brown-share-july-anniversary-date-can-you-believe-brown-warren-share-same-wedding-day/8Hdc2c9xDb5v1DuzrpypjO/story.html.

50   CNN Library, "Oklahoma City Bombing Fast Facts," CNN, last modified March 25, 2018, https://www.cnn.com/2013/09/18/us/oklahoma-city-bombing-fast-facts/index.html.

51   Warren, *A Fighting Chance*, 47.

52   Warren, *A Fighting Chance*, 46.

53   Warren, *A Fighting Chance*, 47.

54   Adam S. Hickey, "Harvard's Top Five Salaries Total More Than $1.5M," *The Harvard Crimson*, September 19, 1997, http://www.thecrimson.com/article/1997/9/19/harvards-top-five-salaries-total-more/.

55   Warren, *A Fighting Chance*, 32.

56   RutgersNewark, "Interview with RU-N Alumna Elizabeth Warren."

Chapter 5

1   Edward W. Said, "The Public Role of Writers and Intellectuals," in Helen Small, ed., *The Public Intellectual* (Oxford: Blackwell Publishers Ltd, 2002), 19–39.

2   Bruce A. Kimball, "The Proliferation of Case Method Teaching in American

Law Schools: Mr. Langdell's Emblematic 'Abomination,' 1890–1915." *History of Education Quarterly* 46, no. 2 (Summer 2006): 227.

3   Kreisler, "Law, Politics, and the Coming Collapse of the Middle Class."

4   Top Law Schools, "Dissecting the Rankings: The U.S. News and World Report," accessed May 3, 2018, http://www.top-law-schools.com/dissecting-the-rankings -news-world-report.html; 7Sage, "Top Law School Rankings from U.S. News, accessed May 3, 2018, https://7sage.com/top-law-school-rankings/.

5   Douglas Peterson, phone interview with the author, February 5, 2018.

6   Peterson, interview.

7   Douglas Moll, phone interview with the author, January 9, 2018.

8   Anthony Flint, "10 Years Later, Did the Big Dig Deliver?" *Boston Globe*, December 29, 2015, https://www.bostonglobe.com/magazine/2015/12/29/years -later-did-big-dig-deliver/tSb8PIMS4QJUETsMpA7SpI/story.html.

9   Chrystin Ondersma, phone interview with the author, January 3, 2018.

10 Ondersma, interview.

11 Elizabeth Warren, "Professor Elizabeth Warren," ElizabethWarren.com email, December 28, 2017.

12 Moll, interview.

13 Ronald J. Mann, phone interview with the author, January 29, 2018.

14 Katherine Porter, phone interview with the author, October 3, 2017.

15 Elizabeth Warren and Jay Lawrence Westbrook, *The Law of Debtors and Creditors: Text, Cases, and Problems* (Gaithersburg: Aspen, 2001), xxiii.

16 Porter, interview.

17 Porter, interview.

18 Porter, interview.

19 Kristie Blunt Welder, interview with the author, April 18, 2018.

20 Warren, *A Fighting Chance*, 52.

21 Warren, *A Fighting Chance*, 48.

22 Federal Register, National Bankruptcy Review Commission, accessed May 3, 2018, https://www.federalregister.gov/agencies/national-bankruptcy-review-commission.

23 Warren, *A Fighting Chance*, 48.

24 David Binder, "Ex-Congressman Mike Synar, Oklahoma Liberal, Dies at 45," *New York Times*, Janary 10, 1996, http://www.nytimes.com/1996/01/10/us/ex -congressman-mike-synar-oklahoma-liberal-dies-at-45.html; and Todd J. Kosmerick, "Synar, Michael Lynn," *The Encyclopedia of Oklahoma History and Culture*, accessed May 3, 2018, http://www.okhistory.org/publications/enc/entry.php?entry=SY001.

25 Warren, *A Fighting Chance*, 49–50.

26 Warren, *A Fighting Chance*, 50.

27 David Binder, "Ex-Congressman Mike Synar, Oklahoma Liberal, Dies at 45."

28 Warren, *A Fighting Chance*, 54.

29 Warren, *A Fighting Chance*, 55.

30 Warren, *A Fighting Chance*, 54.

31 Warren, *A Fighting Chance*, 56.

32 National Bankruptcy Review Commission, "Recommendations to Congress," accessed May 3, 2018, http://govinfo.library.unt.edu/nbrc/report/03recomm.html.

33 Warren, *A Fighting Chance*, 59.

34 Warren, *A Fighting Chance*, 57.

35 Warren, *A Fighting Chance*, 58.

36 Teresa A. Sullivan, Elizabeth Warren, and Jay Lawrence Westbrook, *The Fragile Middle Class: Americans in Debt* (New Haven, CT: Yale University Press, 2000), 135.

37 Robert M. Lawless and Elizabeth Warren, "Shrinking the Safety Net: The 2005 Changes in U.S. Bankruptcy Law," *University of Illinois College of Law*, no. 6 (2006), https://papers.ssrn.com/sol3/papers.cfm?abstract_id=949629.

38 Sullivan, Warren, and Westbrook, *The Fragile Middle Class*, 135.

39 Warren, *A Fighting Chance*, 60–61.

40 Warren, *A Fighting Chance*, 61.

41 Warren, *A Fighting Chance*, 64.

42 Peter Dreier, "Paul Wellstone's Life and Legacy," Huffington Post, October 12, 2012, https://www.huffingtonpost.com/peter-dreier/paul-wellstones-life-and-_b_1961277.html.

43 Paul Wellstone, *The Conscience of a Liberal: Reclaiming the Compassionate Agenda* (New York: Random House, 2001).

44 Elizabeth Warren, Humphrey School of Public Affairs, "The Democratic Party at a Crossroads: The Wellstone Way and Economic Populism," SoundCloud, October 26, 2017, https://soundcloud.com/user-179867903/part-2-the-democratic-party-at-a-crossroads-the-wellstone-way-and-economic-populism.

45 Warren, "The Democratic Party at a Crossroads."

46 Perry Lange, phone interview with the author, December 22, 2017.

47 Lange, interview.

48 John Nichols, "From Paul Wellstone to Elizabeth Warren," *The Nation*, October 25, 2012, https://www.thenation.com/article/paul-wellstone-elizabeth-warren/.

49 Warren, *A Fighting Chance*, 64.

50 Glen Thrush and Manu Raju, "The Outsider," *Politico*, March/April 2015, https://www.politico.com/magazine/story/2015/03/elizabeth-warren-profile-115489.

51 Warren and Tyagi, *The Two-Income Trap*, 126.

52 Tim Haines, "Clinton: Flip-Flop on Bankruptcy Bill 'Had Nothing to Do with Money,' 'It Was about Protecting Women,'" RealClear Politics, February 7, 2016, https://www.realclearpolitics.com/video/2016/02/07/clinton_accuses_sanders_and_warren_of_smear_campaign.html.

53 Dreier, "Paul Wellstone's Life and Legacy."

54 Lange, interview.

55 Perry Lange, personal communications.

56   Nichols, "From Paul Wellstone to Elizabeth Warren."

57   Nichols, "From Paul Wellstone to Elizabeth Warren."

58   Warren, *A Fighting Chance*, 81.

59   Warren, *A Fighting Chance*, 80.

60   Kreisler, "Law, Politics, and the Coming Collapse of the Middle Class."

61   Kreisler, "Law, Politics, and the Coming Collapse of the Middle Class."

62   Sullivan, Warren, and Westbrook, *The Fragile Middle Class*, 7.

63   Sullivan, Warren, and Westbrook, *The Fragile Middle Class*, 15–22.

64   Lisa Kaczke, "Elizabeth Warren's Appearances as a Financial Expert on TV Talk Shows Helped Launch Her Political Career," MassLive, January 26, 2012, http://www .masslive.com/politics/index.ssf/2012/01/elizabeth_warren_appeared_as_f.html.

65   Ryan Grim, "Elizabeth Warren on Her Journey from Low-Information Voter," The Intercept, February 19, 2018, https://theintercept.com/2018/02/19/elizabeth -warren-opens-up-about-her-choices-in-every-presidential-election-since-1972/.

66   Jeff Spross, "Why Elizabeth Warren Left the GOP," ThinkProgress, April 27, 2014, https://thinkprogress.org/why-elizabeth-warren-left-the-gop-e78680711424/.

67   Warren, *A Fighting Chance*, 70.

68   Moffitt, "The Two-Income Trap."

69   Sushil Tyahi LinkedIn, accessed May 3, 2018, https://www.linkedin.com/in /sushil-tyagi-a99138/.

70   Warren, *A Fighting Chance*, 70.

71   Warren and Tyagi, *The Two-Income Trap*, 5.

72   Warren and Tyagi, *The Two-Income Trap*, 71.

73   Stephanie Ebbert, "Daughter of Elizabeth Warren Claims Center Stage," *Boston Globe*, August 11, 2012, https://www.bostonglobe.com/metro/2012/08/11/daughter -elizabeth-warren-claims-center-stage/s92JYWy0MnZkt8ktXVvquL/story.html.

74   Warren and Tyagi, *The Two-Income Trap*, 8.

75   Bradford Plumer, "The Two-Income Trap," Mother Jones, November 8, 2004, https://www.motherjones.com/politics/2004/11/two-income-trap/.

76   Warren and Tyagi, *The Two-Income Trap*, 6.

77   Warren and Tyagi, *The Two-Income Trap*, 169.

78   Warren and Tyagi, *The Two-Income Trap*, 36.

79   Warren and Tyagi, *The Two-Income Trap*, 36.

80   Warren and Tyagi, *The Two-Income Trap*, 132.

81   "The Two-Income Trap," Little, Brown website, accessed May 3, 2018, https:// www.littlebrown.co.uk/books/detail.page?isbn=9780465097708.

82   "The Two-Income Trap," Little, Brown website.

83   Jeff Madrick, "Economic Scene; Necessities, Not Luxuries, Are Driving Americans into Debt, a New Book Says," *New York Times*, September 4, 2003, https://www.nytimes.com/2003/09/04/business/economic-scene-necessities-not -luxuries-are-driving-americans-into-debt-new-book.html.

84 Michele Norris, "Two-Income Ramilies at Risk of Financial Crisis," *All Things Considered*, NPR, September 8, 2003, https://www.npr.org/templates/story/story .php?storyId=1423789.

85 Warren, *A Fighting Chance*, 75.

86 Dr. Phil, "Going for Broke," Dr. Phil, accessed May 3, 2018, https://www.drphil .com/slideshows/going-for-broke-financial-advice/.

87 Sam Brodey, "Andy Slavitt Already Saved Obamacare Once. Can He Do It Again?" MinnPost, March 23, 2017, https://www.minnpost.com/politics-policy/2017/03 /andy-slavitt-already-saved-obamacare-once-can-he-do-it-again.

88 Ebbert, "Daughter of Elizabeth Warren Claims Center Stage."

89 Moffitt, "The Two-Income Trap."

90 Regina E. Herzlinger, ed., *Consumer-Driven Health Care: Implications for Providers, Payers, and Policymakers* (San Francisco: John Wiley & Sons, Inc., 2004), 138.

91 Ebbert, "Daughter of Elizabeth Warren Claims Center Stage."

92 Ebbert, "Daughter of Elizabeth Warren Claims Center Stage."

93 Jody Greenstone Miller and Matt Miller, "The Rise of the Supertemp," *Harvard Business Review*, May 2012, https://hbr.org/2012/05/the-rise-of-the-supertemp.

94 Peter Coy, "The Disposable Worker" BusinessWeek, January 18, 2010.

95 Business Talent Group website, accessed May 3, 2018, https://businesstalentgroup.com.

96 Business Talent Group website, accessed May 3, 2018, https://businesstalentgroup.com.

97 Warren, *A Fighting Chance*, 181.

98 Ebbert, "Daughter of Elizabeth Warren Claims Center Stage."

99 Warren, *A Fighting Chance*, 24.

100 Warren, *A Fighting Chance*, 77.

101 Warren, *A Fighting Chance*, 58.

102 Warren, *A Fighting Chance*, 79.

103 "Bruce H. Mann," Harvard Law School Faculty, accessed May 3, 2018, http://hls .harvard.edu/faculty/directory/10550/Mann.

104 Bruce Mann, *Republic of Debtors: Bankruptcy in the Age of American Independence* (Boston: Harvard University Press, 2009), viii.

105 Mann, *Republic of Debtors*, 261.

106 Mann, *Republic of Debtors*, 8.

107 "Bruce H. Mann," Harvard Law School Faculty.

Chapter 6

1 David Wellstone, Humphrey School of Public Affairs, "The Democratic Party at a Crossroads."

2 Daniel McGinn, "Why a Harvard Professor Is Overseeing the Bailout," *Newsweek*, April 10, 2009, http://www.newsweek.com/why-harvard-professor-overseeing-bailout-77401.

3 Warren, *A Fighting Chance*, 82.

4 Kreisler, "Law, Politics, and the Coming Collapse of the Middle Class."

5   Neva Goodwin et al., *Macroeconomics in Context,* 2nd ed. (New York: Routledge, 2014), 338.

6   Goodwin et al., *Macroeconomics in Context,* 337.

7   Ryan Lizza, "The Virtual Candidate," *The New Yorker,* May 4, 2015, https://www.newyorker.com/magazine/2015/05/04/the-virtual-candidate.

8   Charles Pierce, "What We Learn from Elizabeth Warren," *Esquire,* June 10, 2018, https://www.esquire.com/news-politics/politics/a26352/elizabeth-warren-teacher-0514/.

9   Pierce, "What We Learn from Elizabeth Warren."

10   Pierce, "What We Learn from Elizabeth Warren."

11   Michael Grunwald, "The Real Truth about the Wall Street Bailouts," *Time* magazine, September 30, 2014, http://time.com/3450110/aig-lehman/.

12   Goodwin et al., *Macroeconomics in Context,* 337, 341.

13   Ylan Q. Mui, "Americans Saw Wealth Plummet 40 Percent from 2007 to 2010, Federal Reserve Says," *The Washington Post,* June 11, 2012, https://www.washingtonpost.com/business/economy/fed-americans-wealth-dropped-40-percent/2012/06/11/gJQAllsCVV_story.html?utm_term=.79553e77da67.

14   Nathalie Baptiste, "Them That's Got Shall Get," Prospect.org, October 12, 2014, http://prospect.org/article/staggering-loss-black-wealth-due-subprime-scandal-continues-unabated.

15   Baptiste, "Them That's Got Shall Get."

16   Warren and Tyagi, *The Two-Income Trap.*

17   Warren, *A Fighting Chance,* 43.

18   Harry Reid, interview with the author, November 10, 2017.

19   Warren, *A Fighting Chance,* 94.

20   Congressional Oversight Panel archive, accessed May 3, 2018, https://cybercemetery.unt.edu/archive/cop/20110401223205/http:/www.cop.senate.gov/.

21   Jessica Yellin, "Attorneys: Play Hardball on AIG Bonuses," CNN Politics, March 20, 2009, http://www.cnn.com/2009/POLITICS/03/19/aig.contracts/index.html.

22   C-SPAN, "Elizabeth Warren on Financial Transparency and TARP," YouTube, published December 10, 2009, https://www.youtube.com/watch?v=3dH07-hlXEA.

23   Brady Dennis, "AIG Advised to Limit Its Next Round of Bonuses," *The Washington Post,* October 14, 2009, http://www.washingtonpost.com/wp-dyn/content/article/2009/10/13/AR2009101302504.html.

24   Yellin, "Attorneys: Play Hardball on AIG Bonuses."

25   "Elizabeth Warren Questions Timothy Geithner on TARP Bailout," C-SPAN, September 10, 2009, https://www.c-span.org/video/?c4363808/elizabeth-warren-questions-timothy-geithner-tarp-bailout.

26   Warren, *A Fighting Chance,* 105.

27   Warren, *A Fighting Chance,* 106.

28   Scherer, "The New Sheriffs of Wall Street."

29 Jon Talton, "Sheila Bair on WaMu: 'Was It Fair? Absolutely Not,' *The Seattle Times*, May 5, 2014, https://www.seattletimes.com/nation-world/sheila-bair-on-wamu-was-it-fair-absolutely-not/; Scherer, "The New Sheriffs of Wall Street."

30 Scherer, "The New Sheriffs of Wall Street."

31 Drew DeSilver, "Feds Seize WaMu in Nation's Largest Bank Failure," *The Seattle Times*, last modified September 26, 2008, http://old.seattletimes.com/html/businesstechnology/2008204758_wamu26.html.

32 Scherer, "The New Sheriffs of Wall Street."

33 Scherer, "The New Sheriffs of Wall Street."

34 Congressional Oversight Panel archive.

35 Warren, *A Fighting Chance*, 118.

36 Warren, *A Fighting Chance*, 106.

37 Warren, *A Fighting Chance*, 107.

38 "Elizabeth Warren Pt. 2," *The Daily Show with Jon Stewart*, Comedy Central, April 15, 2009, http://www.cc.com/video-clips/dbjssy/the-daily-show-with-jon-stewart-elizabeth-warren-pt—2.

39 "Elizabeth Warren Pt. 2," *The Daily Show with Jon Stewart*.

40 "Elizabeth Warren Pt. 2," *The Daily Show with Jon Stewart*.

41 "Elizabeth Warren Pt. 2," *The Daily Show with Jon Stewart*.

42 Rebecca Johnson, "Elizabeth Warren: Held to Account," *Vogue*, December 20, 2010, https://www.vogue.com/article/elizabeth-warren-held-to-account.

43 Chris Isidore, "U.S. Ends TARP with $15.3 Billion Profit," CNN Money, December 19, 2014, http://money.cnn.com/2014/12/19/news/companies/government-bailouts-end/index.html.

44 Charles Pierce, "The Watchdog: Elizabeth Warren," *Boston Globe Sunday Magazine*, December 20, 2009, http://archive.boston.com/bostonglobe/magazine/articles/2009/12/20/elizabeth_warren_is_the_bostonian_of_the_year/.

45 Elizabeth Warren, "Unsafe at Any Rate," *Democracy Journal*, no. 5 (Summer 2007): https://democracyjournal.org/magazine/5/unsafe-at-any-rate/.

46 Warren, "Unsafe at Any Rate."

47 Warren, "Unsafe at Any Rate."

48 Warren, *A Fighting Chance*, 131.

49 Warren, *A Fighting Chance*, 134.

50 Warren, *A Fighting Chance*, 134.

51 Warren, *A Fighting Chance*, 135.

52 Warren, *A Fighting Chance*, 139.

53 Warren, *A Fighting Chance*, 138.

54 Warren, *A Fighting Chance*, 139.

55 Theda Skocpol and Lawrence R. Jacobs, *Reaching for a New Deal: Ambitious Governance, Economic Meltdown, and Polarized Politics in Obama's First Two Years* (New York: Russell Sage Foundation, 2011).

56 Barack Obama, "President Barack Obama on 'The Tonight Show with Jay Leno,'" transcript, *New York Times*, March 19, 2009, http://www.nytimes.com/2009/03/20 /us/politics/20obama.text.html.

57 Warren, *A Fighting Chance*, 140.

58 Jeffrey Toobin, "Barney's Great Adventure," *The New Yorker*, January 12, 2009, https://www.newyorker.com/magazine/2009/01/12/barneys-great-adventure.

59 Warren, *A Fighting Chance*, 142; Michael J. Grynbaum, "Barneyt Frank Weds Jim Ready," New York Times, July 7, 2012, http://www.nytimes.com/2012/07/08 /fashion/weddings/barney-frank-wedding-jim-ready.html.

60 Warren, *A Fighting Chance*, 144.

61 Warren, *A Fighting Chance*, 144.

62 Warren, *A Fighting Chance*, 145–146.

63 Dick Trumka, phone interview with the author, January 29, 2018.

64 Warren, *A Fighting Chance*, 147.

65 Suzanna Andrews, "The Woman Who Knew Too Much," *Vanity Fair*, November 2011, https://www.vanityfair.com/news/2011/11/elizabeth-warren-201111.

66 M. B. Pell and Joe Eaton, "Five Lobbyists for Each Member of Congress on Financial Reforms," The Center for Public Integrity, last modified May 19, 2014, https://www.publicintegrity.org/2010/05/21/2670/five-lobbyists-each-member -congress-financial-reforms.

67 Roland S. Martin, "Washington Watch with Roland Martin—Elizabeth Warren Has the Taxpayers' Backs," YouTube, published March 15, 2010, https://www .youtube.com/watch?v=QfFVbF3Ugy8.

68 Arthur Delaney and Ryan Grim, "How Congress Gave Auto Dealers a Pass," Huffington Post, last modified July 25, 2014, https://www.huffingtonpost .com/2014/07/23/car-sales-subprime_n_5614047.html.

69 Nancy Gibbs, "Where Memory and Hope Converge: The Funeral of Edward M. Kennedy," *Time* magazine, August 29, 2009, http://content.time.com/time /nation/article/0,8599,1919484,00.html.

70 Elizabeth Warren, "Remarks at Credit Union National Association Governmental Affairs Conference," Consumer Financial Protection Bureau, March 1, 2011, https://www.consumerfinance.gov/about-us/newsroom/remarks-at-credit-union -national-association-governmental-affairs-conference/.

71 James Surowiecki, "The Warren Court," *The New Yorker*, June 13–20, 2011, https ://www.newyorker.com/magazine/2011/06/13/the-warren-court.

72 CNN Wire Staff, "Protesters Descend on Wall Street, New York City Banks," CNN, April 20, 2012, http://www.cnn.com/2010/US/04/29/banks.protests/index.html.

73 Andy Kroll, "Protesters Swarm Wall St. Lobbyists' Homes," Mother Jones, May 16, 2010, https://www.motherjones.com/politics/2010/05/main-street -battles-wall-street-seiu-npa-gregory-baer-peter-scher-jpmorgan-chase-bank -of-america/.

74 Mary Orndorff Troyan, "Spencer Bachus Finally Gets His Chairmanship," AL.com, December 9, 2010, http://blog.al.com/sweethome/2010/12/spencer_bachus_finally_gets_hi.html.

75 David Corn, "Elizabeth Warren: Passed Over for CFPB Post, But…" Mother Jones, July 18, 2011, https://www.motherjones.com/politics/2011/07/obama-elizabeth-warren-cfpb-cordray-senate/.

76 White House, "President Obama Names Elizabeth Warren Assistant to the President and Special Advisor to the Secretary of the Treasury on the Consumer Financial Protection Bureau," Office of the Press Secretary, White House press release, September 17, 2010, https://obamawhitehouse.archives.gov/the-press-office/2010/09/17/president-obama-names-elizabeth-warren-assistant-president-and-special-a.

77 Warren, *A Fighting Chance*, 172.

78 Harvard Law Today, accessed May 3, 2018, https://today.law.harvard.edu/tag/sacks-freund-award/.

79 Harvard Law Today, "Current Students Endorse Warren for Director of Bureau of Consumer Financial Protection," August 23, 2010, https://today.law.harvard.edu/current-students-endorse-warren-for-director-of-bureau-of-consumer-financial-protection/.

80 Brian Leiter, "Top 25 Law Faculties in Scholarly Impact, 2005–2009," Brian Leiter's Law School Rankings, accessed May 3, 2018, http://www.leiterrankings.com/new/2010_scholarlyimpact.shtml.

81 David A. Skeel Jr., "Bankruptcy's Home Economics," *ABI Law Review* 12, no. 43 (2004): 43.

82 Julie Vorman, "Reform Bill Gives Birth to $550-Million Consumer Bureau," The Center for Public Integrity, last modified May 19, 2014, https://www.publicintegrity.org/2010/07/15/2613/reform-bill-gives-birth-550-million-consumer-bureau.

83 Andy Kroll, "Bogus Attacks on the CFPB," Mother Jones, November 30, 2010, https://www.motherjones.com/politics/2010/11/bogus-attacks-cfpb-elizabeth-warren/.

84 Will Sealy, phone interview with the author, January 18, 2018.

85 Erika Eichelberger, "10 Things Elizabeth Warren's Consumer Protection Agency Has Done for You," Mother Jones, March 14, 2014, https://www.motherjones.com/politics/2014/03/elizabeth-warren-consumer-financial-protection-bureau-2/.

86 Consumer Financial Protection Bureau, "Everyone Has a Story," accessed May 3, 2018, https://www.consumerfinance.gov/consumer-tools/everyone-has-a-story/.

87 Skip Humphrey, "Written Testimony of Hubert H. 'Skip' Humphrey III Before the United States Senate Special Committee on Aging," Consumer Financial Protection Bureau, November 15, 2012, https://www.consumerfinance.gov/about-us/newsroom/written-testimony-of-hubert-h-skip-humphrey-iii-before-the-united-states-senate-special-committee-on-aging/.

88 Jennifer Steinhauer and Binyamin Appelbaum, "Democrats Try to Woo Consumer Advocate to Run," *New York Times*, May 23, 2011, http://www.nytimes.com/2011/05/24/us/politics/24warren.html.

Chapter 7

1 Mikulski, interview.

2 Warren, *A Fighting Chance*, 205.

3 Ylan Q. Mui, "Democrats' Control of Senate Could Hinge on Warren Campaign," *The Washington Post*, September 19, 2011, https://www.washingtonpost.com/business/economy/democrats-control-of-senate-could-hinge-on-warren-campaign/2011/09/16/gIQA1HUYfK_story.html?utm_term=.0e3da2cc799c.

4 Bold Progressives website, accessed May 3, 2018, boldprogressives.org.

5 David Sarasohn, "The Most Underestimated Feminist in DC," Patty Murray Senator web page, June 4, 2013, https://www.murray.senate.gov/public/index.cfm/pattyinnews?ID=A61348FB-38A6-4CE1-9F24-76BD9B15DCD1/.

6 Michael Powell, "Ohio Attorney General Fights Against Wall Street," *New York Times*, October 11, 2010, http://www.nytimes.com/2010/10/12/business/12avenge.html?_r=1&src=busln.

7 Powell, "Ohio Attorney General Fights Against Wall Street."

8 Abby Phillip, "Cordray, Not Warren, to Lead CFPB," *Politico*, July 17, 2011, https://www.politico.com/story/2011/07/cordray-not-warren-to-lead-cfpb-059206.

9 David Nakamura, "Obama Defies Senate, Puts Cordray in Consumer Post," *The Washington Post* via PressReader, January 5, 2012, https://www.pressreader.com/usa/the-washington-post/20120105/289875934337610.

10 Deron Lee, "Obama Picks Cordray Over Warren for Consumer Protection Bureau," *The Atlantic*, July 17, 2011, https://www.theatlantic.com/politics/archive/2011/07/obama-picks-cordray-over-warren-consumer-protection-bureau/352948/.

11 Danielle Douglas, "Senate Confirms Cordray to Head Consumer Financial Protection Bureau," *The Washington Post*, July 16, 2013, https://www.washingtonpost.com/business/economy/senate-confirms-consumer-watchdog-nominee-richard-cordray/2013/07/16/965d82c2-ee2b-11e2-a1f9-ea873b7e0424_story.html?utm_term=.9a79d740c948.

12 Megan Slack, "Senate Confirms Richard Cordray as Consumer Watchdog," The White House, July 17, 2013, https://obamawhitehouse.archives.gov/blog/2013/07/17/senate-confirms-richard-cordray-consumer-watchdog.

13 Warren, *A Fighting Chance*, 210.

14 Elizabeth Warren, "Coming Home," Blue Mass Group, August 11, 2011, http://bluemassgroup.com/2011/08/coming-home/.

15 Warren, *A Fighting Chance*, 335.

16 John Garelick, "Joyce Linehan: The Decider," *Boston Magazine*, December 31, 2013, https://www.bostonmagazine.com/news/2013/12/31/joyce-linehan/.

17 Joyce Linehan, "Elizabeth Warren in My Living Room," *Commonwealth Magazine*, August 17, 2011, https://commonwealthmagazine.org/politics/012 -elizabeth-warren-in-my-living-room/.

18 Linehan, "Elizabeth Warren in My Living Room."

19 Warren, *A Fighting Chance*, 212.

20 Warren, *A Fighting Chance*, 213.

21 LiveSmartVideos, "Elizabeth Warren on Debt Crisis, Fair Taxation," YouTube, published September 18, 2011, https://www.youtube.com/watch?v=htX2usfqMEs.

22 LiveSmartVideos, "Elizabeth Warren on Debt Crisis, Fair Taxation."

23 Josh Freedman and Michael Lind, "The Past and Future of America's Social Contract," *The Atlantic*, December 19, 2013, https://www.theatlantic.com/business /archive/2013/12/the-past-and-future-of-americas-social-contract/282511/.

24 Freedman and Lind, "The Past and Future of America's Social Contract."

25 Elizabeth Warren, Facebook post, June 23, 2016, https://www.facebook. com/ElizabethWarren/photos/pb.38471053686.-2207520000.1468763449./ 10153850113633687/?type=3.

26 Warren, Facebook post.

27 ElizabethforMA, "Elizabeth Warren: My Announcement," YouTube, published September 18, 2011, https://www.youtube.com/watch?v=wx2H31ZgkIQ.

28 Michael Tomansky, "A Woman of the People," Foreign Affairs, September/ October 2014, https://www.foreignaffairs.com/articles/united-states/2014-08-18 /woman-people.

29 Sally Jacobs, "A Lost Boy, Seared By Abuse, He Somehow Found His Way," Boston.com, August 5, 2012, http://archive.boston.com/news/local /massachusetts/articles/2012/08/05/senator_scott_browns_searing_childhood_ and_his_improbable_rise/.

30 Mui, "Democrats' Control of Senate Could Hinge on Warren Campaign."

31 Mui, "Democrats' Control of Senate Could Hinge on Warren Campaign."

32 ElizabethforMA, "Elizabeth Warren: My Announcement."

33 Abby Goodnough, "From the Halls of Harvard into the Street, in Pursuit of a Senate Seat," *New York Times*, September 14, 2011, http://www .nytimes.com/2011/09/15/us/politics/warren-kicks-off-senate-campaign-in -massachusetts.html.

34 Renne Loth, "The Timely Return of Bob Massie," Boston.com, January 16, 2011, http://archive.boston.com/bostonglobe/editorial_opinion/oped /articles/2011/01/16/the_timely_return_of_bob_massie/.

35 Deborah Becker, "WBUR Poll: Undeclared Elizabeth Warren 9 Points Behind Sen. Brown," WBUR, September 6, 2011, http://legacy.wbur.org/2011/09/06 /senate-poll-massachusetts.

36 Warren, *A Fighting Chance*, 233.

37 David Cohen, "Earlier: Akin: 'Legitimate Rape' Rarely Leads to Pregnancy,"

Politico, August 19, 2012, https://www.politico.com/story/2012/08 /akin-legitimate-rape-victims-dont-get-pregnant-079864.

38 Annie Groer, "Indiana GOP Senate Hopeful Richard Mourdock Says God Intented Rape Pregnancies," October 24, 2012, https://www.washingtonpost .com/blogs/she-the-people/wp/2012/10/24/indiana-gop-senate-hopeful-richard -mourdock-says-god-intended-rape-pregnancies/?utm_term=.9ccdcc8ee14b.

39 Roy Blunt, S. 1467 Respect for Rights of Conscience Act of 2011, August 2, 2011, https://www.govtrack.us/congress/bills/112/s1467.

40 Blunt, S. 1467 Respect for Rights of Conscience Act of 2011."

41 Seattle Times Staff, "5 Things to Know about Hobby Lobby's Owners," *The Seattle Times*, last modified July 2, 2014, https://www.seattletimes.com /nation-world/5-things-to-know-about-hobby-lobbys-owners/.

42 Freedom from Religion Foundation, "Freethought Heroine Award," 2014, https ://ffrf.org/outreach/awards/freethought-heroine-award/item/22126-marci-hamilton.

43 Freedom from Religion Foundation, "Freethought Heroine Award."

44 Warren, *A Fighting Chance*, 266.

45 Dan Eggen, "Scott Brown, Elizabeth Warren, Pledge to Curb Outside Campaign Spending," *The Washington Post*, January 23, 2012, https://www.washingtonpost .com/politics/brown-warren-pledge-to-curb-outside-campaign-spending/2012 /01/23/gIQAi4jbLQ_story.html?utm_term=.0288a93c96d9.

46 Thomas Barry, phone interview with the author, January 2, 2018.

47 Jennifer Migliore, phone interview with the author, January 16, 2018.

48 Elizabeth Warren for Senate, https://elizabethwarren.com/compare.

49 Elizabeth Warren, "I'm Gay and I'm Counting on You," Elizabeth Warren for Senate, October 11, 2012, https://elizabethwarren.com/blog/im-gay-and -im-counting-on-you.

50 Diane Masters, "Elizabeth Warren Rally with Rep. John Lewis and Gov. Deval Patrick," Elizabeth Warren for Senate, November 3, 2012, https://elizabethwarren .com/blog/elizabeth-warren-rally-with-rep-lewis-and-gov-patrick.

51 Newsweek Staff, "Elizabeth Warren on Financial Regulatory Reform," *Newsweek*, December 6, 2009, http://www.newsweek.com/elizabeth-warren -financial-regulatory-reform-75759.

52 Scott Wong and John Bresnahan, "Warren Campaign Revises Panel Pay," *Politico*, September 23, 2011, https://www.politico.com/story/2011/09 /warren-campaign-revises-panel-pay-064306.

53 Revg33k, "Forum Post: First Official Release from Occupy Wall Street," Occupy Wall Street, September 30, 2011, http://occupywallst.org/forum /first-official-release-from-occupy-wall-street/.

54 Samuel P. Jacobs, "Elizabeth Warren: 'I Created Occupy Wall Street,'" Daily Beast, October 24, 2011, https://www.thedailybeast.com /elizabeth-warren-i-created-occupy-wall-street.

55 Todd Gitlin, *Occupy Nation: The Roots, the Spirit, and the Promise of Occupy Wall Street* (New York: Harper Collins, 2012), 235.

56 The Young Turks, "Elizabeth warren Occupy Wall Street Attack," YouTube, November 11, 2011, https://www.youtube.com/watch?v=nSGuwU3HSjw.

57 Warren, *A Fighting Chance*, 221.

58 Amy Crawford, "The Estranged Marriage between Elizabeth Warren and Occupy Wall Street," The New Republic, September 4, 2012, https://newrepublic.com/article/106946/estranged-marriage-between-elizabeth-warren-and-occupy-wall-street.

59 Todd Gitlin, phone interview with the author, December 16, 2017.

60 Mikulski, interview.

61 Martin Finucane, "In Crucial First Debate, Scott Brown Challenges Warren's Native American Heritage Claim," Boston.com, September 20, 2012, https://www.boston.com/uncategorized/noprimarytagmatch/2012/09/20/in-crucial-first-debate-scott-brown-challenges-warrens-native-american-heritage-claim.

62 "Massachusetts Senate Debate," September 20, 2012, C-SPAN, https://www.c-span.org/video/?308202–1/massachusetts-senate-debate&start=130.

63 Vine Deloria Jr., *Custer Died for Your Sins: An Indian Manifesto* (Norman: University of Oklahoma Press, 1988), 2.

64 Circe Sturm, *Blood Politics: Race, Culture, and Identity in the Cherokee Nation of Oklahoma* (Berkeley: University of California Press, 2002), 139.

65 Sturm, *Blood Politics*.

66 Linda Geddes, "'There Is No DNA Test to Prove You're Native American,'" New Scientist, February 5, 2014, https://www.newscientist.com/article/mg22129554–400-there-is-no-dna-test-to-prove-youre-native-american/.

67 Tom Holm, phone interview with the author, December 27, 2017.

68 Amy Davidson Sorkin, "Elizabeth Warren's Native American Question," *The New Yorker*, May 8, 2012, https://www.newyorker.com/news/amy-davidson/elizabeth-warrens-native-american-question.

69 Katharine Q. Seelye and Abby Goodnough, "Candidate for Senate Defends Past Hiring," *New York Times*, April 30, 2012, http://www.nytimes.com/2012/05/01/us/politics/elizabeth-warrens-ancestry-irrelevant-in-hiring-law-schools-say.html.

70 Associated Press, "Harvard: Warren Got Job Only on Merits as Teacher," WBUR, May 7, 2012, http://legacy.wbur.org/2012/05/07/elizabeth-warren.

71 Associated Press, "Harvard: Warren Got Job Only on Merits as Teacher."

72 Justin Sink, "Warren Demands an Apology from Opponent in Heritage Controversy," May 31, 2012, http://thehill.com/blogs/blog-briefing-room/news/230315-elizabeth-warren-accuses-scott-brown-of-attacking-parents-over-cherokee-ancestry-demands-apology.

73 Sink, "Warren Demands an Apology from Opponent in Heritage Controversy."

74 Sink, "Warren Demands an Apology from Opponent in Heritage Controversy."

75   Alex Isenstadt, "Warren Gives Fiery Defense of Obama," Politico, September 5, 2012, https://www.politico.com/story/2012/09/warren-gives-fiery-defense-of-obama-blasts-romney-080807.

76   Warren, "Elizabeth Warren's Democratic Convention Speech."

77   Warren, "Elizabeth Warren's Democratic Convention Speech."

78   Warren, "Elizabeth Warren's Democratic Convention Speech."

79   Sean Sullivan, "The Fix's Best Fundraiser of 2012," *The Washington Post*, December 13, 2012, https://www.washingtonpost.com/news/the-fix/wp/2012/12/13/the-fixs-best-fundraiser-of-2012/?utm_term=.42f8a6f0a12f.

80   Warren, *A Fighting Chance*, 271.

81   Michael Levenson, "After Her Record Haul, Warren Slips into Red," *The Boston Globe*, December 5, 2012, https://www.bostonglobe.com/news/politics/2012/12/05/elizabeth-warren-ended-senate-campaign-debt-despite-record-fund-raising/ShWe5K7KzUiVnFHiIxkX5H/story.html.

82   Warren, *A Fighting Chance*, 236.

83   Brian McGrory, "Elizabeth Warren's Private Agony," *The Boston Globe*, November 30, 2012, https://www.bostonglobe.com/metro/2012/11/30/warren-private-sorrow/uwp3BYslrXDgcMgX7xiwPK/story.html.

84   Matthew Q. Clarida and Nicholas P. Fandos, "Warren Handily Defeats Brown in Senate Race," *The Harvard Crimson*, November 6, 2012, http://www.thecrimson.com/article/2012/11/6/warren-wins-senate-election/.

85   Clarida and Fandos, "Warren Handily Defeats Brown in Senate Race."

86   Mikulski, interview.

87   Mikulski, interview.

88   Mikulski, interview.

89   "The Year of the Woman, 1992," United States House of Representatives Office of the Historian, accessed May 3, 2018, , http://history.house.gov/Exhibitions-and-Publications/WIC/Historical-Essays/Assembling-Amplifying-Ascending/Women-Decade/.

90   "The Year of the Woman, 1992," United States House of Representatives Office of the Historian.

91   Jay Newton-Small, *Broad Influence: How Women Are Changing the Way America Works* (New York: Time Books, 2016), 30.

92   "The Year of the Woman, 1992," United States House of Representatives Office of the Historian.

93   Mikulski, interview.

94   Barbara Mikulski, "Senator Barbara Mikulski Farewell Speech," C-SPAN, December 7, 2016, https://www.c-span.org/video/?419740–4/senator-barbara-mikulski-delivers-farewell-speech&start=2583.

95   Michael Scherer, Sam Frizell, and Zeke J. Miller, "Up With People," *Time* magazine, July 20, 2015.

96 Mikulski, interview.

97 Kelly Dittmar et al., "Representation Matters: Women in the U.S. Congress," Center for American Women and Politics, 2017, http://www.cawp.rutgers.edu /sites/default/files/resources/representationmatters.pdf.

98 Dittmar et al., "Representation Matters."

99 Dittmar et al., "Representation Matters."

100 Kirsten Gillibran, "Learn about the Off the Sidelines Campaign," accessed May 3, 2018, https://offthesidelines.org/about/.

101 Barbara Mikulski, "Senator Barbara Mikulski Farewell Speech."

102 Mikulski, interview.

103 Warren, *A Fighting Chance*, 167.

104 Newton-Small, *Broad Influence*, 128.

105 Christina Pazzanese, "The Women Who Questioned Wall Street," *The Harvard Gazette*, May 4, 2015, https://news.harvard.edu/gazette/story/2015/05/the -women-who-questioned-wall-street/.

106 Hillary Rodham Clinton, *What Happened* (New York: Simon & Schuster, 2017), 119.

107 Clinton, *What Happened*, 119.

108 Mark Hensch, "Mike Brzezinski: 'I'm Getting Tired' of Warren," The Hill, November 29, 2016, http://thehill.com/homenews/senate/307932 -mika-brzezinski-im-getting-tired-of-warren.

109 Hensch, "Mike Brzezinski."

110 Kevin Cirilli, "NOW Slams 'Sexist' Warren Buffett over Warren Comments," The Hill, March 5, 2015, http://thehill.com/blogs/blog-briefing-room/234763-now -slams-sexist-warren-buffett-over-warren-comments.

111 Cirilli, "NOW Slams 'Sexist' Warren Buffett over Warren Comments."

112 Clinton, *What Happened*, 119.

113 "The liberal firebrand—who is best known for dressing down Wall Street CEOs": Victoria McGrane, https://www.bostonglobe.com/news/politics/2016/12/14 /warren-gets-spot-armed-services-committee/TR4Xf6TnDn8izaFSlUDJcN /story.html.; While Elizabeth did not immediately throw her hat in the ring: Clinton, *What Happened*, 225.

114 Sarah Mimms, "Is Elizabeth Warren an Effective Senator?" *The Atlantic*, May 26, 2015, https://www.theatlantic.com/politics/archive/2015/05/is-elizabeth -warren-an-effective-senator/449349/.

115 Migliore, interview.

116 Elizabeth Warren, "Senators Warren and Enzi Introduce Bipartisan Bill to Strengthen Genetic Privacy Protections for Research Participants," Elizabeth Warren, April 5, 2016, https://www.warren.senate.gov/newsroom/press-releases /senators-warren-and-enzi-introduce-bipartisan-bill-to-strengthen-genetic -privacy-protections-for-research-participants.

117 Gillian B. White, "One Year after Its Fake-Accounts Scandal, Wells Fargo Isn't a 'Better Bank,'" *The Atlantic*, October 3, 2017, https://www.theatlantic.com /business/archive/2017/10/wells-fargo-fake-accounts-sloan/541875/.

118 Michael Corkery, "Elizabeth Warren Accuses Wells Fargo Chief of 'Gutless Leadership,'" *New York Times*, September 20, 2016, https://www.nytimes .com/2016/09/21/business/dealbook/wells-fargo-ceo-john-stumpf-senate -testimony.html.

119 CNBC, "Senator Elizabeth Warren Grills Wells Fargo CEO John Stumpf on WFC Cross-Selling," YouTube, September 20, 2016, https://www.youtube.com /watch?v=iCLIyXpV5K0.

120 White, "One Year after Its Fake-Accounts Scandal, Wells Fargo Isn't a 'Better Bank.'"

121 David Dayen, "The Elizabeth Warren Model of Political Leadership," The New Republic, February 5, 2018, https://newrepublic.com/article/146952 /elizabeth-warren-model-political-leadership.

122 Dayen, "The Elizabeth Warren Model of Political Leadership."

123 Dayen, "The Elizabeth Warren Model of Political Leadership."

124 Manu Raju and John Bresnahan, "Reid Taps Warren as Envoy to Liberals," *Politico*, last modified November 13, 2014, https://www.politico.com/story/2014/11 /elizabeth-warren-harry-reid-senate-leadership-112847.

125 Lucy McCalmont, "Warren: American Dream Is Slipping Away," Politico, November 19, 2014, https://www.politico.com/story/2014/11/elizabeth -warren-economic-speech-113031.

126 Mark Robert Rank et al., *Chasing the American Dream: Understanding What Shapes Our Fortunes* (Oxford: Oxford University Press, 2014), 2.

127 Rank, *Chasing the American Dream*, 2.

128 Rank, *Chasing the American Dream*, 2.

129 Amanda Marcotte, "Author Courtney Martin Celebrates Millennials Who Are Redefining the American Dream," Salon, September 13, 2016, https://www. salon.com/2016/09/13/author-courtney-martin-celebrates-millennials-who-are -redefining-the-american-dream/.

130 Jared Meyer, "The Economy Is Changing and So Is the American Dream," *Forbes*, March 22, 2017, https://www.forbes.com/sites/jaredmeyer/2017/03/22 /the-economy-is-changing-and-so-is-the-american-dream/#58a2db953cc3.

131 Zoë Henry, "Sorry, Millennials: The 'American Dream' Is Fading, New Study Suggests," Inc.com, December 9, 2016, https://www.inc.com/zoe-henry/is-the -american-dream-fading-children-less-likely-to-out-earn-parents.html.

132 Henry, "Sorry, Millennials: The 'American Dream' Is Fading, New Study Suggests."

133 Roberto Suro, "What Happened on Election Day: Here's What Happened with the Latino Vote," *New York Times*, November 8, 2016, https://www .nytimes.com/interactive/projects/cp/opinion/election-night-2016/heres -what-happened-with-the-latino-vote.

134 Warren and Tyagi, *The Two-Income Trap*, 160.

135 Warren and Tyagi, *The Two-Income Trap*, 160.

136 ElizabethforMA, "Elizabeth Warren's Speech to the National Congress of American Indians."

137 David Wilkins, email correspondence with the author, February 15, 2018.

138 Ali Vitali, "Trump Calls Warren 'Pocahontas at Event Honoring Native Americans," NBC News, November 27, 2017, https://www.nbcnews.com/politics/white-house /trump-calls-warren-pocahontas-event-honoring-native-americans-n824266.

139 Vitali, "Trump Calls Warren 'Pocahontas at Event Honoring Native Americans."

140 Martin Pengelly, "Elizabeth Warren Seeks to Use Trump Pocahontas 'Racial Slur' As Political Tool," *The Guardian*, March 11, 2018, https://www.theguardian .com/us-news/2018/mar/11/elizabeth-warren-donald-trump-pocahontas-native -americans.

141 Bess Levin, "Trump Budget Director Expected to Take Over Agency He Called a 'Sick, Sad Joke,'" *Vanity Fair*, November 16, 2017, https://www.vanityfair.com /news/2017/11/mick-mulvaney-cfpb.

142 Catherine Rampell, "How Mick Mulvaney Is Dismantling a Federal Agency," *The Washington Post*, January 25, 2018, https://www.washingtonpost.com /opinions/mick-mulvaney-cant-legally-kill-the-cfpb-so-hes-starving-it-instead /2018/01/25/4481d2ce-0216-11e8-8acf-ad2991367d9d_story.html?utm_term =.f38ad9489b0c.

143 David Z. Morris, "The Equifax Hack Exposed More Data Than Previously Reported," Fortune, February 11, 2018, http://fortune.com/2018/02/11 /equifax-hack-exposed-extra-data/.

144 Jordan Weissmann, "Mick Mulvaney Says the Consumer Financial Protection Bureau Works for Payday Lenders, Too," Slate, January 23, 2018, https://slate .com/business/2018/01/mick-mulvaney-says-the-consumer-financial-protection -bureau-works-for-payday-lenders-too.html.

145 Liz Goodwin, "Warren's Consumer Dream Dismantled," *The Boston Globe*, March 3, 2018, https://www.bostonglobe.com/news/nation/2018/03/03/warren -responds-mulvaney-cfpb-taunts-this-isn-about/Iv53cIPjzQ6FrSiNblsjfM /story.html.

146 Russell Berman, "Heidi Heitkamp Takes on Elizabeth Warren over the Senate Banking Bill," *The Atlantic*, March 14, 2018, https ://www.theatlantic.com/politics/archive/2018/03/heitkamp-elizabeth -warren-senate-banking-bill-dodd-frank/555524/.

147 Calvin Johnson, interview.

148 Douglas Massey, *Categorically Unequal: The American Stratification System* (New York: Russell Sage Foundation, 2007), 36.

149 D. Stanley Eitzen and Janis E. Johnston, *Inequality. Social Class and Its Consequences* (New York: Routledge, 2007), 45.

150 Cornel West, *Race Matters*, 2nd ed. (New York: Vintage, 2011), 8.

151 Philip Kotler, Confronting Capitalism: Real Solutions for a Troubled Economic System (New York: American Management Association, 2015), 60.

152 Karen Tumulty, "Elizabeth Warren Keeps Pressure on Hillary Clinton and Democrats ahead of 2016," *The Washington Post*, January 17, 2015, https://www .washingtonpost.com/politics/elizabeth-warren-keeps-pressure-on-hillary -clinton-and-democrats-ahead-of-2016/2015/01/17/cc844300-9b49-11e4-a7ee -526210d665b4_story.html?utm_term=.8abdd42b1bcb.

SELECT BIBLIOGRAPHY

INTERVIEWS

Thomas Barry

Patricia Cain

Katrina Cochran

Judy Garrett

Mark Gergen

Todd Gitlin

Bob Hammack

Dennis Hanigan

Jahree Herzer

Tom Holm

Alix James

Calvin Johnson

Karl Johnson

Perry Lange

Joe Mallonee

Ronald Mann

Andrew Mason

Jennifer Migliore

Barbara Mikulski

John Mixon

Douglas Moll

Chrystin Ondersma

Douglas Peterson

Katie Porter

Joe Pryor

Harry Reid

Will Sealy

Bill Toutant

Richard Trumka

Kristie Blunt Welder

David Wilkins

PUBLICATIONS

Alter, Charlotte. "U.S. Women Leadership Ranking is Pathetic Compared to Other Countries." *Time*, January 27, 2015. http://time.com/3684249/u-s-women -leadership-ranking-is-pathetic-compared-to-other-countries/.

American Bar Association. "A Snapshot of Women in the Law in the Year 2000." Accessed October 7, 2017. https://www.americanbar.org/content/dam/aba /marketing/women/snapshots.authcheckdam.pdf.

American Forensic Association. "Founders." Accessed on November 16, 2017. http ://www.americanforensicsassoc.org/founders/.

American Forensic Association. "National Debate Tournament Topics 1946–2012." Accessed November 16, 2017. http://groups.wfu.edu/NDT/HistoricalLists/topics.html.

American Oil and Gas Historical Society. "This Week in Petroleum History, December 4 to December 10." Accessed November 2, 2017. https://aoghs.org /this-week-in-petroleum-history/december-7/.

Andrews, Suzanna. "The Woman Who Knew Too Much." *Vanity Fair*, November 2011. https://www.vanityfair.com/news/2011/11/elizabeth-warren-201111.

Andrews, Wilson, Jason Bartz, and Serdar Tumgoren. "2012 Presidential Election Results." *Washington Post*. Accessed February 1, 2018. http://www.washingtonpost .com/wp-srv/special/politics/election-map-2012/president/.

Appelbaum, Binyamin. "Former Ohio Attorney General to Head New Consumer Agency." *New York Times*, July 17, 2011. http://www.nytimes.com/2011/07/18 /business/former-ohio-attorney-general-picked-to-lead-consumer-agency.html.

Associated Press. "Harvard: Warren Got Job Only on Merits as Teacher." WBUR. May 7, 2012. http://legacy.wbur.org/2012/05/07/elizabeth-warren.

Associated Press. "Read the Text of Elizabeth Warren's Speech to Native American Group." *Boston Globe*, February 14, 2018. https://www.bostonglobe.com/news /politics/2018/02/14/read-text-elizabeth-warren-speech-native-americans /ovAjQq28SbyqiDXnOp1rNK/story.html?event=event25.

Baptiste, Nathalie. "Them That's Got Shall Get." *American Prospect*. October 12, 2014, http://prospect.org/article/staggering-loss-black-wealth-due-subprime-scandal -continues-unabated.

Baskin, Kara. "Elizabeth Warren Was 1966's 'Betty Crocker Homemaker of Tomorrow.'" Grub Street. June 20, 2012. http://www.grubstreet.com/2012/06/elizabeth-warren -betty-crocker.html.

Becker, Deborah. "WBUR Poll: Undeclared Elizabeth Warren 9 Points Behind Sen. Brown." WBUR. September 6, 2011. http://legacy.wbur.org/2011/09/06/ senate-poll-massachusetts.

Berman, Russell. "Heidi Heitkamp Takes on Elizabeth Warren over the Senate Banking Bill." *The Atlantic*, March 14, 2018. https://www.theatlantic.com/politics/archive/2018/03/heitkamp-elizabeth-warren-senate-banking-bill-dodd–frank/555524/.

Berman, Russell. "The Red-State Revolt Spreads to Oklahoma." *The Atlantic*, November 27, 2017. https://www.theatlantic.com/politics/archive/2017/11/the-red-state-revolt-spreads-to-oklahoma/546671/.

Bierema, Laura L. "Women's Leadership: Troubling Notions of the 'Ideal' (Male) Leader." *Advances in Developing Human Resources* 18, no. 2 (2016): 119–136.

Bierman, Noah. "A Girl Who Soared, but Longed to Belong." *Boston Globe*, February 12, 2002. https://www.bostonglobe.com/metro/2012/02/12/for-warren-seeds-activism-forged-plains-oklahoma/rx59B8AcqsZokclyJXkg7I/story.html.

Binder, David. "Ex-Congressman Mike Synar, Oklahoma Liberal, Dies at 45." *New York Times*, January 10, 1996. http://www.nytimescom/1996/01/10/us/ex-congressman-mike-synar-oklahoma-liberal-dies-at-45.html.

Bix, Amy Sue. *Girls Coming to Tech!: A History of American Engineering Education for Women*. Cambridge: MIT Press, 2013.

Block, Melissa. "Expert: Few Clues on How Banks Used TARP Funds." NPR, February 11, 2009. https://www.npr.org/templates/story/story.php?storyId=100597533.

Blunt, Roy. Respect for Rights of Conscience Act of 2011. Govtrack.us, https://www.govtrack.us/congress/bills/112/s1467.

Bowman, Cynthia Grant. "Women in the Legal Profession from the 1920s to the 1970s: What Can We Learn From Their Experience About Law and Social Change?" Cornell Law Faculty Publications. Paper 12 (2009). http://scholarship.law.cornell.edu/facpub/12.

Boxer, Barbara. Remarks at U.S. Senate Tribute to Senator Barbara Mikulski. C-Span Video, 46:30, December 7, 2016, https://www.c-span.org/video/?419740–4/senator-barbara-mikulski-delivers-farewell-speech&start=2583.

Boyd, Dan T. "Oklahoma Oil: Past, Present, and Future." *Oklahoma Geology Notes* 62, no. 3 (Fall 2002): 97–106.

Brand-Williams, Oralandar. "At NAACP Event, Sen. Warren Warns of 'Moment of Crisis.'" *Detroit News*, April 23, 2017. http://www.detroitnews.com/videos/news/local/detroit-city/2017/04/23/elizabeth-warren's-speech-naacp/100831660/.

Braun, Bob. "Head of Congressional Oversight Panel Has New Jersey Roots." *Star-Ledger*, June 21, 2009. http://blog.nj.com/njv_bob_braun/2009/06/head_of_congressional_oversigh.html.

———. "Rutgers Law Professor Pens Centennial History of School." *Star-Ledger*, July 8, 2010. http://blog.nj.com/njv_bob_braun/2010/07/professor_writes _book_on_histo.html.

Brodey, Sam. "Andy Slavitt Already Saved Obamacare Once. Can He Do It Again?" *Minnpost*. March 23, 2017. https://www.minnpost.com/politics-policy/2017/03 /andy-slavitt-already-saved-obamacare-once-can-he-do-it-again.

Brunner, Liz. "At Home with Elizabeth Warren." WCVB.com. YouTube, 2:48, November 5, 2012. http://www.wcvb.com/article/at-home-with-elizabeth-warren /7863078.

Butterfield, Fox. "First Black Elected to Head Harvard's Law Review." *New York Times*, February 6, 1990. https://www.nytimes.com/1990/02/06/us/first-black-elected-to -head-harvard-s-law-review.html.

Butterfield, Fox. "Harvard Law Professor Quits Until Black Woman Is Named." *New York Times*, April 24, 1990. http://www.nytimes.com/1990/04/24/us/harvard-law -professor-quits-until-black-woman-is-named.html?pagewanted=print.

Cardozo Law. "Marci A. Hamilton." Accessed January 3, 2018. Cardozo Law. https ://cardozo.yu.edu/directory/marci-hamilton.

Carmichael, Mary, and Stephanie Ebbert. "Warren Says She Told Schools of Heritage." *Boston Globe*, May 31, 2012. http://archive.boston.com/news/local/massachusetts /articles/2012/05/31/elizabeth_warren_acknowledges_telling_harvard_penn_of _native_american_status/.

Carpenter, Daniel. "The Contest of Lobbies and Disciplines: Financial Politics and Regulatory Reform." In *Reaching for a New Deal: Ambitious Governance, Economic Meltdown, and Polarized Politics in Obama's First Two Years*, eds. Theda Skocpol and Lawrence R. Jacobs, 139–188. New York: Russell Sage Foundation, 2011.

Carter, Kent. *The Dawes Commission and the Allotment of the Five Civilized Tribes, 1893–1914*. Orem: Ancestry Publishing, 1999.

Caryl-Sue, "1899: Oklahoma Land Rush." *National Geographic Society*. Last modified April 11, 2014. https://www.nationalgeographic.org/thisday/apr22 /oklahoma-land-rush/.

Chen, Tim. "The Soft Power of the Consumer Financial Protection Bureau." *Forbes*, June 17, 2011. https://www.forbes.com/sites/moneybuilder/2011/06/17/the-soft -power-of-the-consumer-financial-protection-bureau/#3ae7c5ae3705.

Cherokee Nation. "About the Nation." Accessed September 28, 2017. http://www .cherokee.org/About-The-Nation.

Cirilli, Kevin. "NOW Slams 'Sexist' Warren Buffett over Warren Comments." *The Hill*, March 5, 2015. http://thehill.com/blogs/blog-briefing-room/234763-now-slams -sexist-warren-buffett-over-warren-comments.

Clarida, Matthew Q. and Nicholas P. Fandos. "Warren Handily Defeats Brown in Senate Race." *Harvard Crimson*, November 6, 2012. http://www.thecrimson.com /article/2012/11/6/warren-wins-senate-election/.

Clinton, Hillary Rodham. *What Happened*. New York: Simon & Schuster, 2017.

CNN Wire Staff. "Protesters Descend on Wall Street, New York City Banks." CNN. April 30, 2010. http://www.cnn.com/2010/US/04/29/banks.protests/index.html.

Cohen, David. "Earlier: Akin: 'Legitimate Rape' Rarely Leads to Pregnancy." Politico. August 19, 2012. https://www.politico.com/story/2012/08/akin-legitimate-rape-victims-dont-get-pregnant-079864.

Condon, Stephanie. "Elizabeth Warren Supporters Hound GOP Congressman." CBS News. May 25, 2011. https://www.cbsnews.com/news/elizabeth-warren-supporters-hound-gop-congressman/.

———. "Scott Brown, Elizabeth Warren Make Super PAC Pact." CBS News. January 23, 2012. https://www.cbsnews.com/news/scott-brown-elizabeth-warren-make-super-pac-pact/.

Congress.gov. "H.R.1424." Accessed October 21, 2017. https://www.congress.gov/bill/110th-congress/house-bill/1424/text?overview=closed&r=1.

Congressional Oversight Panel (COP). Archive. April 1, 2011. https://cybercemetery.unt.edu/archive/cop/20110401223205/http:/www.cop.senate.gov/.

Consumer Financial Protection Bureau. "Everyone Has a Story." Accessed January 30, 2018. https://www.consumerfinance.gov/consumer-tools/everyone-has-a-story/.

Corkery, Michael. "Elizabeth Warren Accuses Wells Fargo Chief of 'Gutless Leadership.'" New York Times, September 20, 2016. https://www.nytimes.com/2016/09/21/business/dealbook/wells-fargo-ceo-john-stumpf-senate-testimony.html.

Corn, David. "Elizabeth Warren: Passed Over for CFPB Post, But..." Mother Jones, July 18, 2011. https://www.motherjones.com/politics/2011/07/obama-elizabeth-warren-cfpb-cordray-senate/.

Crawford, Amy. "The Estranged Marriage Between Elizabeth Warren and Occupy Wall Street." New Republic. September 4, 2012. https://newrepublic.com/article/106946/estranged-marriage-between-elizabeth-warren-and-occupy-wall-street.

Crook, Jordan. "Sen. Elizabeth Warren Gets 6M+ Facebook Live Views After Being Silenced by Republicans." Techcrunch.com. February 8, 2017. https://techcrunch.com/2017/02/08/sen-elizabeth-warren-gets-6m-facebook-live-views-after-being-silenced-by-republicans/.

Davis, Angela Y. Women, Race and Class. New Delhi: Navayana, 2011.

Dayen, David. "The Elizabeth Warren Model of Political Leadership." New Republic, February 5, 2018. https://newrepublic.com/article/146952/elizabeth-warren-model-political-leadership.

De Vise, Daniel. "University of Virginia Picks Its First Female President." Washington Post, January 12, 2010. http://www.washingtonpost.com/wp-dyn/content/article/2010/01/11/AR2010011102330.html.

Delaney, Arthur, and Ryan Grim. "How Congress Gave Auto Dealers a Pass." Huffpost,

updated July 25, 2014. https://www.huffingtonpost.com/2014/07/23/car-sales
-subprime_n_5614047.html.

Delgado, Richard and Jean Stefancic. *Critical Race Theory: An Introduction*. New York: New York University Press, 2012.

Deloria, Vine, Jr. *Custer Died for Your Sins: An Indian Manifesto*. Norman, OK: University of Oklahoma Press, 1988.

———. "The Popularity of Being Indian: A New Trend in Contemporary American Society." In The Vine Deloria, Jr., Reader, edited by Barbara Deloria, Kristen Foehner, and Sam Scinta, 79–86. Golden, CO: Fulcrum, 1999.

Dennis, Brady. "AIG Advised to Limit Its Next Round of Bonuses." *Washington Post*, October 14, 2009. http://www.washingtonpost.com/wp-dyn/content /article/2009/10/13/AR2009101302504.html.

Deparle, Jason. "Goals Reached, Donor on Right Closes Up Shop." *New York Times*, May 29, 2005. http://www.nytimes.com/2005/05/29/politics/goals-reached-donor-on -right-closes-up-shop.html.

DeSilver, Drew. "Feds Seize WaMu in Nation's Largest Bank Failure." *Seattle Times*, September 26, 2008. http://old.seattletimes.com/html/businesstechnology /2008204758_wamu26.html.

Dillow, Clay, and Brooks Rainwater. "Why Free Money for Everyone Is Silicon Valley's Next Big Idea." *Fortune*, June 29, 2017. http://fortune.com/2017/06/29 /universal-basic-income-free-money-silicon-valley/.

Dittmar, Kelly, and Kira Sanbonmatsu, Susan J. Carroll, Debbie Walsh, and Catherine Wineinger. *Representation Matters: Women in the U.S. Congress*. New Brunswick: Center for American Women and Politics, Eagleton Institute of Politics, Rutgers, The State University of New Jersey, 2017. http://www.cawp.rutgers.edu/sites /default/files/resources/representationmatters.pdf.

Douglas, Danielle. "Senate Confirms Cordray to head Consumer Financial Protection Bureau." *Washington Post*, July 16, 2013. https://www.washingtonpost .com/business/economy/senate-confirms-consumer-watchdog-nominee-richard -cordray/2013/07/16/965d82c2-ee2b-11e2-a1f9-ea873b7e0424_story.html?utm _term=.5dda25d589a1.

Dreier, Peter. "Paul Wellstone's Life and Legacy." Huffpost. Updated December 12, 2002. https://www.huffingtonpost.com/peter-dreier/paul-wellstones-life-and-_b _1961277.html.

Dr. Phil. "Going for Broke: Financial Advice." n.d. Accessed on February 21, 2018. https://www.drphil.com/slideshows/going-for-broke-financial-advice/.

Dwinell, Joe. "Advocates: Warren's Story is 'Universal.'" *Boston Herald*, October 25, 2017. http://www.bostonherald.com/news/local_coverage/2017/10/advocates_elizabeth _warren_s_story_is_universal.

Ebbert, Stephanie. "Daughter of Elizabeth Warren Claims Center Stage." *Boston Globe*, August 12, 2012. https://www.bostonglobe.com/metro/2012/08/11 /daughter-elizabeth-warren-claims-center-stage/s92JYWy0MnZkt8ktXVvquL /story.html.

Eggen, Dan. "Scott Brown, Elizabeth Warren Pledge to Curb Outside Campaign Spending." *Washington Post*, January 23, 2012.

Eichelberger, Erika. "10 Things Elizabeth Warren's Consumer Protection Agency Has Done for You." *Mother Jones*, March 14, 2014. https://www.motherjones.com /politics/2014/03/elizabeth-warren-consumer-financial-protection-bureau-2/.

Eitzen, D. Stanley, and Janis E. Johnston. *Inequality: Social Class and Its Consequences.* Boulder: Paradigm Publishers, 2007.

"Elizabeth Warren Questions Timothy Geithner on TARP Bailout." C-Span Video, 6:09, September 10, 2009, https://www.c-span.org/video/?c4363808 /elizabeth-warren-questions-timothy-geithner-tarp-bailout.

Elizabeth Warren: Senator for Massachusetts. "Senator Warren Delivers Remarks on Devastating Impact of GOP Tax Plan on Small Businesses." November 14, 2017. https://www.warren.senate.gov/newsroom/press-releases/senator-warren-delivers -remarks-on-devastating-impact-of-gop-tax-plan-on-small-businesses.

Elizabeth Warren for Senate. "Elizabeth Warren vs. Scott Brown On the Issues." Accessed March 9, 2018. https://elizabethwarren.com/compare.

Epstein, Cynthia Fuchs. *Women in Law.* 2nd ed. Urbana: University of Illinois Press, 1993.

Everett, Dianna. "Camp Gruber." Oklahoma Historical Society. 2009. http://www .okhistory.org/publications/enc/entry.php?entry=CA022.

Feldman, Stanley, and Melissa Herrmann. "CBS News Exit Polls: How Donald Trump Won the U.S. Presidency." CBS News. November 9, 2016. https://www.cbsnews .com/news/cbs-news-exit-polls-how-donald-trump-won-the-us-presidency/.

Finucane, Martin. "In Crucial First Debate, Scott Brown Challenges Warren's Native American Heritage Claim." *Boston Globe*, September 20, 2012. https://www .boston.com/uncategorized/noprimarytagmatch/2012/09/20/in-crucial-first -debate-scott-brown-challenges-warrens-native-american-heritage-claim.

Flint, Anthony. "10 years later, did the Big Dig deliver?" *Boston Globe*, December 29, 2015. https://www.bostonglobe.com/magazine/2015/12/29/years-later-did-big-dig -deliver/tSb8PIMS4QJUETsMpA7SpI/story.html.

Franke-Ruta, Garance. "Is Elizabeth Warren Native American or What?" *The Atlantic*, May 20, 2012. https://www.theatlantic.com/politics/archive/2012/05 /is-elizabeth-warren-native-american-or-what/257415/.

Freedman, Josh, and Michael Lind. "The Past and Future of America's Social Contract." *The Atlantic*, December 19, 2013. https://www.theatlantic.com/business /archive/2013/12/the-past-and-future-of-americas-social-contract/282511/.

Freedom from Religion Foundation. "Freethought Heroine Award: Marci Hamilton—2014." Accessed on February 18, 2018. https://ffrf.org/outreach/awards/freethought-heroine-award/item/22126-marci-hamilton.

French, Laurence. *Native American Justice.* Rowman & Littlefield, 2003.

Fullilove, Michael. *Rendezvous with Destiny: How Franklin D. Roosevelt and Five Extraordinary Men Took American into the War and into the World.* New York: Penguin, 2013.

Garelick, Jon. "Joyce Linehan: The Decider." *Boston Magazine*, December 31, 2013. https://www.bostonmagazine.com/news/2013/12/31/joyce-linehan/.

Geddes, Linda. "'There is No DNA Test to Prove You're Native American.'" *New Scientist*, February 2014. https://www.newscientist.com/article/mg22129554-400-there-is-no-dna-test-to-prove-youre-native-american/.

General Mills. "Betty Crocker Homemaker of Tomorrow Test Review 1966." General Mills, 1965.

George Washington University. "Senator Elizabeth Warren Discusses her Time at GW." YouTube Video, 3:00, May 8, 2013, https://www.youtube.com/watch?v=4CBbiZYQ0mg.

Gerber, Eric. "Elizabeth Warren Looks Back at Her Cougar Roots." *University of Houston Magazine*, Spring 2003.

Getman, Julius. *In the Company of Scholars: The Struggle for the Soul of Higher Education.* Austin: University of Texas Press, 1992. E-book.

Gibbs, Nancy. "Where Memory and Hope Converge: The Funeral of Edward M. Kennedy." *Time*, August 29, 2009. http://content.time.com/time/nation/article/0,8599,1919484,00.html.

Gitlin, Todd. *Occupy Nation: The Roots, the Spirit, and the Promise of Occupy Wall Street.* New York: itbooks/HarperCollins, 2012.

Goble, Danney. "Government and Politics." *The Encyclopedia of Oklahoma History and Culture.* Accessed September 5, 2017. www.okhistory.org.

Goodnough, Abby. "From the Halls of Harvard Into the Street, In Pursuit of a Senate Seat." *New York Times,* September 14, 2011. http://www.nytimes.com/2011/09/15/us/politics/warren-kicks-off-senate-campaign-in-massachusetts.html.

Goodwin, Neva, and Jonathan Harris, Julie Nelson, Brian Roach, and Mariano Torras. *Macroeconomics in Context.* 2nd ed. Armonk: M.E. Sharpe, 2014.

Greenstone Miller, Jody, and Matt Miller. "The Rise of the Supertemp." *Harvard Business Review* (May 2012). https://hbr.org/2012/05/the-rise-of-the-supertemp.

Grim, Ryan. "Elizabeth Warren on Her Journey from Low-Information Voter." The Intercept.com. February 19, 2018. https://theintercept.com/2018/02/19/elizabeth-warren-opens-up-about-her-choices-in-every-presidential-election-since-1972/.

Groden, Claire. "Meet Fortune's 2015 Most Promising Women Entrepreneurs." *Fortune*, September 9, 2015. http://fortune.com/2015/09/09/2015-most-promising -women-entrepreneurs/.

Groer, Annie. "Indiana GOP Senate Hopeful Richard Mourdock Says God 'Intended' Rape Pregnancies." *Washington Post*, October 24, 2012. https://www.washingtonpost .com/blogs/she-the-people/wp/2012/10/24/indiana-gop-senate-hopeful-richard -mourdock-says-god-intended-rape-pregnancies/?utm_term=.9ccdcc8ee14b.

Grunwald, Michael. "The Real Truth About Wall Street." *Time*, September 30, 2014. http://time.com/3450110/aig-lehman/.

Grynbaum, Michael J. "Barney Frank Weds Jim Ready." *New York Times*, July 7, 2012. http://www.nytimes.com/2012/07/08/fashion/weddings/barney-frank-wedding -jim-ready.html.

Haines, Tim. "Clinton: Flip-Flop On Bankruptcy Bill 'Had Nothing To Do With Money,' 'It Was About Protecting Women.'" RealClear Politics.com. February 7, 2016. https://www.realclearpolitics.com/video/2016/02/07/clinton_accuses _sanders_and_warren_of_smear_campaign.html.

Hall, Colby. "Video of Elizabeth Warren's Passionate Rebuttal of 'Class Warfare' Goes Viral." Mediaite. September 22, 2011. https://www.mediaite.com/online /video-of-elizabeth-warrens-passionate-rebuttal-of-class-warfare-goes-viral/.

Hall, Mark. "Amazon.com." Encyclopedia Britannica. Accessed January 11, 2018. https://www.britannica.com/topic/Amazoncom.

Harvard Law School. "A Brief Timeline of Our First Two Centuries." Accessed February 19, 2018. http://hls.harvard.edu/about/history/.

———. "HLS Profile and Facts." Accessed February 19, 2018. http://hls.harvard.edu /dept/jdadmissions/apply-to-harvard-law-school/hls-profile-and-facts/.

Harvard Law Today. "Current Students Endorse Warren for Director of Bureau of Consumer Financial Protection." August 23, 2010. https://today.law.harvard.edu/current-students -endorse-warren-for-director-of-bureau-of-consumer-financial-protection/.

Helderman, Rosalind. "Warren to Seek Brown's Senate Seat in Mass." *Washington Post*, September 14, 2011.

Hensch, Mark. "Mika Brzezinski: 'I'm Getting Tired' of Warren." *The Hill*. November 29, 2016. http://thehill.com/homenews/senate/307932-mika-brzezinski -im-getting-tired-of-warren.

Henry, Zoe. "Sorry, Millennials: The 'American Dream' Is Fading, New Study Suggests." *Inc.* December 9, 2016. https://www.inc.com/zoe-henry/is-the-american-dream -fading-children-less-likely-to-out-earn-parents.html.

Herzlinger, Regina E. *Consumer-Driven Health Care: Implications for Providers, Payers, and Policymakers*. San Francisco: Jossey-Bass, 2004.

Hickey, Adam S. "Harvard's Top Five Salaries Total More Than $1.5M." *Harvard*

Crimson, September 19, 1997. http://www.thecrimson.com/article/1997/9/19 /harvards-top-five-salaries-total-more/.

History.com. "FDR Creates Civilian Conservation Corps." Accessed September 20, 2017. http://www.history.com/this-day-in-history/fdr-creates-civilian-conservation-corps.

Humphrey, Skip. "Written Testimony of Hubert H. 'Skip' Humphrey III Before the United States Senate Special Committee on Aging." November 15, 2012. https ://www.consumerfinance.gov/about-us/newsroom/written-testimony-of-hubert -h-skip-humphrey-iii-before-the-united-states-senate-special-committee-on-aging/.

IBM. "The Apollo Missions." IBM.com. Accessed January 27, 2018. http://www-03 .ibm.com/ibm/history/ibm100/us/en/icons/apollo/.

ICT Staff. "Elizabeth Warren's Genealogical Challenge." Indian Country Today. May 15, 2012. https://indiancountrymedianetwork.com/newselizabeth-warrens -genealogical-challenge/.

"ICYMI: Warren's Speech a Hit with Convention Crowd, Brings DNC Hall to Its Feet." Elizabeth Warren for Senate. September 6, 2012. https://elizabethwarren .com/news/press-releases/icymi-warrens-speech-a-hit-with-convention-crowd -brings-dnc-hall-to-its-feet.

"In Remembrance of Allan Axelrod." *Rutgers Law Review*, 61, no. 1 (2008): 13–29.

Investopedia Staff. "Case Study: The Collapse of Lehman Brothers." Updated December 11, 2017. https://www.investopedia.com/articles/economics/09/lehman-brothers -collapse.asp.

———. "Economic Efficiency." Accessed February 2, 2018. https://www.investopedia .com/terms/e/economic_efficiency.asp.

———. "Rational Choice Theory." Accessed February 2, 2018. https://www.investopedia .com/terms/r/rational-choice-theory.asp.

———. "Too Big to Fail." Accessed January 20, 2018. https://www.investopedia.com /terms/t/too-big-to-fail.asp.

———. "Troubled Asset Relief Program—TARP." Accessed February 15, 2018. https ://www.investopedia.com/terms/t/troubled-asset-relief-program-tarp.asp

Isenstadt, Alex. "Warren Gives Fiery Defense of Obama." Politico. September 5, 2012. https://www.politico.com/story/2012/09/warren-gives-fiery-defense-of-obama -blasts-romney-080807.

Isidore, Chris. "U.S. Ends TARP with $15.3 Billion Profit." CNN. December 19, 2014. http ://money.cnn.com/2014/12/19/news/companies/government-bailouts-end/index.html.

Jacobs, Julia, and Victoria McGrane. "This Isn't the First Time Warren Spoke About that Office Incident." *Boston Globe*, October 24, 2017. http://www.bostonglobe. com/news/politics/2017/10/23/warren-view-office-incident-evolved-along-with -society-changing-approach-harassment/qVgXJtPz4s8Imw7bJW034H/story .html?s_campaign=bdc:article:stub.

Jacobs, Sally. "A Lost Boy, Seared by Abuse, He Somehow Found His Way." *Boston Globe*, August 5, 2012. http://archive.boston.com/news/local/massachusetts/articles/2012/08/05/senator_scott_browns_searing_childhood_and_his_improbable_rise/?page=full.

Jacobs, Samuel P. "Elizabeth Warren: 'I Created Occupy Wall Street.'" Daily Beast. October 24, 2011. https://www.thedailybeast.com/elizabeth-warren-i-created-occupy-wall-street.

Johnson, Karl, and Ann Scales. "An Absolutely, Positively True Story: Seven Reasons Why We Sing." *New Mexico Law Review* 16 (1986): 433–478. http://digitalrepository.unm.edu/nmlr/vol16/iss3/3/.

Johnson, Rebecca. "Elizabeth Warren: Held to Account." *Vogue*, December 20, 2010, https://www.vogue.com/article/elizabeth-warren-held-to-account.

Kaczke, Lisa. "Elizabeth Warren's Appearances As a Financial Expert on TV Talk Shows Helped Launch Her Political Career." MassLive. January 26, 2012. http://www.masslive.com/politics/index.ssf/2012/01/elizabeth_warren_appeared_as_f.html.

Kessler, Friedrich. "Contracts of Adhesion: Some Thoughts About Freedom of Contract." (1943). *Yale Law School Faculty Scholarship Series*. 2731. http://digitalcommons.law.yale.edu/fss_papers/2731/.

Khan, Huma, and Caitlin Taylor. "Ted Kennedy's Legislative Accomplishments." ABC News. August 26, 2009. http://abcnews.go.com/Politics/TedKennedy/story?id=7787098.

Kiel, Paul. "Car Dealers Protected from New Consumer Protection Agency." *Mother Jones*, October 27, 2009. https://www.motherjones.com/politics/2009/10/car-dealers-protected-new-consumer-protection-agency/.

Kimball, Bruce. A. "The Proliferation of Case Method Teaching in American Law Schools: Mr. Langdell's Emblematic 'Abomination,' 1890–1915." *History of Education Quarterly*, 46, no. 2 (Summer 2006), 192–247. https://www.jstor.org/stable/20462057?seq=15#page_scan_tab_contents.

Kleefeld, Eric. "Elizabeth Warren On 'Class Warfare': There is Nobody Who Got Rich on His Own." Talking Points Memo. September 21, 2011. https://talkingpointsmemo.com/election2012/elizabeth-warren-on-class-warfare-there-is-nobody-who-got-rich-on-his-own-video.

Kosmerick, Todd J. "Synar, Michael Lynn." *The Encyclopedia of Oklahoma History and Culture*. Accessed January 8, 2018. http://www.okhistory.org/publications/enc/entry.php?entry=SY001.

Kotler, Philip. *Confronting Capitalism: Real Solutions for a Troubled Economic System*. New York: American Management Association, 2015.

Kreisler, Harry. "Conversation with Elizabeth Warren: Law, Politics, and the Coming Collapse of the Middle Class." March 8, 2007. http://globetrotter.berkeley.edu/people7/Warren/warren-con1.html.

Krieg, Gregory J. "What Is a Super PAC? A Short History." ABC News. August 9, 2012. http://abcnews.go.com/Politics/OTUS/super-pac-short-history/story?id=16960267.

Kroll, Andy. "Bogus Attacks On the CFPB." *Mother Jones*, November 30, 2010. https ://www.motherjones.com/politics/2010/11/bogus-attacks-cfpb-elizabeth-warren/.

———. "Protesters Swarm Wall St. Lobbyists' Homes." *Mother Jones*, May 16, 2010. https://www.motherjones.com/politics/2010/05/main-street-battles-wall-street -seiu-npa-gregory-baer-peter-scher-jpmorgan-chase-bank-of-america/.

Krugman, Paul. *The Conscience of a Liberal*. New York: Norton, 2009. Kindle.

Lawless, Robert M., and Elizabeth Warren. "Shrinking the Safety Net: The 2005 Changes in U.S. Bankruptcy Law." University of Illinois Law & Economics Research Paper No. LE06–031(2006). https://ssrn.com/abstract=949629.

Lee, Deron. "Obama Picks Cordray Over Warren for Consumer Protection Bureau." *The Atlantic*, July 17, 2011. https://www.theatlantic.com/politics/archive/2011/07 /obama-picks-cordray-over-warren-consumer-protection-bureau/352948/.

Leiter, Brian. "Top 25 Law Faculties in Scholarly Impact, 2005–2009." Brian Leiter's Law School Rankings. Accessed January 12, 2018.

Levenson, Michael. "After Her Record Haul, Warren Slips Into Red." *Boston Globe*, December 5, 2012. https://www.bostonglobe.com/news/politics/2012/12/05 /elizabeth-warren-ended-senate-campaign-debt-despite-record-fund-raising /ShWe5K7KzUiVnFHiIxkX5H/story.html.

———. "Warren and Brown Share July 12 Anniversary Date." *Boston Globe*, July 12, 2012. https://www.bostonglobe.com/metro/massachusetts/2012/07/11/warren -and-brown-share-july-anniversary-date-can-you-believe-brown-warren-share -same-wedding-day/8Hdc2c9xDb5v1DuzrpypjO/story.html.

Levin, Bess. "Trump Budget Director Expected to Take Over Agency He Called a 'Sick, Sad Joke.'" *Vanity Fair*, November 16, 2017. https://www.vanityfair.com /news/2017/11/mick-mulvaney-cfpb.

Linehan, Joyce. "Elizabeth Warren in My Living Room." *CommonWealth*. August 17, 2011. https://commonwealthmagazine.org/politics/012-elizabeth-warren-in-my-living-room/.

LiveSmartVideos. "Elizabeth Warren on Debt Crisis, Fair Taxation." YouTube Video, 2:05, September 18, 2011. https://www.youtube.com/watch?v=htX2usfqMEs.

Lizza, Ryan. "The Virtual Candidate." *New Yorker*, May 4, 2015, https://www.newyorker .com/magazine/2015/05/04/the-virtual-candidate.

"Local Happenings." Democrat-American (Sequoya County Democrat), April 24, 1925.

Loth, Renee. "The Timely Return of Bob Massie." *Boston Globe*, January 16, 2011, http ://archive.boston.com/bostonglobe/editorial_opinion/oped/articles/2011/01/16 /the_timely_return_of_bob_massie/.

Lowery, Wesley. "Gov. Pence signs revised Indiana religious freedom bill into law." *Washington Post*, April 2, 2015. https://www.washingtonpost.com/news/post

-nation/wp/2015/04/02/gov-pence-signs-revised-indiana-religious-freedom-bill
-into-law/?utm_term=.28e1e88ffd1b.

Madison, Lucy. "Warren Explains Minority Listing, Talks of Grandfather's 'High Cheekbones.'" CBS News. May 3, 2012. https://www.cbsnews.com/news/warren-explains-minority-listing-talks-of-grandfathers-high-cheekbones/.

Madrick, Jeff. "Economic Scene; Necessities, Not Luxuries, Are Driving Americans Into Debt, a New Book Says." *New York Times*, September 4, 2003. http://www.nytimes.com/2003/09/04/business/economic-scene-necessities-not-luxuries-are-driving-americans-into-debt-new-book.html.

Mandel, Seth. "Dems Hope Warren Can Beat the 'Unbeatable' Scott Brown." *Commentary*, August 16, 2011. https://www.commentarymagazine.com/politics-ideas/liberals-democrats/warren-brown-senate/.

Mann, Bruce H. "Failure in the Land of the Free." *American Bankruptcy Law Journal*, 77, no. 1 (Winter 2003): 1–7.

Mann, Bruce H. "Tales from the Crypt: Prison, Legal Authority, and the Debtors' Constitution in the Early Republic." *The William and Mary Quarterly* 51, no. 2 (1994): 183–202. doi:10.2307/2946859.

———. *Republic of Debtors: Bankruptcy in the Age of Independence.* Cambridge: Harvard University Press, 2002.

Marcotte, Amanda. "Author Courtney Martin Celebrates Millennials Who Are Redefining the American Dream." Salon. September 13, 2016. https://www.salon.com/2016/09/13/author-courtney-martin-celebrates-millennials-who-are-redefining-the-american-dream/.

MarketsWiki: "Elizabeth Warren." Updated November 30, 2017. http://www.marketswiki.com/wiki/Elizabeth_Warren.

Martin, Roland. "Washington Watch: Elizabeth Warren Has the Taxpayer's Back." YouTube, 7:10, March 15, 2010. https://www.youtube.com/watch?v=QfFVbF3Ugy8.

Massachusetts Senate Debate. Scott Brown vs. Elizabeth Warren. C-Span Video, 57:27, September 20, 2012. https://www.c-span.org/video/?308202–1/massachusetts-senate-debate&start=130.

Massey, Douglas S. *Categorically Unequal: The American Stratification System.* New York: Russell Sage Foundation, 2008.

Masters, Diane. "Elizabeth Warren Rally with Rep. John Lewis and Gov. Deval Patrick." Elizabeth Warren for Senate, November 3, 2012, https://elizabethwarren.com/blog/elizabeth-warren-rally-with-rep-lewis-and-gov-patrick.

Mayer, Jane. *Dark Money: The Hidden History of the Billionaires Behind the Rise of the Radical Right.* New York: Anchor Books, 2017.

McCalmont, Lucy. "Warren: American Dream Is Slipping Away." Politico. November 19, 2014. https://www.politico.com/story/2014/11/elizabeth-warren-economic-speech-113031.

McGinn, Daniel. "Why a Harvard Professor is Overseeing the Bailout." *Newsweek*, April 10, 2009. http://www.newsweek.com/why-harvard-professor-overseeing -bailout-77401.

McGrane, Victoria. "Religion Is Constant Part of Elizabeth Warren's Life." Boston Globe, September 2, 2017. https://www.bostonglobe.com/news/nation/2017/09/02/ religion-constant-part-warren-life/ndGztmfK5veAGMI6A4OKEI/story.html.

———. "Warren Raises Foreign Policy Profile with Armed Services Assignment." *Boston Globe*, December 14, 2016. https://www.bostonglobe .com/news/politics/2016/12/14/warren-gets-spot-armed-services-committee /TR4Xf6TnDn8izaFSlUDJcN/story.html.

McGrory, Brian. "Elizabeth Warren's Private Agony." *Boston Globe*, November 30, 2012. https://www.bostonglobe.com/metro/2012/11/30/warren-private-sorrow /uwp3BYslrXDgcMgX7xiwPK/story.html.

Mecoy, Don. "Elizabeth Warren: An Okie in Washington Riles Wall Street." *Oklahoman*, August 1, 2010. http://newsok.com/article/3481388.

Meyer, Jared. "The Economy Is Changing And So Is the American Dream." Forbes, March 22, 2017. https://www.forbes.com/sites/jaredmeyer/2017/03/22/the- economy-is-changing-and-so-is-the-american-dream/#4436c73b3cc3.

Meyer, Jared. "Embracing the Millennial American Dream." Prepared for the Manhattan Institute for Policy Research. November 18, 2015. https://www.jec.senate.gov /public/_cache/files/4d096d89-6273-4b7d-be2c-cf968521cc15/jec-meyer-written -testimony.pdf.

Mirk, Sarah. "These Letters About Sexual Harassment from the 1970s Could Be About Trump Today." October 19, 2016. https://www.bitchmedia.org/article /these-letters-about-sexual-harassment-1970s-could-be-about-trump-today.

Mimms, Sarah "Is Elizabeth Warren an Effective Senator?" *The Atlantic*, May 26, 2015. https://www.theatlantic.com/politics/archive/2015/05/is -elizabeth-warren-an-effective-senator/449349/.

Mixon, John. *Autobiography of a Law School*. Houston: University of Houston Law Foundation, 2012. http://www.law.uh.edu/history/mobile/index.html#p=2.

———. "Neoclassical Economics and the Erosion of Middle-Class Values: An Explanation for Economic Collapse." Notre Dame Journal of Law, Ethics & Public Policy, 24, no. 2 (2012): 327–378. https://scholarship.law.nd.edu/ndjlepp/vol24/ iss2/4/.

Mize, Richard. "Sequoya Convention." Oklahoma Historical Society. 2009. http://www .okhistory.org/publications/enc/entry.php?entry=SE021.

Moffitt, Nancy. "The Two-Income Trap." *Wharton Magazine* (Fall/Winter 2017). http://whartonmagazine.com/issues/fall-2003/the-two-income-trap/#sthash .nisAOOOP.dpbs.

Morgenson, Gretchen. "From Outside or Inside, the Deck Looks Stacked." *New York Times*, April 26, 2014. https://www.nytimes.com/2014/04/27/business/from-outside-or-inside-the-deck-looks-stacked.html.

Morris, David Z. "The Equifax Hack Exposed More Data Than Previously Reported." *Fortune*, February 11, 2018. http://fortune.com/2018/02/11/equifax-hack-exposed-extra-data/.

Mui, Ylan Q. "Americans Saw Wealth Plummet 40 Percent from 2007 to 2010, Federal Reserve Says." *Washington Post*, June 11, 2012. https://www.washingtonpost.com/business/economy/fed-americans-wealth-dropped-40-percent/2012/06/11/gJQAllsCVV_story.html?utm_term=.79553e77da67.

———. "Democrats' Control of Senate Could Hinge on Warren Campaign." Washington Post, September 19, 2011. https://www.washingtonpost.com/business/economy/democrats-control-of-senate-could-hinge-on-warren-campaign/2011/09/16/gIQA1HUYfK_story.html?utm_term=.e19ea1ee50fd.

———. "In Mass. Race, A Watchdog to Watch." *Washington Post*, September 21, 2011.

———. "Senate Blocks Richard Cordray Confirmation to Head Consumer Watchdog Agency." *Washington Post*, December 8, 2011. https://www.washingtonpost.com/blogs/2chambers/post/senate-republicans-block-cordray-as-obama-consumer-watchdog-nominee/2011/12/08/gIQA6j9BfO_blog.html?utm_term=.fd856ce5f11f.

Myers, Dee Dee. *Why Women Should Rule the World*. New York: Harper, 2008.

Nakamura, David, and Felicia Sonmez. "Obama Defies Senate, Puts Cordray in Consumer Post." *Washington Post*, January 5, 2012. https://www.pressreader.com/usa/the-washington-post/20120105/289875934337610.

"National Bankruptcy Review Commission." Federal Register. Accessed December 3, 2017. https://www.federalregister.gov/agencies/national-bankruptcy-review-commission.

National Weather Service. "Norman, Oklahoma Tornadoes (1890-Present)." Accessed on December 20, 2017. https://www.weather.gov/oun/tornadodata-city-ok-norman.

National Weather Service. "Tornadoes in the Oklahoma City, Oklahoma Area Since 1890." Accessed on December 20, 2017. https://www.weather.gov/oun/tornadodata-okc.

NBC News. "Women Senators Say #MeToo, Reveal Stories of Sexual Harassment." YouTube Video, 6:27, October 23, 2017, https://www.youtube.com/watch?v=Q5fhDShPCvA.

NeJaime, Douglas, and Reva B. Siegel. "Conscience Wars: Complicity-based Conscience Claims in Religion and Politics." *Yale Law Journal*, 124, no. 7 (May 2015): 2202–2679. https://www.yalelawjournal.org/feature/complicity-based-conscience-claims#_ftnref196.

Neumann, Richard K., Jr. "Women in Legal Education: What the Statistics Show." *Journal*

of Legal Education, 50 (2000): 313–357. https://scholarlycommons.law.hofstra
.edu/cgi/viewcontent.cgi?referer=https://www.google.com/&httpsredir=1&article
=1882&context=faculty_scholarship.

Newsweek Staff. "Elizabeth Warren on Financial Regulatory Reform."
Newsweek, December 6, 2009. http://www.newsweek.com/elizabeth-warren
-financial-regulatory-reform-75759.

Newton-Small, Jay. *Broad Influence: How Women Are Changing the Way America Works.*
New York: Time Books, 2016.

Nichols, John. "Elizabeth Warren Says She'll Consider Massachusetts Senate
Run." *The Nation*, July 19, 2011. https://www.thenation.com/article/elizabeth
-warren-says-shell-consider-massachusetts-senate-run/.

———. "From Paul Wellstone to Elizabeth Warren." *The Nation*, October 25, 2012.
https://www.thenation.com/article/paul-wellstone-elizabeth-warren/.

Norris, Michele. "Two-Income Families at Risk of Financial Crisis." "All Things
Considered," National Public Radio. Audio, 5:40, September 8, 2003. https://www
.npr.org/templates/story/story.php?storyId=1423789.

O'Brien, Kathleen. "How Elizabeth Warren's Rutgers Roots Forged her Future VP
Prospects." Updated June 26, 2016. http://www.nj.com/news/index.ssf/2016/06
/sen_elizabeth_warren_-_her_jersey_years.html.

Obama, Barack. "Remarks by the President on the Confirmation of Richard Cordray
as Director for CFPB." White House. July 17, 2013. https://obamawhitehouse
.archives.gov/the-press-office/2013/07/17/remarks-president-confirmation
-richard-cordray-director-cfpb.

Obituary of Gregory B. Millard, *New York Times*, October 7, 1984. https://www.nytimes
.com/1984/10/07/obituaries/gregory-b-millard-37-arts-official-with-city.html.

"Oklahoma City Bombing Fast Facts." CNN. March 29, 2017. https://www.cnn
.com/2013/09/18/us/oklahoma-city-bombing-fast-facts/index.html.

Orndorff Troyan, Mary. "Spencer Bachus Finally Gets His Chairmanship." AL.com,
December 9, 2010.

Osborn, Billy J. *Wetumka: A Centennial History.* San Jose: Writers Club Press, 2002.

Pasvogel, Glenn E., Jr. "The Bankruptcy Reform Act of 1978—A Review and Comments."
University of Arkansas at Little Rock Law Review, 13, no. 3 (1980): 13-73.

Pazzanese, Christina. "The Women Who Questioned Wall Street." *Harvard Gazette*,
May 4, 2015. https://news.harvard.edu/gazette/story/2015/05/the-women-who
-questioned-wall-street/.

PBS.org. "Battlefield: Vietnam." Accessed September 18, 2017. http://www.pbs.org
/battlefieldvietnam/timeline/index1.html

———. "Timeline of World War II." September 2007. http://www.pbs.org/thewar
/at_war_timeline_1940.htm

Pearlstein, Steven. "How the Cult of Shareholder Value Wrecked American Business." *Washington Post*, September 9, 2013. https://www.washingtonpost.com/news /wonk/wp/2013/09/09/how-the-cult-of-shareholder-value-wrecked-american -business/?utm_term=.57f2911c182a.

Pell, M. B., and Joe Eaton. "Five Lobbyists for Each Member of Congress on Financial Reform." Center for Public Integrity. May 21, 2010, https://www.publicintegrity .org/2010/05/21/2670/ five-lobbyists-each-member-congress-financial-reforms.

Pengelly, Martin. "Elizabeth Warren Seeks to Use Trump Pocahontas 'racial slur' as Political Tool." *The Guardian*, March 11, 2018, https://www.theguardian.com/us-news/2018 /mar/11/elizabeth-warren-donald-trump-pocahontas-native-americans.

Perlow, Jason. "IBM and Univac in the Apollo Program." ZDNet.com, July 13, 2009. http://www.zdnet.com/pictures/ibm-and-univac-in-the-apollo-program/.

Phillip, Abby. "Cordray, Not Warren, to Lead CFPB." Politico.com. July 17, 2011. https ://www.politico.com/story/2011/07/cordray-not-warren-to-lead-cfpb-059206.

Phillips, Kate. "The Kennedy Funeral." *New York Times*, August 29, 2009. https ://thecaucus.blogs.nytimes.com/2009/08/29/the-kennedy-funeral/

Pierce, Charles. "The Watchdog: Elizabeth Warren." *Boston Globe*, December 20, 2009. http://archive.boston.com/bostonglobe/magazine/articles/2009/12/20/elizabeth _warren_is_the_bostonian_of_the_year/.

———. "What We Learn from Elizabeth Warren." *Esquire*, June 10, 2016. https://www .esquire.com/news-politics/politics/a26352/elizabeth-warren-teacher-0514/.

Plumer, Bradford. "The Two-Income Trap." *Mother Jones*, November 8, 2004. https ://www.motherjones.com/politics/2004/11/two-income-trap/.

"Population of Wetumka, Oklahoma." Population.us. Accessed November 18, 2017. http://population.us/ok/wetumka/.

Powell, Michael. "Ohio Attorney General Fights Against Wall Street." *New York Times*, October 11, 2010. http://www.nytimes.com/2010/10/12/business/12avenge.html? _r=1&src=busln.

"President Barack Obama on 'The Jay Leno Show.'" March 19, 2009. http://www .nytimes.com/ 2009/03/20/us/politics/20obama.text.html.

Protess, Ben. "Consumer Watchdog Hires Former Bankers." *New York Times*, February 17, 2011. https://dealbook.nytimes.com/2011/02/17/consumer-watchdog-hires-former-bankers/.

Raju, Manu, and John Bresnahan. "Reid Taps Warren as Envoy to Liberals." Politico. November 12, 2014. https://www.politico.com/story/2014/11/elizabeth-warren -harry-reid-senate-leadership-112847.

Rampell, Catherine. "How Mick Mulvaney Is Dismantling a Federal Agency." *Washington Post*, January 25, 2018. https://www.washingtonpost.com/opinions/mick-mulvaney -cant-legally-kill-the-cfpb-so-hes-starving-it-instead/2018/01/25/4481d2ce-021 6–11e8–8acf-ad2991367d9d_story.html?utm_term=.f38ad9489b0c.

Rank, Mark Robert, Thomas A. Hirschl, and Kirk A. Foster. *Chasing the American Dream: Understanding What Shapes Our Fortunes.* New York: Oxford University Press, 2014.

Rappeport, Alan. "Payday Rules Relax on Trump's Watch After Lobbying by Lenders." *New York Times,* February 2, 2018. https://www.nytimes.com/2018/02/02/us /politics/payday-lenders-lobbying-regulations.html?ribbon-ad-idx=5&rref=home page&module=Ribbon&version=context&region=Header&action=click&conten tCollection=Home%20Page&pgtype=article.

Reid, Jim. "What's New in School?" *Daily Oklahoman* (Oklahoma City, OK), July 17, 1965.

Reston, Maeve. "Elizabeth Warren, In Spotlight, Hits 'Late Show with David Letterman.'" September 4, 2014. http://www.latimes.com/nation/politics/politicsnow/la-pn-elizabeth -warren-late-show-david-letterman-20140904-story.html.

Reuters Staff. "Bair: Regulators Clashed Ahead of WaMu Crash." April 16, 2010. https://www.reuters.com/article/financial-bair/bair-regulators-clashed-ahead -of-wamu-crash-idUSN1614676320100416.

Roller, Emma. "Elizabeth Warren's 11 Commandments of Progressivism." *The Atlantic,* July 18, 2014. https://www.theatlantic.com/politics/archive/2014/07 /elizabeth-warrens-11-commandments-of-progressivism/455955/.

Rostochil, Lynne. "From Civil Rights to the Who: A Look at Wedgewood Village Amusement Park." Accessed December 2, 2017. http://okcmod.com/2014/07 /in-celebration-of-wedgewood/.

Rubin, Paul H. "Law and Economics." *The Concise Encyclopedia of Economics.* Accessed February 2, 2018. http://www.econlib.org/library/Enc/LawandEconomics. html#abouttheauthor.

Rubino, Kathryn. "Which Law Schools Have Been the Very Best Over the Last 10 Years?" Above the Law. August 30, 2017. https://abovethelaw.com/2017/08/which-law -schools-have-been-the-very-best-over-the-last-10-years/?rf=1.

Rutgers in Newark. "Interview with RU-N Alumna Elizabeth Warren." YouTube Video, 9:59, November 9, 2011, https://www.youtube.com/watch?v=NItCGcV84GM&t =203s.

Sandberg, Sheryl. *Lean In: Women, Work, and the Will to Lead.* New York: Knopf, 2013.

Sarasohn, David. "The Most Underestimated Feminist in DC." United States Senator Patty Murray. June 4, 2014. https://www.murray.senate.gov/public/index.cfm/ pattyinnews?ID=A61348FB-38A6–4CE1–9F24–76BD9B15DCD1.

Scherer, Michael. "The New Sheriffs of Wall Street." *Time,* May 24, 2010. http://content .time.com/time/magazine/article/0,9171,1989144,00.html.

Sherer, Michael, Sam Frizell, and Zeke J. Miller. "Up With People." *Time,* July 20, 2015.

Schrems, Sue and Vernon Maddux. *Images of America: Norman: 1889–1949.* Charleston: Arcadia Publishing, 2013.

Seattle Times Staff. "5 Things to Know About Hobby Lobby's Owners." *Seattle Times,* July

1, 2014, https://www.seattletimes.com/nation-world/5-things-to-know-about-hobby-lobbys-owners/.

Seelye, Katharine Q., and Abby Goodnough. "Candidate for Senate Defends Past Hiring." *New York Times,* April 30, 2012. http://www.nytimes.com/2012/05/01/us/politics/elizabeth-warrens-ancestry-irrelevant-in-hiring-law-schools-say.html.

Seitz-Wald, Alex. "Oklahoma: The Unlikeliest Democrat Battle State." NBC.com. February 24, 2016. https://www.nbcnews.com/politics/2016-election/oklahoma-unlikeliest-democratic-battleground-state-n524866.

"Sessions Attorney General Nomination." C-Span Video, 30:36:01, February 6, 2017, https://www.c-span.org/video/?423606-103/us-senate-confirms-jeff-sessions-takes-tom-price-nomination&start=30611.

Shelden, Darla. "Oklahoma Debate Champion and Advocate for Middle Class Families Becomes Senate Hopeful." *City Sentinel* (Oklahoma City), December 14, 2011. http://city-sentinel.com/2011/12/oklahoma-debate-champion-and-advocate-for-middle-class-families-becomes-senate-hopeful/.

Shopkow, Leah. "'Arthur': From the *History of the Kings of Britain*." Indiana University. http://www.indiana.edu/~dmdhist/arthur_gm.htm.

Sink, Justin. "Warren Demands an Apology from Opponent in Heritage Controversy." *The Hill,* May 31, 2012. http://thehill.com/blogs/blog-briefing-room/news/230315-elizabeth-warren-accuses-scott-brown-of-attacking-parents-over-cherokee-ancestry-demands-apology.

Skeel, David A., Jr. "Bankruptcy's Home Economics." *ABI Law Review,* 12, no. 43 (2004): 43–58.

Slack, Megan. "Senate Confirms Richard Cordray as Consumer Watchdog." White House. July 17, 2013. https://obamawhitehouse.archives.gov/blog/2013/07/17/senate-confirms-richard-cordray-consumer-watchdog.

Smith, Aaron. "Shared, Collaborative and On Demand: The New Digital Economy." Pew Research Center. May 19, 2016. http://www.pewinternet.org/2016/05/19/the-new-digital-economy/.

Sorkin, Amy Davidson. "Elizabeth Warren's Native American Question." *New Yorker,* May 8, 2012. https://www.newyorker.com/news/amy-davidson/elizabeth-warrens-native-american-question.

Spross, Jeff. "Why Elizabeth Warren Left the GOP." ThinkProgress. April 27, 2014, https://thinkprogress.org/why-elizabeth-warren-left-the-gop-e78680711424/.

Steinhauer, Jennifer, and Binyamin Applebaum. "Democrats Try to Woo Consumer Advocate to Run." *New York Times,* May 23, 2011. http://www.nytimes.com/2011/05/24/us/politics/24warren.html.

Sturm, Circe. *Blood Politics: Race, Culture, and Identity in the Cherokee Nation of Oklahoma.* Berkeley: University of California Press, 2002.

Sullivan, Sean. "The Fix's Best Fundraiser of 2012." *Washington Post*, December 13, 2012. https://www.washingtonpost.com/news/the-fix/wp/2012/12/13/the-fixs-best -fundraiser-of-2012/?utm_term=.6fb918481173.

————. *As We Forgive Our Debtors: Bankruptcy and Consumer Debt in America.* New York: Oxford University Press, 1989.

Sullivan, Teresa A., Elizabeth Warren, and Jay Lawrence Westbrook. *The Fragile Middle Class: Americans in Debt.* New Haven: Yale University Press, 2000.

————. "Laws, Models, and Real People: Choice of Chapter in Personal Bankruptcy." *Law & Social Inquiry*, 13, no. 4 (Autumn 1988): 661–706.

Suro, Robert. "Here's What Happened with the Latino Vote." *New York Times*, November 9, 2016. https://www.nytimes.com/interactive/projects/cp/opinion /election-night-2016/heres-what-happened-with-the-latino-vote.

Surowiecki, James. "The Warren Court." *New Yorker*, June 13 & 20, 2011. https://www .newyorker.com/magazine/2011/06/13/the-warren-court.

Taft, Isabelle. "How a Decade in Texas Changed Elizabeth Warren." *Texas Tribune*, July 13, 2016. https://www.texastribune.org/2016/07/13/how-decade-texas-changed -elizabeth-warren/.

Talton, Jon. "Sheila Bair on WaMu: 'Was it Fair? Absolutely Not.'" *Seattle Times*, May 5, 2014. https://www.seattletimes.com/nation-world/sheila-bair-on-wamu-was-it -fair-absolutely-not/.

Texas Divorce Index, 1968–2014. https://search.ancestry.com/search/db.aspx ?dbid=8794.

Thrush, Glenn, and Manu Raju. "The Outsider." Politico.com. March/April 2015. https://www .politico.com/magazine/story/2015/03/elizabeth-warren-profile-115489 ?paginate=false.

Tomasky, Michael. "A Woman of the People: Elizabeth Warren and the Future of the American Left." *Foreign Affairs*, September/October 2014. https://www.foreignaffairs .com/articles/united-states/2014-08-18/woman-people.

Toobin, Jeffrey. "Barney's Great Adventure." *New Yorker*, January 12, 2009. https://www .newyorker.com/magazine/2009/01/12/barneys-great-adventure.

————. "The Professor: Elizabeth Warren's Long Journey Into Politics." *New Yorker*, September 17, 2012. https://www.newyorker.com/magazine/2012/09/17/the -professor-5.

Top Law Schools. "Dissecting the Rankings: The U.S. News and World Report." Accessed February 18, 2018. http://www.top-law-schools.com/dissecting-the -rankings-news-world-report.html.

Tractenberg, Paul. *A Centennial History of Rutgers Law School in Newark: Opening a Thousand Doors.* Charleston: The History Press, 2010. Kindle.

Tumulty, Karen. "Elizabeth Warren Keeps Pressure on Hillary Clinton and Democrats

Ahead of 2016." *Washington Post*, January 17, 2015. https://www.washingtonpost
.com/politics/elizabeth-warren-keeps-pressure-on-hillary-clinton-and-democrats
-ahead-of-2016/2015/01/17/cc844300–9b49–11e4-a7ee-526210d€65b4_story
.html?utm_term=.8abdd42b1bcb.

Ulen, Thomas S. "Rational Choice Theory in Law and Economics." In *Encyclopedia of Law and Economics*, edited by Boudewijn Bouckaert and Gerrit De Geest, 790–818. Cheltenham: Edward Elgar, 2000. http://reference.findlaw.com /lawandeconomics/0710-rational-choice-theory-in-law-and-economics.pdf.

United States House of Representatives Office of the Historian. "The Year of the Woman, 1992." 2007. Accessed March 4, 2018. http://history.house.gov/Exhibitions-and-Publications /WIC/Historical-Essays/Assembling-Amplifying-Ascending/Women-Decade/.

University of Chicago Law School. "Henry G. Manne, '52, 1928–2015." Accessed September 3, 2017. https://www.law.uchicago.edu/news/henry-g-manne-52-1928-2015.

University of Houston. "Department of Communication Sciences and Disorders: Undergraduate Program Student Handbook 2017–2018." Accessed November 16, 2017. http://www.uh.edu/class/comd/_docs/handbooks/current_undergradhandbook.pdf.

University of Houston Law Center. "Irene Merker Rosenberg." Accessed October 3, 2017. http://www.law.uh.edu/faculty/main.asp?PID=37.

University of Pennsylvania Law School et al. "Appointments." *Law Alumni Journal*. University of Pennsylvania Law School, XXV, no. 3. (Spring 1990). http://scholarship .law.upenn.edu/cgi/viewcontent.cgi?article=1060&context=plj.

Vennochi, Joan. "Consolation Prize: The Senate." *Boston Globe*, July 14, 2011. http://archive .boston.com/bostonglobe/editorial_opinion/oped/articles/2011/07/14/consolation _prize_the_senate/.

Vitali, Ali. "Trump Calls Warren 'Pocahontas' at Event Honoring Native Americans." NBC News. Updated November 27, 2017. https://www.nbcnews.com/politics/white-house/trump-calls-warren-pocahontas-event-honoring-native-americans-n824266.

Vorman, Julie. "Reform Bill Gives Birth to $550-million Consumer Bureau." Center for Public Integrity, July 15, 2010. https://www.publicintegrity.org/2010/07/15/2613 /reform-bill-gives-birth-550-million-consumer-bureau.

Waits, Wallace F., Jr. "Hatbox Field." Oklahoma Historical Society. 2009. http://www .okhistory.org/publications/enc/entry.php?entryname=HATBOX%20FIELD.

Warren, Elizabeth and Amelia Warren Tyagi. *All Your Worth: The Ultimate Lifetime Money Plan*. New York: Free Press, 2005.

———. *The Two-Income Trap: Why Middle-Class Mothers and Fathers Are Going Broke*. New York: Basic Books, 2003.

———, and Jay Lawrence Westbrook. *The Law of Debtors and Creditors: Text, Cases, and Problems*. Gaithersburg: Aspen, 2001.

———. "Bankruptcy Policy." *University of Chicago Law Review*. 775 (1987): 885–814.

———. "Bankruptcy Policymaking in an Imperfect World." *Michigan Law Review,* 42, no. 2 (November 1993): 336–387.

———. "Busing: Supreme Court Restricts Equity Powers of District Court to Order Interschool Busing." *Rutgers Law Review,* 28 (1975).

———. "Coming Home." Blue Mass Group (blog). August 11, 2011. http://bluemassgroup .com/2011/08/coming-home/.

———. CV. http://www.law.harvard.edu/faculty/ewarren/Warren%20CV%20062508.pdf

———. "Election 2012: Elizabeth Warren Wins Massachusetts Senate Race." YouTube Video, 4:37, November 6, 2012. https://www.youtube.com/watch?v=BVuOaCO4RmE.

———. "Elizabeth Warren on Financial Transparency and TARP." C-Span Video, 2:46, December 10, 2009. https://www.youtube.com/watch?v=3dH07-hlXEA.

———. "Elizabeth Warren Part 2." Interview by Jon Stewart, *The Daily Show with Jon Stewart,* April 15, 2009. Video, 5:11. http://www.cc.com/video-clips/dbjssy /the-daily-show-with-jon-stewart-elizabeth-warren-pt—2.

———. "During the debate on whether to make Jeff Sessions the next Attorney General…" Facebook, February 8, 2017. https://www.facebook.com/senatorelizabethwarren /videos/724337794395383/.

———. "Regulated Industries' Automatic Cost of Service Adjustment Clauses: Do they increase or decrease cost to the consumer?" *Notre Dame Lawyer* 55 (1980): 333–355.

———. "Remarks at Credit Union National Association Governmental Affairs Conference." March 1, 2011. https://www.consumerfinance.gov/about-us/newsroom/remarks-at -credit-union-national-association-governmental-affairs-conference/

———. "Rutgers School of Law Commencement Address." May 27, 2011. https://www .consumerfinance.gov/about-us/newsroom/rutgers-school-of-law-commencement -address/.

———. "Senator Elizabeth Warren Interview." HuffPost Show. YouTube Video, 28:10, April 4 2015. https://www.youtube.com/watch?v=47gYlZ4EDAc.

———. "Senators Warren and Enzi Introduce Bipartisan Bill to Strengthen Genetic Privacy Protections for Research Participants." Senate website. April 5, 2016. https://www .warren.senate.gov/newsroom/press-releases/senators-warren-and-enzi-introduce -bipartisan-bill-to-strengthen-genetic-privacy-protections-for-research-participants.

———. "Speech at the Democratic National Convention." Politico.com. September 5, 2012. https://www.politico.com/story/2012/09/elizabeth-warren-dnc-speech -text-080802.

———. "Speech to the National Congress of American Indians." Elizabeth Warren for Massachusetts. YouTube Video, 17:47, February 14, 2018. https://www.youtube .com/watch?v=eAxHa92QmTc.

———. "The Economics of Race: When Making it to the Middle Isn't Enough." *Washington & Lee Law Review* 61 (2005): 1777–1799.

————. "The Market for Data: The Changing Role of Social Sciences in Shaping the Law." *Wisconsin Law Review*, no. 1 (2002): 1–42.

————. "Trade Usage and Parties in the Trade: An Economic Rationale for an Inflexible Rule." *Pittsburgh Law Review* 42 (1981): 515–582.

————. "Tax Accounting in Regulated Industries: Limitations on Rate Base Exclusions." *Rutgers Law Review*, 31 (1978): 187–204.

————. "Unsafe at Any Rate." *Democracy: A Journal of Ideas*, Summer 2007, no. 5. https://democracyjournal.org/magazine/5/unsafe-at-any-rate/.

————. "Warren: Congress Has Responsibility to DACA Recipients." Interview by Ali Velshi, *All In*, February 7, 2018. Video, 9:01. https://www.msnbc.com/all-in/watch /warren-congress-has-responsibility-to-daca-recipients-1156319811588.

————. *A Fighting Chance*. New York: Picador, 2014.

————. Remarks at Center for American Progress event, November 14, 2017. Senator Elizabeth Warren website. https://www.warren.senate.gov/newsroom/press -releases/senator-warren-delivers-remarks-on-devastating-impact-of-gop-tax -plan-on-small-businesses.

————. Remarks at "The Democratic Party at a Crossroads: The Wellstone Way and Economic Populism." Audio, 58:27–1:25:45, October 22, 2017. Center for the Study of Politics and Governance, Humphrey School of Public Affairs, University of Minnesota. https://soundcloud.com/user-179867903/part-2-the-democratic -party-at-a-crossroads-the-wellstone-way-and-economic-populism.

————. *This Fight Is Our Fight: The Battle to Save America's Middle Class*. New York: Metropolitan Books, 2017.

Washington, Jesse. "Candidate's Ancestry Debate." Indian Country Today online. May 26, 2012. https://indiancountrymedianetwork.com/news/elizabeth-warrens -genealogical-challenge/.

Weissmann, Jordan. "Mick Mulvaney Says the Consumer Financial Protection Bureau Works for Payday Lenders, Too." Slate, January 23, 2018. https://slate.com /business/2018/01/mick-mulvaney-says-the-consumer-financial-protection -bureau-works-for-payday-lenders-too.html.

Wellstone, David. Remarks at "The Democratic Party at a Crossroads: The Wellstone Way and Economic Populism." Audio, 58:27–1:25:45, October 22, 2017. Center for the Study of Politics and Governance, Humphrey School of Public Affairs, University of Minnesota. https://soundcloud.com/user-179867903/part-2-the -democratic-party-at-a-crossroads-the-wellstone-way-and-economic-populism.

Wellstone, Paul. *The Conscience of a Liberal: Reclaiming the Compassionate Agenda*. New York: Random House, 2001.

West, Cornell. *Race Matters*. 2nd ed. New York: Vintage. 2001.

Wetumka Gazette Staff, "Herring-Reed." *Wetumka Gazette*, January 8, 1932.

Wetumka Gazette Staff. "J. H. Herring Dies Today." *Wetumka Gazette*, March 23, 1932.

White, Gillian B. "One Year After Its Fake-Accounts Scandal, Wells Fargo Isn't 'A Better Bank.'" *The Atlantic*, October 3, 2017. https://www.theatlantic.com/business /archive/2017/10/wells-fargo-fake-accounts-sloan/541875/.

White House. "President Obama Names Elizabeth Warren Assistant to the President and Special Adviser to the Secretary of the Treasury on the Consumer Financial Protection Bureau." September 17, 2010. https://obamawhitehouse .archives.gov/the-press-office/2010/09/17/president-obama-names-elizabeth -warren-assistant-president-and-special-a.

Wilstein, Matt. "Mika Brzezinski Turns on Elizabeth Warren: 'I'm Getting Tired of This Act.'" Daily Beast. November 29, 2016. https://www.thedailybeast.com /mika-brzezinski-turns-on-elizabeth-warren-im-getting-tired-of-this-act.

Wong, Scott, and John Bresnahan. "Warren Campaign Revises Panel Pay." Politico. September 23, 2011. https://www.politico.com/story/2011/09/warren-campaign -revises-panel-pay-064306.

Wysong, Earl, Robert Perrucci, and David Wright. *The New Class Society: Goodbye American Dream?* 4th ed. Lanham: Rowman & Littlefield, 2014.

Yale Law School. "Entering Class Profile." Accessed February 19, 2018. https://law.yale .edu/admissions/profiles-statistics/entering-class-profile.

Yellin, Jessica. "Attorneys: Play Hardball on AIG Bonuses." March 20, 2009. http:// www.cnn.com/2009/POLITICS/03/19/aig.contracts/index.html.

INDEX

H

ACKNOWLEDGMENTS

Writing this book has been one of the most enriching journeys of my life, bringing me in conversation with dozens of extraordinary people. My gratitude runs deep for all of you. I'll start with Barbara Mikulski, senator-turned-professor—speaking to you about your distinguished decades in the Senate was a life event in itself. Thank you for your generous time and zeal. Extended thanks also to Senator Harry Reid for a delightful interview and warm, thoughtful discussion. Thank you, Dick Trumka, for sharing your enthusiastic stories about Elizabeth Warren, and hearty thanks to Perry Lange, whose insights about working closely with Senator Paul Wellstone contributed new material for the record about the late, great senator from Minnesota.

This book would not be possible without the voices from Oklahoma who so generously welcomed me to Norman and Oklahoma City and spoke about their memories. Bob Hammack's contribution, both in reaching out to his network to provide sources and offering his own insights and memories, was invaluable to my work. It was also a pleasure and very productive opportunity to meet with Joe Pryor, and my heartfelt thanks go to Katrina Cochran, Judy Garrett, Joe Mallonee, and Andrew Mason for their interviews. Deep thanks to Warren's high school debate partner, Karl Johnson, now an eminent attorney specializing in Indian law. It is an honor to know you. Warm thanks also to Northwest Classen High School Principal Jahree Herzer for your insights and for opening your school archives to me.

Thank you, scholars and former students whose lives have intersected with Warren, for the generous insights that made such a substantial contribution to this book: Katherine Porter, Bill Toutant, Mark Gergen, Calvin Johnson, Patricia Cain, Alix James, Chrystin Ondersma, John Mixon, Ronald Mann, and Douglas Moll. Thomas Barry provided over-the-top assistance and first-person material for which I am most grateful, and many thanks also to Will Sealy and Jennifer Migliore for your stories and memories, and to Shanti Fry for schooling me on some of the finer points of political campaigning.

My thanks to Todd Gitlin for a lively discussion about Occupy; Douglas Peterson for his expertise on the Ivy Leagues of law education; and Denis Hanigan for what turned out to be a moving look back at his father's leadership of George Washington University's debate team. Many thanks to genealogist Yona-tli Nokose for crafting a tree that provided a very helpful road map throughout the writing of this book. And heartfelt appreciation to and admiration for Native American scholars David Wilkins and Tom Holm for sharing your wisdom and perspectives.

Thank you to the librarians who provided so much expert assistance, and always with tireless generosity: Tammi Pierce at the

Norman Public Library, Laura Martin at the Oklahoma Historical Society, Eric Edwards at the Illinois State Library, and Meghan Harmon with the Abraham Lincoln Presidential Library. Many thanks also to Stephanie Hixon at the Moore-Lindsay House in Norman for your kind guidance. And for her invaluable research assistance and cheerful, always-on-call spirit, my warmest thanks and appreciation go to Lavanya Sunkara.

I could not have done this work without the love and support of my family and friends, including my husband, Stanford; my mother, Phyllis Berg; my mother-in-law, Trudy Felix; my beloved sister-in-law, Audrey Schindler, and her mother, Lynn; my dear and brilliant friend, David Frank; the ever-constant political go-to man, Steven Jacques; and the women who keep my heart and soul alive, Marla Fries, Mary Veronica Sweeney, Jodi Weber, and Tara Gilfillan. I am also indebted to the wisdom, energy, and groundbreaking work of everyone on the faculty of the department of educational leadership at Minnesota State University–Mankato. It is an honor to journey with you as I develop my skills as a researcher. Your work in social equity is changing the world.

Finally, my deep thanks to my agent, Esther Margolis, former publisher extraordinaire who invited me to lunch one afternoon to ask if I had any book ideas. After telling her about my long interest in Elizabeth Warren and handing her the twenty-page book proposal I just happened to have in my bag, the rest is history. And to my editor at Sourcebooks, Grace Menary-Winefield: words fail me when I need them most to express my gratitude for your expert guidance, endless patience, and meticulous professionalism in every step of this process. Thank you for every phone call, email, edit, and ounce of glorious championing you have done for this book.

ABOUT THE AUTHOR

Antonia Felix is author of eighteen nonfiction books, including *Michelle Obama: A Photographic Journey, Sonia Sotomayor: The True American Dream, Condi: The Condoleezza Rice Story,* and *Wesley K. Clark: A Biography.* Her work also includes short fiction published in the acclaimed anthology *Fracture: Essays, Poems, and Stories on Fracking in America, Fatal Remedy: A Thriller,* and *La Divina,* a play about Maria Callas that debuted at Minnesota Concert Opera. Felix has taught in graduate programs at Hamline University, and she and her husband live near Minneapolis, Minnesota.